Introducing Information Management:

an *Information Research* reader

Introducing Information Management:

an *Information Research* reader

Edited by

Elena Macevičiūtė and T. D. Wilson

facet publishing

Published by
Facet Publishing, 7 Ridgmount Street,
London WC1E 7AE
www.facetpublishing.co.uk

Facet Publishing is wholly owned by CILIP: the Chartered Institute of Library and
Information Professionals.

First published 2005

British Library Cataloguing in Publication Data
A catalogue record for this book is available from the British Library.

ISBN 1-85604-561-7

Typeset from editors' disks by Facet Publishing in 10/13 pt NewtonB and
Humanist 521.
Printed and made in Great Britain by MPG Books Ltd, Bodmin, Cornwall.

Contents

Editors and contributors

Suliman Al-Hawamdeh is Professor at the School of Library and Information Studies, University of Oklahoma, USA, where he teaches courses in a variety of areas including information retrieval, the information and knowledge society and knowledge management. His research has concerned aspects of information retrieval, the development of Singapore as a knowledge economy and other knowledge management issues. He is a former member of the Editorial Board of *Information Research*. His e-mail address is suliman@ou.edu.

David Allen is Senior Lecturer in Information Management at the Leeds University Business School, UK, and Director of the AIMTech Research Group. His research deals with information systems and their implications for work, information management and organizations, particularly at the strategic level. He is currently working on a number of funded research projects on applications of mobile technologies in e-government and in emergency services such as police forces. David is a member of the Editorial Board of *Information Research*. His e-mail address is david.k.allen@gmail.com.

France Bouthillier is Associate Professor and Director of the Graduate School of Library and Information Studies, McGill University, Montreal, Canada. She teaches on aspects of business information and the management of information services, and her research relates to business information needs, competitive intelligence and knowledge management. Her current funded research project investigates the use and value of competitive intelligence software applications in the private and public sectors in Canada. Her e-mail address is france.bouthillier@mcgill.ca.

Judith Broady-Preston is a Lecturer in the Department of Information Studies, University of Wales, Aberystwyth, UK and Chair of the Knowledge Management Research Group. Her research interests include strategy formulation, information flow and scorecard models in organizations; performance measurement and quality issues; intellectual capital/business value; the development of competitive advantage by organizations; and CRM, e-CRM and communities of practice. She has managed several funded research projects, and is currently working on the applications of the balanced scorecard and philosophical aspects of knowledge management. Her e-mail address is jbp@aber.ac.uk.

Chun Wei Choo is Professor at the Faculty of Information Studies, University of Toronto, Canada. He was previously Director of Planning at the National Computer Board of Singapore and Manager, Research Planning, of the Board's Information Technology Institute. His main research interests are information management, organizational learning, environmental scanning and the management of information technology. He is a member of the Editorial Board of *Information Research*. His e-mail address is choo@fis.utoronto.ca.

Cheryl Marie Cordeiro is an affiliate of the Gothenburg Research Institute, and is currently in a PhD programme at the Department of Linguistics, Gothenburg University, Sweden, where she is working on a project entitled 'Asia Lite: a linguistic analysis of the adaptation of the Scandinavian management style in the Asian business environment'. She was previously in the Master of Science (Information Studies) programme at the Nanyang Technological University of Singapore. Her e-mail address is cheryl.cordeiro@gri.gu.se.

Zita Correia is a Senior Researcher at the Centro de Informação Técnica para a Indústria, Instituto Nacional de Engenharia, Tecnologia e Inovacão, Lisbon, Portugal. She holds a PhD in information management from the University of Sheffield and is experienced in contract research, mainly funded by European programmes. Her research interests are in competitive intelligence in business, organizational information strategies and government information policies, and extend to the impact of information society developments on the condition of citizenship, particularly relating to the citizen's access to and use of information. Her e-mail address is zita.correia@ineti.pt.

Shrianjani 'Gina' de Alwis is Head of Library Services at the Singapore Institute of Management and currently pursuing her PhD with the Division of Information Studies at Nanyang Technological University, Singapore. Her main research interest concerns managers' information behaviour. Her e-mail address is ginaalwis@sim.edu.sg.

Susan Higgins is Assistant Professor at the School of Library and Information Science, University of Southern Mississippi, USA. She teaches in the areas of collection development and library services to children and young adults, and has researched topics as varied as international issues in information studies education and the value of print literacy in the education of young children. Her e-mail address is susan.e.higgins@usm.edu.

Maija-Leena Huotari is Professor of Information Studies in the Department of Finnish, Information Studies and Speech Therapy at the University of Oulu, Finland. She holds a PhD in information science from the University of Sheffield and her research interests focus on the strategic management of organizational information and knowledge, organizational information behaviour and information seeking. She is currently Chair of the Finnish University Network for Communication Sciences, and a member of the Editorial Board of *Information Research*. Her e-mail address is maija-leena.huotari@oulu.fi.

Joyce Kirk is Professor and Pro-Vice Chancellor (Students) at RMIT University, Melbourne, Australia. She was previously Dean of the Faculty of Humanities and Social Sciences at the University of Technology Sydney. Her research interests include information seeking behaviour in organizations and the application of information management methods. Her e-mail address is joyce.kirk@rmit.edu.au.

Louise Limberg is Professor at the Swedish School of Library and Information Science, University College of Borås, Sweden. Her research is concerned with aspects of information seeking behaviour, especially in relation to teaching and learning. She is currently involved in a major project in this area and has a particular interest in the application of phenomenographic research techniques to information behaviour research. Her e-mail address is louise.limberg@hb.se.

Elena Macevičiūtė is Senior Lecturer at the Swedish School of Library and Information Science, Borås University College, Sweden, and Professor at the Faculty of Communication of Vilnius University, Lithuania. Her research interests cover aspects of information management and information resources as well as international and intercultural communication. She is a member of the Editorial Board of *Information Research* and its Book Reviews Editor. Her e-mail address is elena.maceviciute@hb.se.

Hugh Preston is a Lecturer in the Department of Information Studies, University of Wales Aberystwyth, UK. His research interests cover management information, organizational information systems, business decision making and management science, with a particular focus on health services. He is a former member of the Editorial Board of *Information Research*. His e-mail address is hjp@aber.ac.uk.

Kathleen Shearer is a Research Associate with the Canadian Association of Research Libraries (CARL). She is the coordinator of the CARL Institutional

Repository Project and is actively involved in monitoring new developments in scholarly communication. She is also one of the lead investigators for the research study, 'Optimizing the Transformation of Knowledge Dissemination: towards a Canadian research strategy'. In the past, she has worked as a freelance information professional for organizations such as Bombardier Aerospace, Bristol-Myers Squibb and Library and Archives Canada. Her other research interests include the assessment of information systems and knowledge management. Her e-mail address is mkshearer@videotron.ca.

Aiki Tibar is a Researcher in the Tallinn University of Technology Library, Estonia. She is also in the PhD programme at the Department of Information Studies, University of Tampere, Finland, where she is working on a project entitled 'Information needs and information-seeking behaviour of scientists'. Her previous project was on information needs in industry. Her e-mail address is tibar@lib.ttu.ee.

Gunilla Widén-Wulff is a Lecturer in the Department of Information Studies, Faculty of Economics and Political Science, Åbo Akademi University, Turku, Finland. Her research is on social capital from an information science perspective and networking in the fields of science, technology, education, and business. She is currently Chair of the Finnish Association of Information Studies. Her e-mail address is gunilla.widen-wulff@abo.fi.

T. D. (Tom) Wilson is Professor Emeritus of the University of Sheffield, UK, and Visiting Professor at the University of Leeds Business School, UK, and at Borås University College, Sweden. His research has ranged widely over aspects of information management, from work in the field of information seeking behaviour, through studies of information overload and the relationship between company performance and information culture, to recent work on the role of mobile technologies in e-government. He is also publisher and Editor-in-Chief of *Information Research*. His e-mail address is t.d.wilson@shef.ac.uk.

Preface

Information management (IM) is a field of wide scope which is also related to other fields, such as information systems, computer science, artificial intelligence research, information science, documentation and more. From a disciplinary point of view research in the field has become increasingly diversified and increasingly specialized, with areas such as laboratory IM and health IM constituting virtually separate fields of investigation and publication. In addition one should mention diverse levels of IM: research is done on personal, organizational and state-wide IM. Organizational IM is the major subject of research in this reader; however, the body of research on the other two levels is growing.

Preparing a Reader on such a field, therefore, is rather difficult, especially having in mind the variety of traditions of education for information throughout the world. Our answer has been to refer to a source of contributions which enables us to check the demand for work in specific areas from those working and studying in the field. That source is the electronic journal *Information Research*, which was established in 1995, at the beginning of the world wide web revolution in information delivery. The 'hit counters' on the papers in the journal provide a useful, though crude, indication of use and we have asked the authors of the papers that appear to have been most used to revise or re-write their papers as contributions to this volume. Thus, the chapters are not simply the original papers re-issued: they have all been revised to some degree and many have been almost completely re-written to take into account developments since the original paper appeared.

Thus, the material addresses a wider audience than was originally intended. It might be interesting not only for the students on various information-related programmes, but also for researchers following the development of the discipline and practitioners, who constituted a large part of the 'hitting' audience. We also believe that the Reader can be used creatively by lecturers and students for a variety of purposes:

- to study various aspects of information management
- to find ideas for projects and research papers

- to get acquainted with a variety of research methods in the IM field
- to follow the traditions and topics of IM research in different countries and areas of activity
- to compare the chapters with original articles and see how a single researcher develops ideas and research over time.

The book is divided into five sections: the general scope of IM, information behaviour, environmental scanning and decision making, 'knowledge management' and information strategy. As a result, there are areas within IM that are not covered, but we believe that the chapters represent those aspects of IM that are most likely to be required by a wide range of students – they represent, in our opinion, the core of the field. Besides, some authors provided rather comprehensive literature reviews that reflect most influential works on IM, as the cumulated reference list indicates; consequently, the Bibliography at the end of the book is, in itself, a valuable resource for the student of the field. In addition, each section of the book starts with a short introduction that characterizes the chapters within it and also provides tips for further reading.

We have been lucky to have a group of very supportive authors, all of whom agreed on the need for a reader of this kind. But they did not only agree, they also worked on their papers and, in large measure, met the deadlines that were set. They have also foregone any payment for the work and agreed that all royalties should go to support *Information Research* as an open access journal. Both editors would like to thank them for their creative co-operation, fruitful communication and support for the journal and the idea of this Reader.

The editors had opportunities to meet regularly and resolve any problematic issues. The work was divided equally and we both share responsibility for any mistakes introduced into the original works during the editing process.

We would like to thank Facet Publishing, and Rebecca Casey in particular, for the encouragement we received in the production of this volume.

Professor Elena Macevičiūtė
Professor T. D. Wilson

Acronyms and initialisms

BPR	business process re-engineering
BSC	balanced scorecard
CCO	Clatterbridge Centre for Oncology
CD-ROM	compact disc (read-only memory)
CEO	chief executive officer
CHI	Commission for Health Improvement
CIDA	Canadian International Development Agency
CIS/R	Clinical Interview System, Revised, a patient administration system
CKO	Chief Knowledge Officer
CoPs	communities of practice
CSF	critical success factors
DAB	Direkt Anlage Bank AG
DKR	dynamic knowledge repository
EC	European Commission
EDB	Economic Development Board
ELIS	everyday-life information seeking
EPR	electronic patient records
EPS	employee purchase scheme
EU	European Union
GDP	gross domestic product
GIIC	Global Information Infrastructure Committee
GP	general practitioner
HEIs	higher education institutions
HER	electronic health records
HoD	heads of departments
HRGs	health resource groups
I&M	*Information & Management*

IAPMEI	Instituto de Apoio às Pequenas e Médias Empresas e ao Investimento (Institute for the Assistance of Small and Medium-size Businesses and on Investment)
ICT	information and communication technology
IDA	Infocomm Development Authority
IEP	*Information Economics and Policy*
IJIM	*International Journal of Information Management*
IM	information management
IM&T	information management and technology
IO	*Information and Organization*
IRM	information resource management
IS	information systems
ISO	International Organization for Standardization
IT	information technology
JSIS	*Journal of Strategic Information Systems*
KBE	knowledge-based economy
KM	knowledge management
LearnLib	*Learning through the School Library project*
LIS	library and information science
LISA	*Library and Information Science Abstracts*
MIS	management information systems
MITA	Ministry of Information and the Arts
MNC	multinational company
MOE	Ministry of Education
MQ	*Management Information Systems (MIS) Quarterly*
MRT	mass rapid transit
N3	the new national network of the National Health Service in the UK
NASA	National Aeronautics and Space Administration
NCB	National Computer Board
NeLH	National Electronic Library for Health
NHS	National Health Service
NHSIA	NHS Information Authority
NHSnet	NHS Network
NII	national information infrastructure
NIIG	National Information Infrastructure Group
NLB	National Library Board
NPfIT	NHS National Programme for Information Technology
NSTB	National Science and Technology Board
NTU	Nanyang Technological University
OECD	Organization for Economic Co-operation and Development

PACS	picture archiving and communication system
PC	personal computer
PEDIP	Strategic Programme for the Development of Portuguese Industry
PwC	PricewaterhouseCoopers
QMAS	quality management and analysis system
R&D	research and development
SIC	standard industrial classification
SIM	strategic information management
SME	small and medium enterprise
SMT	senior management team
SUS	Secondary Uses Service
TAS	Telecommunications Authority of Singapore
TCS	Tata Consultancy Services
TV	television
UK	United Kingdom
USA	United States of America
USAID	US Agency for International Development

Part A
General papers

Introduction

We have already noted that information management (IM) is a wide-ranging subject area: consequently, identifying general papers that help us to understand that diversity and that place the authors' perceptions of the subject in a more general framework is difficult. One general introduction to the field is that presented by Wilson (2003), where the scope of the field is taken to include: information requirements, the information life-cycle, information resources, the economics of information, tools such as information and communication audits and information mapping, information access, networks and intranets, legal aspects of access and privacy, information policy and strategy, and strategic information systems. This view reflects the organizational perspective on information management and was employed in selecting articles for this chapter. However, even within the organizational perspective there are different approaches to information in organizations and to IM. Moreover, there are different paradigms underlying IM research. The most influential and widely used are the structural-functional and the cognitive. During the last 20 years an increasing variety of interpretative perspectives have been used in organizational and IM research.

The three chapters presented here are more limited in their scope, but offer useful refinements of different recent perspectives.

First, Joyce Kirk focuses on the strategic aspect of information management and the issue of relating information management strategies to business strategies, particularly in small- and medium-sized companies. Her chapter summarizes a variety of approaches to information, management and organizations, and outlines their implications and propositions for information management.

Then, Elena Macevičiūtė and T. D. Wilson update their 2002 paper to report upon the scope of research on information management as revealed by an analysis of the papers in a number of core journals. They provide an outline of changes in research trends from 1989 to 2004 and conclude that the boundary between information management and information systems becomes ever fuzzier. The chapter also reveals the variety of research methods characteristic of authors publishing in the field.

Finally, Gunilla Widén-Wulff reports on a study of 15 insurance companies in Finland, in which she explored the concept of information culture. She identifies three groups of companies with different information cultures and shows how these different cultures relate to the business success of the companies.

There are, of course, a number of texts that deal with information management from the point of view presented here, perhaps the best known of which are Choo (2002) and a collection of 'classic' works on IM edited by Ethel Auster and Chun Wei Choo (1996).

1

Information in organizations: directions for information management

Joyce Kirk

Introduction

Information management (IM) is practised in organizations. Yet information is used by individuals in those organizations. The counterpoint between the organization and its individual members has particular relevance to IM because of its responsibilities to both the organization at one level and to individuals at another level. This counterpoint means that we need to consider both the organization and its members in information terms as a starting point for developing strategies for effective IM in small- and medium-sized enterprises (SMEs).[1] This chapter develops some general guidelines for effective information management under three headings:

* information and organizations
* information and managers
* information management in SMEs.

Information and organizations

This discussion of organizations and information has two parts. The first provides an overview of organizations by examining images used to describe them and then drawing some implications for IM. The second outlines a hierarchy of definitions of information which are appropriate for organizations and draws further

[1] SMEs, according to the standard EU definition, employ no more than 249 people, have less than 40 million euro turnover and no more than 25% ownership or control by one or more enterprises which are not SMEs.

implications for IM. The discussion concludes with a set of propositions about information management.

Images of organizations

Machines, organisms, political systems and cultures (Morgan, 1986): these are familiar and conventional images of organizations. Senge (1990) added a fifth image: learner. Each image represents a perspective on the nature of organizations. The machine image suggests that information keeps the cogs ticking over and the task of IM is to ensure that information is delivered where and when it is needed through clearly defined and understood communication channels. The organism image implies that information from internal and external sources is required to keep the organization in a state of equilibrium. The image of the political system recognizes that because different groups in organizations have different interests they will need and use information differently in the exercise of power and influence, in seeking support and negotiating conflict; it brings to mind the political and social context of IM. The image of the organization as culture is particularly powerful with its suggestions of shared beliefs, values, norms and meaning, and its emphasis on ritual, myth, language and symbol. It suggests that the use of information in an organization will have cultural aspects, in contrast to the assumption that the use of information is a rational human activity. IM has a clear role in making meaning and will embody, through its practice, the beliefs and values of the organizations. The image of the organization as learner suggests a community which regenerates itself through the creation of knowledge – the outcome of learning. IM ensures that the organization has the information and information capabilities necessary to adapt continuously to its changing internal and external environments.

Although none of these five images is by itself an adequate representation, together they highlight the complexity of organizations and the processes which sustain them. It is this complexity which is part of the context of IM in organizations and informs IM practice.

What are some of the implications for IM that emerge from these images of organizations?

1   IM has the potential to contribute to the achievements of organizations.
2   IM has different purposes in different organizations. These purposes will be influenced by the organization's goals, its culture and its stance on information.
3   IM is practised in a political, social and cultural context which shapes both what IM does and how it does it.
4   IM practice is value laden and so it has an ethical dimension. The ethics of IM practice are most often implicit.

5 Organizational learning concepts and theory are applicable to IM in some organizations. Not all organizations are ready for this development, nor is it an appropriate direction for all organizations.

Some definitions of information

Organizations are aware of the potential of information to provide competitive advantage and sustain their success (Porter, 1985), as evidenced in a number of published case studies (Grimshaw, 1995; Owens et al., 1996) and commentaries (Broadbent, 1977). Descriptions of information as an asset and a resource (Best, 1996; Burk and Horton, 1988) are usual. However, the origin of these descriptions in classical economics ignores the place of information in the fabric of the political system and culture of an organization. If information is to provide competitive advantage then its full potential needs to be considered.

A very useful hierarchy of definitions of information (Braman, 1989) has been developed in the area of information policy studies. The hierarchy is applicable to organizations for a number of reasons: first, it recognizes the qualitative differences among definitions of information; second, its macro view is more appropriate to organizations than definitions based only on the individual as an information user; third, it provides a range of definitions which are useful in different situations; and fourth, it foreshadows the need for information policy in organizations.

The hierarchy consists of four levels, each based on a category of definitions drawn from many different fields:

1 Information as a resource. 'Information, its creators, processors and users are viewed as discrete and isolated entities. Information comes in pieces unrelated to bodies of knowledge or information flows into which it might be organized' (Braman, 1989, 236).
2 Information as a commodity. The notion of information as a commodity incorporates 'the exchange of information among people and related activities as well as its use' (Braman, 1989, 238) and implies buyers, sellers and a market. Information as a commodity has economic power.
3 Information as perception of pattern. Here the concept of information is broadened by the addition of context. Information 'has a past and a future, is affected by motive and other environmental and casual factors, and itself has effects' (Braman, 1989, 238). Information has a power of its own although its effects are isolated.
4 Information as a constitutive force in society. Information has a role in shaping context. 'Information is not just affected by its environment, but is itself an actor affecting other elements in the environment' (Braman, 1989, 239).

The traditional view of IM has focused very much on information as a resource and as a commodity and on IM as providing a service to the organization. That service has taken the form of providing access to information in a range of sources. The definition of information as perception of pattern transfers IM into a constitutive force and gives it a place in achieving the goals of an organization. IM shifts from service provision to strategy formation.

What conclusions can be drawn for IM in organizations from this hierarchy of definitions of information?

1   IM needs to encompass the full range of information, from a resource to a force for change and development.
2   Information can be integrated into organizational processes and so it can influence organizational culture, structure and work patterns.
3   IM can properly address information products, services, information flow and use in an organization.
4   Useful measures of the effectiveness of IM can be based on the impact of information on the organization.

Our consideration of organizations, information and IM can be drawn together in a number of propositions:

Proposition 1

Information and IM contribute to the achievement of organizational goals.

Proposition 2

IM is contextualized by the organization.

Proposition 3

To be as effective as possible IM must assume a broad view of information.

Proposition 4

Information can be value-laden; so too can IM practice.

Information and managers

Managers are responsible for strategy development and implementation and for enabling organizations to meet their goals. Therefore, it is appropriate to investigate their attitudes towards information and IM. The first part of this discussion deals with the nature of managerial work and draws a number of implications for IM. The second considers the nature of information from the point of view of individual users and is based on work in information science and management. Again, implications for IM are drawn.

The work of managers

The classic view of managerial functions as planning, organizing, communicating, coordinating and controlling (Fayol, 1949) suggests a rational and ordered approach to management activities. Yet studies of managers in their workplaces present a picture of managerial activities that is quite different. A brief overview of a number of studies of managers highlights the active, informal, fragmented and chaotic nature of managerial work.

Mintzberg (1975) identified ten different roles for managers. The roles were categorized into three groups:

1 The interpersonal roles of figurehead, leader and liaison.
2 The informational roles of monitor, disseminator and spokesperson.
3 The decisional roles of entrepreneur, disturbance handler, resource handler and negotiator.

This approach to management acknowledges the action-oriented, outward-looking and ritualistic aspects of managerial work as well as managers' preferences for oral communication in finding information.

Kotter (1982) identified three major processes in which managers are engaged: agenda setting, network building and implementing their agendas through networks. The key challenges for general managers relate to the demands of these processes: 'figuring out what to do (making decisions) in an environment characterized by uncertainty, great diversity, and an enormous quantity of potentially relevant information' and 'getting things done (implementation) through a large and diverse group of people despite having relatively little control over them' (Kotter, 1982, 20).

Luthans et al. (1988) identified four other managerial activities: networking, routine communication, traditional management and human resources management. Networking includes interaction with outsiders and socializing and politicking inside and outside the organization; routine communication activities include exchanging information and handling paperwork; traditional management activities consist of planning, decision-making and controlling; and human resources management includes motivating and reinforcing, disciplining or punishing, managing conflict, staffing, and training or developing. This study distinguished between successful and effective managers, i.e., between those who are promoted and those who have 'satisfied, committed subordinates and produce organizational results' (Luthans et al., 1988, 62). The categories of activity contribute differently to success and effectiveness. Networking had the strongest relationship with success, whereas routine communication was the strongest for effectiveness. Human resource management had the weakest relationship with success, and networking with effectiveness.

The final study considered here explores the work of middle managers. It suggests that managing relationships, finding innovation, creating a mindset and facilitating learning (Floyd and Wooldridge, 1996) are integral to creating competitive advantage. The study of middle managers focused on strategy formation and moved away from the overly rational, command-and-control model of strategy as a two-stage process of formulation and implementation to a model that has 'more to do with learning than planning' (Luthans et al., 1988, 39). Four distinct roles in strategy for middle managers were identified: championing strategic alternatives; synthesizing information; facilitating adaptability; and implementing deliberate strategy. By engaging in these roles, middle managers link strategic purpose and organizational action.

What are some implications for IM that emerge from this overview of managerial work?

1   IM has the potential to contribute to the effectiveness of managers in their diverse organizational roles.
2   IM should seek to meet the information needs of managers and enhance their information capabilities.
3   IM must recognize informal and formal information sources and flows both internal and external to the organization.
4   IM should enable managers to integrate business strategy and information.

Some definitions of information

Because information is integral to the work of managers we should indicate what information is at the level of individual users of information. There are two perspectives which are useful to a consideration of IM in organizations: one from the field of information and communication, the other from management.

The first is central to the user-oriented paradigm (Dervin and Nilan, 1986) in information studies. This perspective posits that information is a process that applies to adaptive and creative behaviour. It relies on *Information₁*, or 'information which describes reality, the innate structure or pattern of reality' (Dervin, 1977, 22) and *Information₂* or 'ideas, the structures or pictures imputed to reality by people' (Dervin, 1977, 22). Individuals move between *Information₂* (subjective, internal information) and *Information₁* (objective, external information) by *Information₃*, a set of behaviours, or the 'how' of the information process.

Similar categories of information have been derived from an analysis of dictionary definitions (Buckland, 1991): information-as-thing, information-as-knowledge and information-as-process. Information-as-knowledge is intangible and to be communicated needs to be expressed or represented in some physical way, so becoming tangible information-as-thing. The point is made that information-as-thing has a 'fundamental role' in information systems (Buckland, 1991, 352) − not only computer-based systems but also libraries, museums, etc.

The second perspective, based on an analysis of successful companies in Japan, is centred on the individual as a creator of new knowledge (Nonaka, 1991). It draws a distinction between explicit and tacit knowledge. Explicit knowledge is formal, systematic and codified rather like *Information₁* or information-as-thing. Tacit knowledge is highly personal, consisting of technical skills and 'know-how'; it has cognitive dimensions such as implicit mental models and beliefs which shape our perceptions of the world. There are similarities among *Information₂*, information-as-knowledge and tacit knowledge.

This perspective links individual and organizational knowledge. New knowledge always begins with an individual and it is this individual's personal knowledge which is transformed into organizational knowledge. There are four patterns suggested for creating knowledge in an organization, and some indications of the creation process through the spiral of knowledge (Nonaka, 1991, 97−9) are given. These are similar to *Information₃* and information-as-process.

These two perspectives on information present a contrast between information-as-object and information-as-construct. Both kinds of information are necessary for managers in organizations. Not only do managers use information as one of the resources available to them but they also have a role in knowledge creation for themselves, their co-workers and their organizations.

What implications for IM can be drawn from a discussion of information as used by individuals?

1 If information in organizations is conceptualized as a process it can then be integrated into strategy formation.
2 IM needs to encompass information-as-object and information-as-construct as well as interactions between them.
3 IM has a role in enhancing the information capabilities of individuals in organizations.
4 Almost all managerial activities have an information component. Therefore, IM practice should be responsive to the needs of managers as information users and as information producers or knowledge creators.

Implications for IM that emerged from this overview serve to elaborate and clarify the scope of IM in organizations. Some propositions about IM are:

Proposition 1

Managers are in a unique position to integrate information and organizational strategy.

Proposition 2

A process approach to information supports the integration of information and business strategy and is a foundation for IM.

Proposition 3

IM must adopt a broadly-based approach to information that includes information-as-object and as a user construct, formal and informal flows of information inside and outside organizations, internal and external sources of information, and enhancing the information capabilities of individuals in organizations.

Proposition 4

The effectiveness of IM can be measured by the impact of information on the organization.

These propositions underpin a shift in IM, away from the provision of information that emphasizes technology and access towards strategy focused on information use and its integration into business strategy

Information management in SMEs

Though tentative, the propositions about IM are based on a range of perspectives, the most central of which regards information as potentially sustaining an organization's competitive position. The links among the perspectives on information are shown in Figure 1.1.

Broad guidelines for IM have been developed from the propositions and each one will now be explored. The guidelines fall into categories related to the purpose, scope and implementation of IM:

1   Purpose of IM
  • Information and IM contributes to the achievement of organizational goals.
  • A process approach to IM supports the integration of information and strategy.

2   Scope of IM
  • IM is contextualized by the organization and is value-laden.
  • IM must adopt a broadly-based approach to information and encompasses:
    — information-as-object and as a user construct
    — formal and informal flows of information inside and outside organizations
    — sources of information internal and external to organizations
    — enhancing the information capabilities of individuals in organizations.

3   Implementation of IM
  • Managers are in a unique position to integrate information and business strategy.
  • The effectiveness of IM can be measured by the extent of knowledge creation or innovation in organizations.

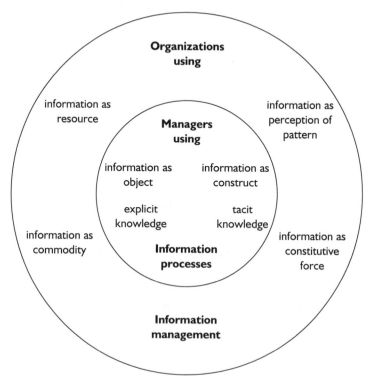

Figure 1.1   The information environment of organizations

Purpose

IM contributes to the achievement of organizational goals

Information can contribute to the success of organizations and to the achievement of organizational goals, whether information is regarded as a resource or as a force for change and development. The assumptions are made that the goals of an organization are explicit and known throughout the organization, and there is some way to determine the extent to which the goals have been met.

Concern about the need to link business strategy and information is shared by managers in countries in the Western world (Broadbent et al., 1992). A key factor in linking or aligning business strategy and information has been IT, a tool essential for business success in a global economy. The potential for IT and information to transform organizations is evident in those companies which have redesigned their business processes. Information and IT have acted as enabling and integrating tools for survival and growth in rapidly changing environments (e.g., Johannessen and Olaisen, 1993).

A process approach to IM supports the integration of strategy and information

The calls for integration come from at least three different communities: IM, information systems and management. Successful companies are those that adapt to and shape their environments and do so by using and creating information in a process of continuous improvement and innovation.

IM has been described by Choo (2002, 24–5) as a continuous cycle of related activities encompassing the information value chain. The activities in the cycle are:

- identification of information needs defined by subject requirements and situation
- information acquisition involving evaluation and assessment of sources and matching sources to needs
- information organization and storage of the organization's memory
- information products and services aimed at enhancing the quality of information
- information distribution through sharing information informally or formally
- information use in the creation and interpretation of information, and in decision-making processes.

Identification of information needs and information use are not always regarded as components of IM. Yet it is these two activities which require the integration of business strategy and information. Information needs will arise in the context of the organization's goals and the objectives of work teams, and it is this context which surrounds the use of information.

The integration of business strategy and information also suggests different ways of organizing work and designing the organization. In the learning organization there are three groups of experts who need to work together as partners in strategy formation teams (Choo, 2002): domain experts, information experts and information technology experts.

The focus of each group of experts is different. Organizational effectiveness is the focus of the domain expert, enlightenment is the focus of the information expert and process efficiency is the focus of the information technology expert. As partners in the strategy formation teams they will create, organize and use knowledge. The partners will engage in learning and in furthering the organization's objectives. They will assume information responsibility within the team and for themselves.

Key factors for success in SMEs reinforce the need for integration of business strategy and information. These key factors are:

- relationships with customers and suppliers
- flatter management structures and better use of resources
- training and quality
- environmental issues (Abell, 1994, 236).

Each of these factors rests on information: its use, creation, storage and distribution. Issues regarding the quality of information (i.e., accuracy, validity, timeliness), its accessibility, availability, presentation, ease of use, organization and storage are the concern of teams or task forces developing strategy or engaging in projects in relation to any one of these factors.

Scope

IM is contextualized by the organization and is value-laden

The earlier discussion of images of organizations suggests different approaches to IM in organizations. While the objectives of IM will be linked to the effectiveness of organizations, its practice will vary across organizations. For example, in the 'machine' organization, the IM function might be centrally located in a unit established to control internally generated information. This unit would have links to an IT unit. There might also be a library which provides information services based on externally generated information. Depending on the industry sector, the marketplace, the culture and the nature of work in the organization, this structural arrangement for IM might be appropriate. The objectives and priorities for IM will be framed within this context.

By contrast, in a learning organization, IM might be decentralized in a federal structure which supports teams but locates some IM functions centrally. Each team will be responsible for providing information to know-how databases accessible through the organization's intranet. Compared to the previous example, the objectives of IM and priorities for services will be quite different. Some differences will be seen in:

- distinctions made between internally and externally generated information
- the re-use and sharing of information arising from activities in each organization
- the relationships between library, IM and IT staff
- the applications of IT
- the value attributed to information
- the information ethos
- measures of success used by the organization and by information management.

It needs to be recognized that both these examples are valid. There is no single approach to IM which is inherently more effective than any other.

An important element in IM is information politics, which indicate the assumptions made about how people generate and use information in organizations. Some models of information politics (Davenport et al., 1996a) include:

- technocratic utopianism: a heavily technical approach to IM stressing categorization and modelling of information assets
- anarchy: the absence of any overall IM policy, leaving individuals to obtain and manage their own information
- feudalism: the management of information by individual business units defining their own information needs and reporting only limited information or none
- federalism: an approach to IM based on consensus and negotiation of the key information elements and reporting structures.

It is possible that a number of models could co-exist in an organization. The models reinforce the point that the context of the organization influences IM and remind us that it may include barriers to the development of sound IM practice. The issue of context is applicable to SMEs as well as large organizations.

IM must adopt a broadly-based approach to information

From the hierarchy of definitions of information it is possible to derive a hierarchy of definitions of information management (see Table 1.1).

Table 1.1   Possible hierarchy of definitions of IM

Definitions of information*	Definitions of IM
Information as resource	IM as IT systems
Information as commodity	Information resource management
Information as perception of pattern	IM as aligning information strategy and business strategy
Information as constitutive force	Information and knowledge management integrating strategy formation and information

* Definitions of information based on Braman (1989).

If IM is to influence the development of the organization then it should recognize as many categories of information as possible, as broad a range of sources and media as possible, and as broad a range of uses of information as possible.

Information experts have a role in enhancing the information capabilities of individuals in organizations. Efforts to adapt human behaviour to information systems have not been successful. IT offers some potential for developing interactive systems which should be capable of adapting to human behaviour, but systems capturing information needs and use patterns are needed.

There are a number of approaches to adding value to information already in use but there is room for further development. Information experts might discuss with managers their media preferences, information use strategies and any barriers they have encountered in using and applying knowledge, and then tailor information products and services to enable managers to perform their work roles better. Taylor (1986) sees adding value to information as helping users to match the information provided by a system with their needs. The added values include ease of use, noise reduction, quality, adaptability, time savings and cost savings. Another approach is directed toward reducing information overload for managers (Simpson and Prusak, 1995) by increasing the quality of information.

SMEs can adopt a broadly-based approach to information and ensure that the information they need in order to maintain their competitive advantage is accessible and usable.

Implementation

Managers are in a unique position to integrate information and business strategy

Successful implementation of information strategy presupposes senior management support, expressed most visibly in funding priorities and through information-related activities and projects. The integration of information and business strategy presupposes a learning team-based organization.

Davenport et al. (1996b, 54) refer to 'activities using individual and external knowledge to produce outputs characterised by information content'. Activities such as education, accounting, research and development, law, and management processes of strategy and planning belong to knowledge work (Davenport et al., 1996b). This view suggests that there are five different processes in knowledge work:

- finding existing knowledge, understanding knowledge requirements, searching for it among multiple sources and passing it on to a user
- creating new knowledge
- packaging knowledge created externally to the processes
- applying existing knowledge
- revising knowledge.

These five processes are used by managers and all are dependent on information. They also enable managers to integrate information and business strategy. These knowledge work processes are possible in SMEs. The task of IM is to enable managers to engage effectively in knowledge work. Key contributions by IM include:

- developing information filters so that the volume of information is contained
- enhancing the quality of information
- building know-how databases
- facilitating information sharing across teams.

Managers in SMEs supported by effective IM and information experts, like their colleagues in large organizations, are well placed to integrate information and business strategy.

The effectiveness of IM can be measured by the extent of knowledge creation or innovation in organizations

Evaluation of IM has to take into account different views on information. Evaluation based solely on information-as-object will be misleading. The focus of evaluation needs also to include information-as-construct and information processes. One approach to the evaluation of IM could be based on the processes of IM discussed earlier. Another approach might be based on innovations in the organization and might include consideration of the information capabilities of managers and their co-workers. The measures of the effectiveness of IM will be very similar in SMEs and large organizations.

Conclusion

IM has multiple meanings. Its meanings are shaped by different perspectives on information, on organizations and on the work of managers. IM has the potential to transform organizations but only when information and business strategies are integrated. Managers in SMEs and large organizations have a key role in putting information to productive use and ensuring that their organizations are successful.

In organizations, IM is the key to systematic innovation and to the benefits that innovation brings.

Acknowledgement

The author would like to acknowledge Elena Macevičiūtė's contribution to the paper in editing it for publication.

2

The development of the information management research area

Elena Macevičiūtė and T. D. Wilson

Introduction

Ideas regarding the information society and of information as the key resource for the development of new industries emerged in the 1970s and 1980s but, as Black and Brunt (1999) point out, the development of information systems is a feature of modern organizations from the 19th century onwards. In the late 1970s, the US Paperwork Reduction Act (Commission on Federal Paperwork, 1977) led to recognition that the production of information by bidders for government contracts was an unbearable cost, and the cost of handling that information at the federal government level was also onerous.

Out of this emerged the idea that *information is a resource*: it has potential value for an organization and, therefore, the organization should know its information resources (information mapping became a buzz-phrase of the time) and the costs of acquiring, storing, manipulating and using information. Organizational budgets should recognize these costs.

The consequences of the emergence of information management for research were significant. The economics of information, which, until then, had been a relatively insignificant part of economics, attained a new importance. Previously, economics had factored information out of its equations – in the market, everyone was assumed to have perfect information about that market. That is manifestly untrue, and a new field – asymmetric information – was introduced into economics.

Second, the information content of information systems became important: previously, databases were just that; they consisted largely of the numbers management needs to control an organization, such as production figures. The recognition that most information produced in an organization is text rather than numbers led to building systems that could handle text, and to a greater interest in the information systems community of information retrieval.

Third, it was recognized that effective systems need to be built according to the needs of the information user, rather than the convenience of the information producer, to present and organize information in the most accessible fashion.

Finally, information policy and information strategy became key terms and the need to have such policies and strategies, at national, local and organizational level, was recognized.

Four decades have passed since the emergence of IM as a research field. During this period it has been developed by scholars and practitioners all over the world. In addition, a tremendous change in information handling and communication technology has occurred. Empirical research in the areas of economics, management, organizational theory, information systems, and library and information science served as a basis for further theoretical development in these fields. All this had a significant influence on IM work and research. The last decade has been especially interesting as many changes that have been accumulating throughout the years have manifested themselves explicitly and taken root in the academic environment.

The aim of our chapter is to reveal changes in IM research during the decade 1989–2000, updated for the period 2000–2004.

Background

The content and scope of IM has been under close scrutiny by researchers and practitioners from several fields (business and management, organization research, information systems, information and communication technology, public administration, communication, information and librarianship) for a long time. Lately, authors trying to draw a line between information management and knowledge management renewed the discussions (Davenport and Prusak, 2000; Kirk, 1999; Rowley, 1998). The change in the profession under the impact of new technology, globalization of markets, and increasing social and economic pressures is evident in the writings of library and information science (LIS) professionals, but it is expressed practically in the same words by representatives of the business and computer fields. The LIS representatives advocate stronger orientation towards the perspective of management in new flexible organizations and their use of technology (Dresang and Robbins, 1999). In the business field information management is seen as a higher management level function, especially when it is labelled as knowledge management. Mintzberg (1998) has described the information roles of managers and sees management as an information-intensive job. There is a growing understanding of IM's significance to all kinds of senior executives in a vast range of business and management related literature. Information management programmes are found in business and management schools as well as in schools and departments of librarianship and information science. Moreover, computer professionals, information systems designers and (IT) specialists for businesses are now more concerned about information content, patterns of information use, users' needs and strategic thinking.

There have been numerous attempts to define the framework for IM. The concepts largely depend on the contents put into the words *information management*. It depends on not only the concept of *information* as such, but the multiple meanings of the phrase, the emphasis of its elements, or the word order as well as the scientific perspective. The phrase is also used to mean something other than what the LIS field considers to be the management of information resources. It is used as an abbreviation for the management of IT, information systems management, management information systems, etc.

Rowley (1998) proposes four different levels of information management: information retrieval, information systems, information contexts and information environments. Effective information management needs to address issues at all of these levels. Choo (2002, 24) defines information management as 'a continuous cycle of six closely related activities [so that the organization learns and adapts to its changing environment]: identification of information needs, information acquisition, information organization and storage, developing information products and services, information distribution, and information use'.

Kirk (1999) developed a hierarchy of the definitions of IM based on Braman's (1989) concepts of information developed in the area of information policy studies as follows: IT systems, information resource management, IM as aligning information strategy and business strategy, and integrating strategy formation and information.

The diversity of the field is illustrated by a visualization tool, RefViz, which uses term–term association measures and is an add-on to EndNote. In all, 492 references to papers published between 1999 and 2004 with the term *information management* in the title were downloaded from Web of Science. Of these, 462 had sufficient information for RefViz to use: Figure 2.1 shows the results.

The clustering of papers is not particularly tight and many groups have very few associated papers. The largest groups are: 18, dealing with information systems development aspects of IM; 13, information systems modelling; 12, health information management; 17, user services development; and 8, medical patients' databases. Schlögl (2003), employing multidimensional scaling in a bibliometric study to find the structure of the information management field, mapped three main areas: IT management, information content management and knowledge management.

Several authors have discussed IM in research and education. Anderton (1986), Lytle (1988) and Wilson (2003) present reflections on the subject and note the confusion over the educational base of IM as well as the distinct differences from the traditional LIS and information science education. Fairer-Wessels (1997), through

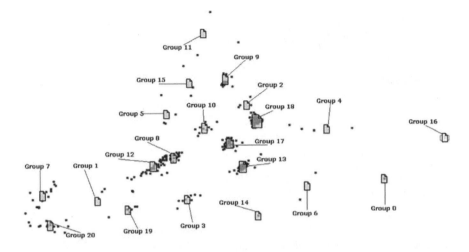

Figure 2.1   Visualization of the IM literature

an extended review of literature on the educational issues, comes to the conclusion that the present paradigm of information management 'over-specialization' has resulted in a fragmented approach with various focuses on one or another component: information processing, management information systems or managing IT. She argues for a more holistic paradigm in IM studies to reflect the interdisciplinarity of the field. Macevičiūtė (2002) discovered two approaches to IM education in the UK, Scandinavia and the Baltic States: one is holistic, enabling the acquisition of the core competencies of at least three professional groups (domain expert, information expert, IT expert and management expert); the other is an integrating approach, focusing on development of the competence of one professional group and including elements that allow communication with the other professionals. More recently, Maes (2003) has described the integration of IM teaching into the programmes of the Graduate Business School at the University of Amsterdam, pointing to the necessary relationship between research and teaching.

The definition of *information management* chosen for this study is that proposed by Wilson (2003):

The application of management principles to the acquisition, organization, control, dissemination and use of information relevant to the effective operation of organizations of all kinds. 'Information' here refers to all types of information of value, whether having their origin inside or outside the organization, including data resources, such as production data; records and files related, for example, to the personnel function; market research data; and competitive intelligence from a wide range of sources. Information management deals with the value, quality, ownership, use and security of information in the context of organizational performance.

Data collection

In 1989 Wilson reviewed the three main journals publishing articles on IM. At that time the core journals in the field were:

*   *International Journal of Information Management*
*   *Management Information Systems Quarterly*
*   *Information Management Review.*

This work inspired our 2000 study into changes that occurred in the field during the decade 1989–2000. A follow-up study in 2004 assessed the period 2000–2004. The easiest way to establish the changes would be to compare the categories that emerged in 1989 with the categories that emerge in any new study. Consequently, a survey of the contents of the core journals was repeated in 2000 and 2004. However, the group of journals has changed considerably. First, *Information Management Review* ceased publication. Therefore, other publications were included in the core group. The main criterion for selection was the profile of research articles. It had to match more or less the profile of the three 1989 journals, i.e., most of the articles should deal with information activity in organizations. Therefore, journals such as *Information Management and Processing* were not included as the bulk of its articles are on information retrieval issues and only approximately 5% deal with other information-related topics.

Six journals published in 2000 and 2004 were selected:[1]

*   *Information Economics and Policy* (IEP; vol. 12, issues 1–4; vol. 16, issues 1–4)
*   Information & Management (I&M; vol. 37, issues 1–6; vol. 38, issues 1–4; vol. 41, issues 3–8; vol. 42, issue 1)
*   *Information and Organization* (IO; before 2001 *Accounting, Management and Information Technologies*; vol. 10, issues 1–4; vol. 14, issues 1–4)
*   *International Journal of Information Management* (IJIM; vol. 20, issues 1–6; vol. 24, issues 1–6)

---

[1] The journal *Information & Management* displays an irregular pattern of publication: a volume can consist of four or eight issues, cover a part of the year or spread over two years. A full volume of *Information & Management* in 2000 consists of six issues, but two issues of volume 38 were also published in 2000; the articles received in 1999 and the beginning of 2000 appear in the next two issues (nos 3 and 4). In 2004, issues 3–8 of volume 41 and the first issue of volume 42 appeared. The *International Journal of Information Management* appears bi-monthly; the rest are quarterlies.

- *Journal of Strategic Information Systems* (JSIS; vol. 9, issues 1–4; vol. 12, issue 4; vol. 13, issues 1–3)
- *MIS Quarterly* (MQ; vol. 24, issues 1–4; vol. 28, issues 1–4).

The contents of the research articles in 2000 were analysed using the headings that emerged in 1989 and the resulting indexing list was used for analysis of the articles in 2004. Book reviews and editorials were omitted. New headings or sub-headings were added when necessary. Both authors indexed all articles in 2004 and, on a six-point scale, found an average agreement in the indexing of 4.75. Further discussion resolved the differences. The headings indicate the main subjects of the article. Not more than three headings were assigned to an article if the subject was complex. In addition, the research methods and the institution of the authors were studied, paying attention to affiliation, country, and number of authors of the article. A total of 150 papers was chosen for analysis in 2000, while the same journals gave rise to 190 papers in 2004. The distribution of papers over journals is shown in Table 2.1.

Table 2.1 The number of articles in selected journals

Title	Number of articles	
	2000	2004
Information Economics and Policy (IEP)	20	29
Information & Management (I&M)	48	72
Information and Organization (IO)	11	15
International Journal of Information Management (IJIM)	33	35
Journal of Strategic Information Systems (JSIS)	15	17
MIS Quarterly (MQ)	23	22
Total	150	190

Results and discussion

Contents

The review of the research field in the 1980s revealed five main categories (the full list can be found in Wilson, 1989:

- economics of information
- information management practice
  — application areas
- information systems and technology
  — artificial intelligence
  — systems theory

- information policy and strategy
- information use and users.

The comparison of subject categories found in 2000 and 2004 with those from the 1989 study reveals new or expanded areas. Most of the research areas present in the 1980s remain. There is a significant reduction in attention to systems theory, although a systemic approach is often applied, and the interest in AI applications declined considerably (only two articles were found in 2000 and none in 2004). Also, in 2004 articles on education for IM totally disappear.

The main changes can be summarized as follows:

1 In the economics of information a shift to market economics is evident. In 2000 the greatest attention was paid to ways of increasing competitive advantage, aiding business strategies through IT, commercial and corporate usage of information networks, and the economic implications of information systems. In 2004 e-commerce is the research topic that shows the biggest increase (from 11 articles in 2000 to 36 in 2004). The economic aspect is present in at least one-third (34%) of all articles in 2000 and 2004.

2 In 2004 interest in IM functions and in strategic issues of IM in general has declined; papers on strategic issues are now more widely distributed over specialized areas, such as ICT (including networks and the telecommunications industry) and information systems. Papers on this topic are found in all of the journals.

3 An increasing concern with organizational culture, environment and human issues was visible in 2000. Organizational environment and learning were investigated as the factors influencing IT usage (five articles). In 2004 interest in these issues was decreasing (three articles vs. 13). As with IM functions, these areas are now present mainly as the second categories in articles on information systems or information technology.

4 Different aspects of information users' behaviour gained priority over the previously dominating information needs research (no articles with the primary category of information needs were found in 2000). In 2004 research focused on consumer behaviour on the internet and information sharing.

5 An entirely new category has emerged: information professionals. Researchers have realized that the professional behaviour of information systems and software developers, IT officers, information managers, librarians, etc. can influence the quality of products and services and has to be taken into account.

6 The information systems area is changing in the same direction: human factors, the impact of organizational environment and culture, and users' involvement and satisfaction gain more attention than previously. IS evaluation and quality issues, users' satisfaction and information usage interest

researchers of database systems, decision support systems, group support systems and other software (especially groupware, which emerges as a new category). The conclusions of Claver et al. (2000, 186) that 'there is decreasing interest in subjects focusing on systems development in favour of managerial topics, which have received the most attention since 1996' is also supported.

7 Information networking, the internet and intranets gain attention on various levels (from individual users' behaviour to macroeconomic issues). This category naturally did not exist in 1989 and is the only one of the new categories that by 2000 had expanded to almost the same size as the categories of information systems or IM functions. It also grew considerably between 2000 and 2004 (75 articles vs. 30). E-commerce, internet usage, issues regarding websites, internet-based systems, and consumer behaviour are major topics within this category.

8 Telecommunication policies are the main concern of information policy research with a strong emphasis on the telecommunications market and services regulation. An issue of *IEP* that published material from a *Symposium on Universal Service Obligation and Competition* introduced this topic into the analysis in 2000 (vol. 12, issue 3). In 2004 articles on telecommunication policy and industry also appeared in IJIM.

9 Application areas have proliferated significantly. In 1989 only six application areas were listed. Most of them remain, although interest in government applications appears to have declined, and banking and the financial sector in general has become the area of greatest interest. Health care and medicine still appears as a dominant area in the general IM periodicals, though many specialized journals are published for this sub-field. In addition, interest in the book trade, commerce, education, engineering and construction, environmental policy, heritage preservation, manufacturing, port and post office applications, share trading, the air force and the airline industry has emerged or strengthened.

10 Knowledge management emerged as a new term rather than a new field in 2000 – the papers generally concern the influence of human factors or organizational cultures on information transfer, etc. Most of these papers concentrate on issues of human resources and organizational learning and were given a different primary category. The number of articles on knowledge management (even with the original titles given by authors) significantly declined in 2004. Only four articles were indexed with a secondary category of knowledge management that year (vs. nine in 2000).

11 There are also several cross-category headings that indicate researchers' interest in security issues (ten articles), outsourcing strategies (eight articles), information sharing (six articles), and virtual technologies (five articles).

Each of the selected journals has, of course, its area of interest. The dominating subjects are listed in Table 2.2. In many cases the articles deal with complicated subjects that cannot be described by one category; therefore, the number of articles in dominating areas may be higher than the overall number of articles in the journal.

Table 2.2   Profiles of analysed journals

Title	Dominating subjects	
	2000	2004
Information Economics and Policy	Information policy: telecommunications (13 articles) Economics of information (4 articles)	Telecommunication industry: market (13) Economics of information: intellectual property (7)
Information & Management	Information systems (22) Information networks (7) Information management functions (5) Information use and users (3)	Information networks: e-commerce (24) Information systems: human and organizational factors (12) Information use and users (10) Information technology: strategy (7)
Information and Organization	Organizational learning and culture (7) Information systems (3)	Theory and research methods (6) Information systems: research (5)
International Journal of Information Management	Information management functions (9) Information systems (8) Information networks (4) Information use and users (4) Education for information (3)	Information networks (22) (Information networks: internet: e-commerce – 10) Information systems (17) Information technology (9)
Journal of Strategic Information Systems	Information systems (6) Information technology (4) Organizational culture (2)	Information technology (10) Information systems (7) Information management functions (4)
MIS Quarterly	Information systems (9) Information technology (7) Information professionals (4)	Information systems (15) Information technology (5) Information networks (4) Information professionals (4)

Table 2.2 shows also that most of the journals tend to retain their profile though certain subjects may shift positions in different years. It seems that one of the major factors that determines these shifts is publication of issues on special topics. Thus the theory and research methods category gains first position in IO in 2004 because of its issue 3 being devoted to action research; intellectual property strongly dominates in IEP because of issue 1 (special issue on Innovation, Competition, Standards and Intellectual Property); and JSIS vol. 12, no. 4 is devoted to the LEO conference on business computing. The journal that has a considerably changed profile between 2000 and 2004 is IJIM, which appears to have stopped publishing papers on IM functions and use. E-commerce and information systems were the dominating topics in 2004 in this journal.

Research methods

- Overall, 32 research methods were listed as used in research presented in the analysed journals.
- In 2000 a shift in methodology from positivist to qualitative methods was reg- istered. Case studies pervaded the areas of information systems, IT and IM functions research, with major application of unstructured and semi-structured interviews, document analysis, ethnographic observation and other qualitative methods of data collection. This is no longer the case, as the analysis of 2004 shows. Economic modelling and questionnaire surveys with consequent sta- tistical analysis prevail. Qualitative methods such as case studies are still popular (32 articles) but not used as frequently as earlier.
- The increasing interest in organizational cultures resulted in more cross-cul- tural studies in 2000. In 2004 this trend declined in the analysed journals. Instead, laboratory experiments and online data analysis occur more often.

Authors

The investigated articles were written by 315 authors in 2000 and by 383 in 2004 (see Table 2.3 on next page).

In 2000, 38 articles (25%) were published by a single author, the rest by two or more authors. In 2004 a more detailed analysis of the authorship was made. It shows that 41% of all the articles are written by two authors, 31% by one author and 28% by three or more authors. Table 2.3 shows the numbers and percentages of differ- ent authorship patterns in each journal. Single author articles dominate in 2004 in JSIS (53%), while two author articles dominate MQ (59%) and the largest num- ber of articles by three and more authors appears in IJIM (34%). The overall pattern of publishing in this respect is consistent with the pattern that usually occurs in social science journals (cf. Endersby, 1996).

Table 2.3   Number of authors per article

Title	Number of authors 2000		2004			
	1	2+	1	2	3	4+
Information Economics and Policy	10	10	12	14	2	1
	(50%)	(50%)	(42%)	(48%)	(7%)	(3%)
Information & Management	7	41	15	34	15	8
	(15%)	(85%)	(21%)	(47%)	(21%)	(11%)
Information and Organization	4	7	7	5	1	2
	(37%)	(63%)	(47%)	(33%)	(7%)	(13%)
International Journal of Information Management	10	23	13	10	10	2
	(30%)	(70%)	(37%)	(29%)	(29%)	(5%)
Journal of Strategic Information Systems	2	13	9	3	4	1
	(13%)	(87%)	(53%)	(18%)	(23%)	(6%)
MIS Quarterly	5	18	2	13	4	3
	(22%)	(78%)	(9%)	(59%)	(18%)	(14%)
Total	38	112	58	79	36	17
	(25%)	(75%)	(31%)	(41%)	(19%)	(9%)

The majority of the authors are affiliated to universities. Some come from business-based research units and from other research institutions. Most of those affiliated to universities come from business, management, finance and economic departments (55%) and from computing and information systems departments (32%); approximately 7% of authors belong to information management or LIS departments. In fact, there is no big difference between the journals as far as the subject affiliation of the authors is concerned. The only exception may be IJIM, which in 2000 published more articles written by staff from information studies and LIS departments; however in 2004 only three of their authors came from this field.

Regarding country of origin of the authors, there are two American-dominated journals: MQ (77% authors from the USA in 2000 and 73% in 2004), I&M (57% in 2000 and 54% in 2004). In JSIS, 53% of authors were from the USA in 2000 but in 2004 the USA contributions dropped to 16%. Less US dominated is IO (38% in 2000 and 43% in 2004) and IEP (21% in 2000 and 28% in 2004). Authors from the UK are more frequently published in IJIM (48% in 2000 and 32% in 2004) and JSIS (26% in 2004). However the range of the representatives from different countries is increasing. In 2000 the authors were affiliated to institutions in 22 different countries; in 2004 this rose to 29 different countries.

There are some interesting changes in the top ten countries in 2000 and 2004, as shown in Table 2.4 – particularly, the rise of the Netherlands to third place from eighth and Taiwan to fourth place from tenth. Several countries such as Australia, Canada and Singapore keep a similar level of publication in the analysed journals. Norway, New Zealand, Denmark and Italy appeared on the top list in 2004, while Finland, South Korea and Hong Kong disappeared. It is clear why not a single article was published by Hong Kong authors in 2004 (there are six authors from China on the list), but much more difficult to understand why Finnish authors have disappeared from the list totally. There are also 12 new countries in the total list in 2004 while five have disappeared.

Table 2.4   Ten countries with the highest number of authors

Rank	2000 Country	Authors No.	%	2004 Country	Authors No.	%
I	USA	143	45.4	USA (1)	172	40.1
2	UK	46	14.6	UK (2)	57	20.5
3	Australia	16	5.1	Netherlands (8)	21	4.9
4	South Korea	15	4.8	Taiwan (10)	18	4.2
5	Singapore	14	4.4	Canada (7)	17	4.0
6	Hong Kong	13	4.1	Australia (3)	14	3.3
7	Canada	12	3.8	Norway (–)	9	2.1
8	Netherlands	10	3.2	Singapore (5)	9	2.1
9	Finland	10	3.2	New Zealand (–)	8	1.9
10	Taiwan	7	2.2	Denmark and Italy (–)	7	1.8

Note: No. in parentheses by the country name in 2004 is the 2000 ranking

In 2004 I&M published articles written by authors from 15 countries, IJIM from 14, IEP from 13, JSIS from 10, MQ from six, and IO from four countries.

Thus, we see that the authors come not only from more diverse disciplines (e.g., management, computer science, information retrieval, information systems, library and information science, consultancy sectors, economics, etc.) but from a wider geographical spread (in addition to those in the list we found India, Brunei, Malaysia, Saudi Arabia, Nigeria, Venezuela, Switzerland, Belgium, Brazil, Israel, South Africa, Egypt, France, Germany, Greece, Japan, Spain, Sweden and Turkey). However, US and UK researchers continue to dominate.

Conclusion

In the 1980s IM was emergent and perceived by some to be a re-write of traditional librarianship. However, it has continued to thrive and much of what is now included is far removed even from modern information science, although IM draws upon ideas from both librarianship and information science. In one form or another it is likely to persist in the future, since information problems are likely to persist in organizations. The means for resolving the problems may change, but the need to understand those problems and develop solutions will remain.

At present there is a visible subordination of IM functions to the information systems, information networks and information technology areas in the analysed journals. This may be attributed to a number of factors: the increasing significance of technology in the management of information, resulting from the development of the internet, the world wide web, digital libraries and the like; a change of focus in research financing by international and national bodies; and changes in priorities in research, especially in the UK, as a result of institutions seeking to satisfy the demands of the Research Assessment Exercise. Whatever the changes and whatever the reasons, however, the journals seem to draw on very similar research production and begin to lose their originally distinctive profiles.

3

Business information culture: a qualitative study of the information culture in the Finnish insurance industry

Gunilla Widén-Wulff

Introduction

Information as a resource in an organization should be supported by an open and active information culture. This project is a study of different information cultures existing in a selection of Finnish insurance businesses. The study explores how different information cultures are structured and how they function, and brings forth some answers to the question, 'When does information become a resource in a business company?' Companies are often aware of the fact that information is an important resource, but only a few concrete measures of how to use this resource exist. In this study, the companies are evaluated according to the hypothesis that a company with a rich and active information culture and with the different parts of the learning organization integrated is also a financially successful business (Widén-Wulff, 2001).

Information culture is difficult to define and is often described in the context of information technology (IT), suggesting that organizations solve their information problems by buying IT equipment. In fact, IT is only part of the whole information culture, and effective IM is about helping people to make effective use of the information, rather than the machines (Davenport, 1994).

An understanding of information culture must be built on several cornerstones: first, the information environment must be explored, as information culture can be seen as a part of the whole organizational culture. In short, the function of organizational culture is to keep up the corporate identity and make it possible for employees to understand and be committed to organizational aims. Its function is also to keep the balance in the social system and create meaning and contents (Juuti, 1994, 23). The information environment is shaped by the behaviour, attitudes and openness to information among the employees. However, evaluation of and attitudes towards information also depend on the organization's situation (Ginman, 1987, 222). The information profile must be officially confirmed so that the executive becomes aware of the importance of information (Ginman, 1987, 231).

Second, information culture is about managing the substance and the knowledge base of the organization, that is, supporting a learning organization. An organization analyses the environment, interprets what is observed and frames its own opinions. Cronin and Davenport (1993) define these processes as *social intelligence*. Social intelligence is a multi-faceted concept composed of activities (locating, validating, analysing), content (tacit knowledge, rumour), and capabilities (information infrastructure, literacy). The raw material comprises publications, reports, oral texts, etc. but the important part is to be able to interpret the material. Social intelligence is about life-long learning where the participants are active instead of passive (Ginman, 1995).

Finally, information culture is about having access to and using information as a resource for the knowledge base throughout the organization. The individual is the most important part in this multidimensional knowledge processing (cf. Nonaka, 1994; Senge, 1990). Knowledge creation happens when information is anchored in the information holder's conviction and understanding. It is an interaction between information, experience and rationality. From the organizational point of view, teamwork and middle management have a special role in this interaction (Nonaka, 1994). Information culture is responsible for unwritten, unconscious behaviour and fills the gap between what has officially happened and what really happened (Ginman, 1987, 24).

In this study, information culture is described as a context in which needed information is communicated so that the company has the greatest possible use of internal and external information. This culture consists of individuals, traditions, systems and values. The aim is to show how these factors together create the context in which the information is regarded as an important resource for fulfilling corporate goals.

Empirical analysis

When studying information culture it is advantageous to look at companies from the same field. Grönhaug and Haukedal (1988) give an example of two companies in the shipping business; they have the same environment, with the same trends, risks, etc. It was shown that the two companies interpreted environmental influences very differently, devised very different strategies and, therefore, their results were also very different from each other. It was concluded that internal factors affected their business behaviour more than external factors: that is, the information culture, the attitudes and the traditions of the company.

The material for this study consists of interviews in 15 Finnish insurance businesses, which is a representative number of companies for the whole insurance business market in Finland. Two or three people in each company were interviewed. Managers at the top level, the marketing level and the production level were interviewed. Questions covered: individuality, company aims, motivation, communication, information technology, knowledge creation, innovation and information management. The insurance business was selected because these companies are information-intensive in their activities, in which information management is very important. The people working in such organizations are often specialists and experts. The activities and products of insurance companies are built on specialist knowledge and, therefore, it is interesting to look at how the information culture is structured in this field.

The case study method was used to analyse the material, in order to ground the analytical concepts in the material. Case studies are used to interpret a particular set of events in a believable manner, where the events are put into a social or historical complexity (Andersen, 1997, 19; Gummesson, 1988, 75). In this study, theory is used as a base and a tool for the interpretation of the material; it is important to have a clear theoretical model as a frame when the research process and analysis has so few standardized rules (Andersen, 1997, 20). The companies are studied as different cases, and from these cases a broader view and understanding of the insurance business information culture is created.

The analysis was conducted in five stages.

- Stage 1: Analysis of information environment
- Stage 2: Analysis of the learning organization
- Stage 3: Analysis of information as a resource
- Stage 4: From stages 1–3 the picture of different information cultures has been built up
- Stage 5: Comparison of information cultures and business performance.

Information environment

The information environment constitutes the first cornerstone of the analysis of information culture. The dimension of open vs. closed organization environments was chosen as the starting point in this analysis, because information aspects are best seen in this dimension of organizations (cf. Blackler, 1995; Correia and Wilson, 1997; Dewhirst, 1971; Hofstede, 1991; Miller, 1994). Dividing the companies into the categories of open or closed environments makes the material more manageable for further analysis. This study was conducted through an analysis of six factors as measures of how open or closed the organizations were. The six factors were: the scale of change in the company, co-operation, teamwork, education, company aims and middle management's role in the company.

These factors are further divided into two, open vs. closed, with a scale of 1—5 representing the following levels of openness in the information environment: 1 = closed, 2 = fairly closed, 3 = middle, 4 = fairly open and 5 = open. Table 3.1 shows the measures adopted for these factors.

Table 3.1   Scales used for the measurement of open and closed organizations

	Closed	Open
1 Scale of change in the company	No reorganizations	Reorganization in processes Reorganization in structures New employees in central positions
2 Co-operation between units	Low information exchange Protection of one's preserves Very few forms of co-operation	Actively work for co-operation Tools: teamwork, groups based on people from different units, process thinking, customer friendly thinking, open office landscape, seminars and training
3 Teamwork	Uncritical of teamwork Not inclined to go in for it in full	Team learning Developing knowledge, expert groups and team training Look at how the teamwork fits into own organization
4 Education	Training suggestions made mainly by the personnel Shortage of time for training Falls behind developments	The training is planned, multifaceted and supported at all levels Open interest from the personnel
5 Company aims	Company aims are not very well known	Company aims are well known
6 Middle management's role	Looks only at own operative activities	Active role as an information and communication link Experts Creators of a motivating environment

The result of this analysis was that the companies were divided into three groups: closed environments (three firms), open environments (four firms) and a group of eight firms lying between these extremes. It must be remembered, however, that the companies are individual and their internal environments cannot be generalized, but some description of the defined keys for analysis (the six factors) can be made.

The overall picture of the companies with a closed environment is that they struggle with an old and more traditional company culture. It is commonly a fact that these companies' aims are formulated in general terms and disseminated on only a few occasions. With unclear corporate aims, the possibilities for shared values are poor and internal co-operation, teamwork and education become less effective.

The open companies have gone through major organizational changes and the company aims, therefore, have been stressed more explicitly. The personnel seem to be more a part of the organization as individuals, and the functioning teamwork and co-operation is a result of many years of work.

The learning organization

The second cornerstone of information culture is concerned with how organizations manage to build up their knowledge base and social intelligence. Organizational learning is a result of motivation and interest. In order to achieve successful organizational learning there must be both opportunity and willingness to learn and develop (Ruohotie, 1998, 132), and mutual understanding where needs and opportunities correspond. Organizational learning takes place through individuals and the learning activities of the individual must then correspond to the organizational aims (Argyris et al., 1996, 123).

Thus, individual visions are important and, at the same time, these have to be incorporated into the organizational visions and aims (Cronin and Davenport, 1993; Koenig, 1998; Nonaka and Takeuchi, 1995; Senge, 1990).

The theoretical key for the analysis of the learning organization is constructed from aspects of human and intellectual capital. In this study, human capital is divided into the following categories: creativity, motivation and development. Intellectual capital is described through the company's individuality (core competencies) and how the company views knowledge creation and how that can be supported by technology, communication networks and information management.

It was found that the different parts of the learning organization function quite differently in the three groups of internal environments. Co-operation is valued differently, which is described through the internal environment. It is not valued in closed environments whereas it is a key factor in open environments. Parts of the learning organization such as creativity, individual learning and communication networks are more visible in the open environments.

The theoretical framework suggests that creativity, motivation and learning are processes that need support from many levels in the organization. Support from management is especially important, but the creation of common strategies and values and interesting staff in these processes is also underlined in the theoretical framework (cf. Andreau and Ciborra, 1995; Ruohotie, 1998).

Table 3.2 gives a short summary of the support of the learning organization in the three different groups of internal environments.

Table 3.2   Learning organization attributes in different information environments

Closed environments ($n = 3$)	Human capital is difficult to use in closed environments when the aims of the processes are vague, resulting in isolated processes. Knowledge is valued as ideal and, at the same time, it is concluded that knowledge organization should be more effective. Details are focused on, rather than communication of a broader view. Core competencies are well defined, but there are only a few measures to value and develop them. An integrated basis for knowledge creation is missing. Instead, there are several isolated processes. This applies also to technology, communication networks and information management efforts in the companies.
Open environments ($n = 4$)	Creativity is a very strong component. There are official channels for creativity, but these companies underline even further the creative atmosphere in the company. Interactivity and active communication support the creativity and motivation processes. Knowledge is strongly emphasized. The versatility of knowledge is underlined as well as its content and communication in the company. The core competencies are well defined and so are the measures for evaluating and developing them. Continuity, technology and the ability to change are the most central factors in these processes.
Middle group ($n = 8$)	Middle companies have come into an active phase, defining their core competencies and developing tools for their maintenance. The work with individuality is even more active than in the open companies. The tools for evaluating the core competencies exist, but in order to use the core competencies even more effectively, the middle companies need multidimensional co-operation.

Information as a resource

Information culture is about the role of information as a resource, evaluated through its use in different business processes, such as strategic planning, marketing and production (see Table 3.3). It is also about gaining access to the knowledge held by individuals in the company, since those individuals are the 'knowledge processors' of the organization. Discovering what people know and incorporating that knowledge into the strategic planning process is especially difficult (cf. Houser and Shamir, 1993; Nonaka, 1994).

Table 3.3   Information as a resource in different information environments

Closed environments (n = 3)	The different business processes involve some key persons, but an overall communication of these processes is missing.
	Strategic planning is a normative process and does not involve levels other than the top management. The result of the process is discussed from the top down. This also applies to the marketing and the production processes.
	The responsibility for communicating the processes is unclear, and the networks are not built for systematic communication. Different projects to develop communication and improve knowledge of these processes exist (e.g., quality projects, different meeting cultures and better internal education). These projects are still in their beginning phase or in a planning phase, and their results were unclear.
Open environments (n = 4)	Communication regarding business activities has existed for a long period of time.
	When new company guidelines are drawn up, several channels are used in order to involve individuals in this planning. It has been concluded that it is very difficult to use the individual level of knowledge in this process, but interest and willingness among the personnel (regarding themes of interest directly for the personnel) were mentioned as important ingredients. Further value discussions and evaluation of the processes are important. Finally, a common language for both the management and the personnel is needed. The information that is produced in these processes is important for the whole company.

Continued on next page

Table 3.3   *(continued)*

	The open companies see themselves as expert organizations where everyone is an expert. For example, product development is a part of the strategic planning and is communicated in that way. In these companies, internal education is underlined as a communication channel.
Middle group (*n* = 8)	The middle group has similar difficulties to the closed companies when it comes to communicating business activities. Though these companies underline the role of units and departments in communication and evaluation, strategic planning is the responsibility of the top management. The aims of the different business processes are pointed out and clarified for all personnel. Education and interactive communication are pointed out in the communication processes.

The perspective taken on business activities has also been shown to be an important factor in other studies. In the dissertation by de Heer (1999, 241) Finnish log-house exporters were interviewed, and the study shows that the motivated and experienced companies emphasized proactive behaviour, integrating the opinions of customers in their own activities and information behaviour. Motivation is a very important factor for open information behaviour. Furthermore, an outward organizational culture and integration of the socio-cultural values in the export country with the producer country culture were needed. In general, a hermeneutic way of thinking in a company was thought of as an important starting point for being able actively to map the threats and opportunities. This is underlined by Alfino (1998), who points out that collective responsibility and a shared perspective by decision-makers in a company reduces the hindrances to the communication of information. This is probably the case for all processes in the company.

Different information cultures

The aim of this study was to explore how different information cultures are structured and to see when information becomes a resource in a business organization. Information culture was reviewed by looking at aspects of the information environment and the learning organization, and how information is communicated in different work processes. It is concluded that there exist three kinds of information culture in Finnish insurance companies: see Table 3.4.

Table 3.4	Different information cultures in the studied insurance companies, and which part of the knowledge capital (Koenig, 1998) they emphasize
Supportive information culture	A supportive company culture strives to create a safe environment for personnel where there is no need to be afraid of changes (Wallach, 1983). The closed companies have a supportive information culture where tradition and safety are underlined. These emphasize knowledge in different parts of the infrastructure. They handle the information in the processes but not interactively between them.
Innovative information culture	An innovative culture is alert to changes and flexibility (Wallach, 1983). The open companies with an innovative information culture underline change and continuity. Social capital is the part of knowledge capital that is emphasized, as well as the networking aspects of human and intellectual capital and learning.
Administrative information culture	An administrative culture is based on systematic thinking and clear division of responsibility and power, with old traditions in business activities (Wallach, 1983). The companies in the middle have mostly an administrative information culture. They point out their core competencies and a systematic development of them where the role of the units is underlined. Knowledge resources are the part of knowledge capital that is underlined, i.e. communication channels, and the measures for core competencies and their development.

Information culture and business success

But what is the role of information culture in connection with financial solidity?

In 1998, when the empirical material for this study was collected, the market for the Finnish insurance business was generally good. Consequently, differences in the business success of the companies were small, and the critical success factors were not so visible. The measurement of business success was based on the companies' annual reports from 1996–1998. It was difficult to compare the financial figures between the 15 different insurance companies exactly because they are different in size and insurance trades. Therefore, five key criteria were used for the analysis of the business success:

1 Market share: the share of the total market for insurance products.
2 Solvency: an insurance company should have a solvency position that is sufficient to fulfil its obligations to policyholders and other parties. Regulations

to promote solvency include minimum capital and surplus requirements, statutory accounting conventions, limits to insurance company investment and corporate activities, financial ratio tests and financial data disclosure.

3   Expense ratio: the percentage of each premium euro that goes to insurers' expenses including overheads, marketing and commissions.
4   Net investment income: income generated by the investment of assets.
5   Difference between current and book values on investment activities.

The key figures were assessed on a three-point scale (0–2 points) relating to how successful the key criterion was for the company (not successful, rather successful and very successful). The maximum score of a company's business success was 10.

Figure 3.1 shows that the innovative information cultures show a common pattern of high business success. However, it is important to remember that the external environment plays an important role, and a more passive, supportive information culture suits a stable external environment, whereas the role of the information culture grows in change-intensive environments. The insurance business in Finland is in a turbulent phase, but in this field of business there are also more and less turbulent markets in which the companies operate.

Information culture and business success

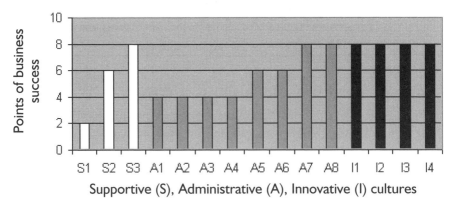

Figure 3.1   Information culture and business success

Conclusions

Earlier studies concluded that the success factors of a business lie in several areas. Owens and Wilson (1997), who have analysed corporate success and information use, point at several external factors (market, branch nature, changes in legislation and competitor profiles) and several internal factors (internal politics, effective information systems, technology, knowledge base, information ethos, quality, profitability, productivity and export success). This study gives some complements to Owens and Wilson's factors. The manageability and especially the interaction of the factors highlighted from the information culture are important. It is also important to underline how this interaction functions in the organization. An active information culture seems to be an ingredient of financial stability, although it is not possible to say clearly that an active information culture is a given success factor.

While there are different kinds of information culture among the insurance businesses and they adapt differently, it is important to know what kind of culture exists in a company in order to adjust information work and planning accordingly. Open, changing companies can more easily shape an active information culture, because the integration of processes and functions is working well. This means that the planning of processes is strongly integrated and solutions can be created for the whole company. Because of the integration of processes, more active communication between the units is created.

However, all insurance companies are information-intensive organizations, and the management of intellectual capital is especially important. Intellectual capital was underlined by all the companies analysed and it seems that today's trend is to strive for an active information culture in order to be able to handle better the demands of change and the rich information flow (e.g., Koenig, 1998; Owens and Wilson, 1997). The insurance business as a whole is in an active development phase, which brings changes at several levels (products, technology, laws, economy, etc.). Because of these changes, time loss is a common problem in insurance companies and becomes a hindrance to developing a more active information culture. At the same time, those companies which are better suited to change are in a better position.

An active information culture can have many advantages. Communication of information becomes more effective in the company and, in the long run, there will be sizeable effects on customer contacts also. Companies naturally strive to maintain as good a relationship as possible with their customers. The common language in the company is mirrored in customer relations, and in the insurance business it is especially important to use a common and straightforward language with customers. In an active information culture, where processes and activities are integrated, the possibilities for creating and communicating a common language are improved. An active information culture can also have negative effects. It is more difficult to keep up a unified picture if the company goes through rapid changes. An active information culture provides the potential to change quickly, but if the whole organization is affected, the organization's culture is a factor that cannot be changed so quickly. Therefore, contradictions easily occur, something which is often problematic for the personnel.

It is important to consider the information culture in information-intensive companies such as insurance companies. There is no strong economic connection, but it probably has financial implications in the long run. Information culture and success require integrated planning activities in the whole organization, as well as well-communicated aims. Information and the knowledge base must be used effectively through co-operation between individuals, units and management, resulting in good synergy. The even more specialized business world of today needs an information culture in which it is possible to keep together the knowledge base and the social capital. Integrated thought – involving everyone – is important, leading to good results.

Part B
Information behaviour

Introduction

Within information science, the field of information behaviour has emerged as a significant sub-discipline in terms of volume of research and publication. The area has been defined as:

> the totality of human behavior in relation to sources and channels of information, including both active and passive information seeking, and information use. Thus, it includes face to face communication with others, as well as the passive reception of information as in, for example, watching TV advertisements, without any intention to act on the information given. (Wilson, 2000)

It includes information-seeking behaviour, information search behaviour and information use. Researchers look into various types of information-seeking, use and searching within certain situations and contexts. They try to distinguish not only certain stages and components of behaviour, but also find the external and internal factors influencing these as well as the variables that are determined by certain information behaviour characteristics. This effort to reveal the interactions between individual, group or organizational information behaviour and internal and external conditions and factors distinguishes the newest trend in the area from earlier investigations of users' interactions with information systems only.

The field is diverse, with investigations of subjects as different as primary school children, law students and senior business managers. The methods used are equally diverse, but there is a strong focus on qualitative methods and analytical techniques based on the tools of 'grounded theory'.

The chapters presented here have been selected because they deal with different areas of investigation and, to some extent, use different tools and methodological perspectives.

The first chapter, 'Determining organizational information needs: the critical success factors approach', by Maija-Leena Huotari and T. D. Wilson, illustrates the application of a well-established technique from the management field to understanding information needs in a variety of different settings: university heads of departments, a pharmaceutical company, a publishing firm and the management structure of a university. The work, over several projects, illustrated the value of the CSF technique in eliciting information needs.

Aiki Tibar applied the same technique in her study, 'Critical success factors and information needs in industry: an Estonian study', which investigated 16 manufacturing companies. Tibar found that Huotari's findings relating to the emergence of information management as a critical success factor were supported in her work.

Finally, 'Experiencing information seeking and learning: research on patterns of variation' by Louise Limberg examines information behaviour in the context of a task undertaken by students in a Swedish school, using the qualitative research techniques of phenomenography. The approach here is very different from that of the previous two chapters and serves to illustrate that research purpose and research method are inextricably linked.

These three chapters only touch upon the information behaviour field and an excellent overview of the field can be found in *Looking for Information*, by Donald O. Case (Academic Press, 2002). The field is also supported by an excellent conference series, *Information Seeking in Context*, the published proceedings of which can be found in Vakkari et al. (1997), Wilson and Allen (1999), *The New Review of Information Behaviour Research* volumes 1, 2, 3 and 4, and *Information Research* volume 10, issues 1 and 2 (available at http://informationr.net/ir/).

4

Determining organizational information needs: the critical success factors approach

Maija-Leena Huotari and T. D. Wilson

Introduction

Human information behaviour is human activity that enables people to access, organize and use information. It includes steps taken to gain access as well as passive reception of information which then, or later, turns out to be of use (Wilson, 1999). We define organizational information behaviour in the same way: organizations design systems and services to acquire, share and disseminate information of all kinds, from production data from factories to events in the marketplace. However, information also reaches the organization by many routes that are not designed for information acquisition. For example, the salesman in the field collects information on competing firms, and the CEO learns of the market difficulties of competitors when playing golf. In other words, organizational (or corporate) information behaviour embraces not only the formal systems set up to manage internal information flows, but also the systems – including libraries and information centres designed to access external information, as well as the organizational and personal communication systems – through which information reaches the organization and is disseminated.

In relation to this complex of interacting systems and habits, the literature on corporate information needs is noticeably less extensive than the literature on individuals' information needs and information-seeking behaviour (e.g., as noted by Dervin and Nilan, 1986; Hewins, 1990; Wilson, 1994a). Studies on organizational information needs are restricted almost entirely to work using critical success factors (CSF).

This paper describes four case studies of the use of the CSF approach carried out in the UK and in Finland.

Critical success factors

Critical success factors as a basis for determining the information needs of managers were proposed by Daniel (1961) and popularized by Rockart (1979). The idea is that, in any organization, certain factors will be critical to success, in the sense that, if objectives associated with the factors are not achieved, the organization will fail – perhaps catastrophically (e.g., Boynton and Zmud, 1984; Goldsmith, 1991; Leidecker and Bruno, 1984).

The CSF approach was applied in case studies carried out in UK universities (Greene et al., 1999; Pellow and Wilson, 1993) and as a component of a strategic information management (SIM) methodology put forward by Wilson (1994b, 1994c). The CSF approach was combined with the value chain concept (Porter, 1985) to form an information audit (Buchanan and Gibb, 1998; Ellis et al., 1993; see also Goldsmith, 1991). More recently, the CSF approach has been applied in a study of the use of electronic information systems in UK higher education (Armstrong et al., 2001).

The case studies in UK universities, using a qualitative research strategy, were followed by cases testing the SIM methodology in the pharmaceutical and publishing sectors in Finland, which are reported here. Qualitative, open-ended interviews were conducted to identify the critical areas, related information needs and the use of information systems. Grounded theory methods (Glaser and Strauss, 1967; Strauss and Corbin, 1990) were applied to define the CSF in both sets of studies. An understanding of the production, marketing and managerial processes within the Finnish companies and the market conditions within which they operated was gained from relevant documentation.

The SIM methodology was elaborated further in a pilot study carried out in higher education in Finland, also reported here. Social network analysis (Granovetter, 1973; Mizruchi, 1994; Wasserman and Faust, 1994) was combined with the CSF approach and proved useful for discovering deeper structures in actors' information-seeking behaviour. The approach allows deeper analysis of the complexity of organizational information behaviour (Huotari, 1998; 1999). The methodology was developed further by replacing the concept of the value chain with the framework of Normann and Ramírez's (1994) value constellation concept (Huotari, 2000). The conceptual base was strengthened with the concept of a strategic partnership (Huotari and Iivonen, 2001). Moreover, concepts from Chatman's everyday-life information-seeking (ELIS) theory were included to define a comprehensive conceptual base for the proposed SIM theory (Huotari and Chatman, 2001).

Relating CSF to information needs

Academic heads of departments

The results of a pilot study (Pellow and Wilson, 1993) led to a more extensive examination of CSF and related information needs in universities which aimed at:

- a better understanding of the developing range of managerial information needs of academic departments in universities
- a clearer picture of the present role of university libraries in the development of campus-wide information systems and the potential for university library involvement in meeting departmental management information needs
- the extension of university administrators' understanding of academic perceptions of CSF and the administrative and managerial services needed to ensure their achievement
- the identification of areas in which communications between the central university administrative and academic support services, as far as management information provision is concerned, might be improved.

The final report of the project (Greene et al., 1999) showed that, while there was some reluctance among some heads of departments (HoD) to attempt to identify CSF and, in some cases, misunderstanding of what the term meant, it was eventually possible to elicit useful lists of factors. Among those identified, a clear distinction existed between internal and external factors, the balance of which depended on four key factors: political and economic environment; institutional setting; relative position of the department both within the university and vis-à-vis comparable departments; and departmental culture. While these factors interacted it was evident that successful research-led departments in older universities were more likely to be externally focused than largely teaching-oriented departments in newer universities. In the former, HoDs placed great emphasis on maintaining and defending 'traditional virtues' such as academic freedom and autonomy. This was less evident in newer universities where there was a generally more managerial culture.

Additionally, one common factor was HoD reliance for management information on extensive networks of informal contacts. This was supplemented by information from more formal sources.

HoDs generally felt that they were poorly served by the providers of financial management information, which was seen as often inaccurate, too intricate or cumbersome to use and out of date. Some HoDs suggested that improved management and financial information systems within their university would allow them to concentrate more on their primary activities and spend less time meeting the bureaucratic needs of the university. They felt that such needs were not being adequately met by the university because the main central administrative departments were not addressing them.

The administrative officers, particularly those more senior, tended to agree on the poor quality and timeliness of management information. They felt, however, that their main role was to meet the needs of their institution's senior management team and external bodies rather than those of HoDs. However, they made efforts to improve HoDs' awareness of external funding opportunities, the policies of the research and funding councils, and the provision of financial and management information. Many university administrators reported difficulties with identifying the needs of the HoDs because they are a disparate group, with individual interests, concerns and priorities. It was difficult for administrators to identify and focus closely on HoDs' needs in a consistent and helpful way. Moreover, there was a distinct cultural dissonance between administrators and HoDs, since neither group sufficiently understood or appreciated the pressures under which the other worked. In a rapidly changing environment, with strong external pressure for accountability, and the need to manage corporately, administrators, despite academic departments' being the 'productive' parts of the university, did not have time or resources to devote to what to them seemed second-order information needs.

Thus, in this instance, adoption of the CSF approach proved to be very fruitful in uncovering management information needs, thereby providing universities with information which their administrators had previously had difficulty in establishing. Consequently, it would be possible to take direct action to target those needs for which known information resources existed.

The pharmaceutical company

A case study using the SIM methodology was carried out in a Finnish pharmaceutical company, which was a division of a group with more than 10,000 employees in over 30 countries. It was a medium-sized company with its domestic market in the Nordic countries. The company was sold two years after the study reported here was completed. A total of 28 interviews were conducted in 1992 (Huotari, 1995, 2001; Huotari and Wilson, 1996).

Information and knowledge were seen as the life-blood of the company's activities in this industrial sector. Therefore, it was not a surprise that information management (IM) and human resources played the most critical role, followed by marketing, research and development (R&D), resources in general, production and quality assurance, general management and finance.

IM as a CSF

The critical areas of IM related to the role of the information systems (IS) and the infrastructure. This covered computerized IS, setting up a competent infrastructure and, in particular, achieving the planned performance in the functions of documentation, marketing, finance and personnel. Additionally, co-operation in interactive IS development, cost-efficiency of IS, and the speed of information storage, retrieval and dissemination were also significant.

Similarly, the quality of IM involved the accuracy of information processed and provided by internal accounting and planning; the quality of information provided for top management decision making; the ability to keep top management up to date on legislation; and sufficient current IS resources to provide information for reports. The IS's ability to acquire external information upon which actions were based was seen as important.

Overall, internal information flows were seen as critical. Analysis of the information needs of the R&D organization and the speed of the R&D-related processes were critical to the performance of the IM function for R&D. High quality documentation, speed in carrying out R&D-related activities, and knowledge of intellectual property rights were crucial for drug registration. Data processing and computer programming for the marketing accounting service, an improved graphics service for the marketing staff, and communication involving two-way information transfer with the marketing department and market research were all crucial to marketing and customer service.

The significance of the IM function appears to be strongly related to the industrial sector of the organization. A central task when undertaking pharmaceutical R&D processes is documentation. It was a critical area of IM because documentation processes are determined by external legislation and guidelines set by health and safety authorities, who guide all the R&D registration and operation activities. Thus, information and records management systems are needed to provide essential external information, and for organizing (filing, storing and retrieving) all documentation produced during the basic research, product development, clinical trials, quality assurance and production required in drug development (Huotari, 2001, 74).

The most strategic activity of the pharmaceutical company was R&D and 14 interviews were carried out at this level. Areas critical to the achievement of the strategic aims of the R&D division fell into ten main themes and demonstrated the strategic role of IM and human knowledge in this sector of industry. Furthermore, efficiency and speed, differentiation, resources, co-operation, decision-making and planning, research, marketing and finance were perceived as critical. There were many varied information needs relating to these factors.

The publishing case

The publishing company was part of a group and, at one time, the third largest publishing house in Finland. It was active in three sectors: non-fiction for the general public; business literature; and educational materials. Following the study it was sold to its major competitor, the biggest publisher in Finland.

A total of 27 interviews was carried out in 1993, and full support provided by top management (Huotari, 1997; Huotari and Wilson, 1996). Of these, 15 interviews were carried out at the top level of the company and the critical issues proposed fell into eight themes.

However, the executives were not as ready to define the essential information needed to monitor performance of these areas as those in the pharmaceutical sector. Human resources, products and marketing were seen as critical to ensure the financial base to continue the business. These were followed by IM, customer relations, efficiency and speed, and general management.

CSF and value chain analysis revealed the necessary crucial interaction between the activities involved in the publishing decision/publication design and marketing/sales, whose performance was based on market needs. This interaction is essential for an organization in the publishing sector: actions are taken on a very short-term basis (the shortest period for producing a book was five months).

IM as a CSF

IM was important to ensure the achievement of all planned primary activities (but not as critical as in the drug company). In addition, it had a minor role in the publishing decision, in publication design, in marketing and sales, and in customer relations and distribution.

Quality of information was crucial — acquiring accurate information and disseminating accurate internal information. Better information flows were needed, as well as high quality information systems in general and, in particular, for the provision of customer services. Acquisition of external information was crucial. The IS staff's ability to define organizational information needs and their quality of service were both stressed.

In addition, the IS infrastructure was a critical area, especially for maintaining a customer database for editorial work, for making publishing decisions and for designing business books. Further development of a strategic IS was crucial to the performance of marketing and sales.

The critical areas fell into nine themes which stressed the crucial role of human knowledge as vital both to create and to sell products. These CSF were followed by IM, finance and marketing activities: knowledge of marketing and marketing channels, of marketing communication, of customers, and the ability to serve them. These critical areas had a crucial role in the performance of all activities: sales, customer service and the primary activity of advertising and marketing material design. The information needs clustered around these critical areas.

Information sources and channels used in the private sector

The findings of these two case studies showed that people were the most frequently used information sources (see also Auster and Choo, 1994b; McKinnon and Bruns, 1992). In the drug company, meetings and face-to-face contacts were most often used to obtain internal and external information at the level of the company and in the most strategic activity, R&D. In the publishing company, meetings and personal contacts were used to obtain internal information and external information at the level of the company. Telephone and fax were used in marketing and sales to get external information. This aroused interest in the nature of social aspects of information behaviour.

These studies also demonstrated that IM and IS have become critical to the performance of pharmaceutical and publishing companies.

The University of Tampere study

A pilot test of the elaborated SIM methodology was carried out at the University of Tampere, Finland (Huotari, 1999). Mintzberg's (1983) model of the elements of organizational structure (the strategic apex, the middle level, the support staff, the technostructure and the operative core), excluding the operative core, was used as a basis for selecting interviewees. IM was included to allow more detailed examination of this function. The analysis was carried out in three phases, the first of which was concerned with analysis of the CSF.

The second level analysis of CSFs strongly emphasized immaterial, intellectual and social factors as crucial to the achievement of the strategic aims and goals of the University. The critical roles of people, collaboration at local, national and international levels, and strategic management demonstrate that knowledge is the base of all activity. Additionally, the performance of research and teaching as basic activities of a university is based on knowledge and its delivery. In this, IM has a vital role. Furthermore, the recruitment of students and satisfaction of their education needs were perceived as critical factors.

These CSFs prompted an interest in elaborating the conceptual base towards strategic value creation in the context of networked enterprises in order to propose a new SIM theory. The concepts of social types (i.e., insider–outsider typology), worldview, social norms, information behaviour and trust, which had been combined in Chatman's theory of everyday-life information seeking theory, and the concepts of homogeneity, density and content from social network theory, were invoked. A closer analysis of the nature of the critical information needs allowed a deeper examination of the value structure underlying the contacts and collaborative activities of the university and its internal and external stakeholders.

IM as a CSF

In the University, IM seemed to have a supportive rather than a strategic role, with a focus on the development of the infrastructure for IM, production of information for the needs of researchers and lecturers and the development of network services. There was a strong emphasis on internal, factual information. These information needs focus mostly on IM infrastructure – perceived as a critical area in central administration, the finance department, the student advisor's office, the international unit and the computer centre. Performance monitoring focused primarily on aspects such as the number of claims, network capacity and use, use of network services, problems with network use and information provision for the recruitment of foreign students. In addition, information on the system's output, planning and quality was essential.

The role of social contacts in information seeking

Social network analysis was applied as a component of SIM methodology in order to deepen understanding of the actors' information seeking patterns. It provided a tool to examine the complexity of organizational information behaviour, by analysing the role of formal and informal social contacts of the key players in acquiring wanted internal and external information.

The analysis indicates that internal formal contacts were most actively used by the middle level and most of these contacts took place at the same organizational level or inside the faculties. The strategic apex and the support staff were utilized as information sources. The strategic apex had most of its contacts with the support staff, the middle level and within top management. The support staff interacted most frequently with the middle level and with staff of other support units. Strikingly, those responsible for IM had only one information exchange relationship of a reciprocal nature: with the support staff. IM was also quite markedly focused on itself, and reported information contacts with the strategic apex, the technostructure, the middle level, the operative core and some contacts with the middle level, whereas these parts did not refer to IM at all.

The nature of these contacts shows that information seeking was partly limited to one-way contacts, which are inadequate when aiming at strategic information systems development. Of all parts of the university, the actors responsible for IM referred most often to the operative core.

These contacts, and the problems they revealed, reflect to some extent the hierarchical organizational culture of higher education. Whether the development of electronic IS, such as e-mail, network services, feedback systems, discussion groups, etc., would change this traditional culture would be interesting to examine (e.g., Lucas, 1998).

Internal informal contacts played a minor role in the actors' information behaviour in this context. Most of these contacts took place at the middle level, inside the faculties. The strategic apex and the support staff also used informal internal contacts for information seeking to a certain extent. The analysis revealed a number of problems linked to the limited interaction between IM and other parts of the University, which further stressed the lack of two-way-communication between IM and the other parts of the University.

External formal contacts were most frequently used by the middle level (the deans) and the strategic apex. Colleagues in other universities and higher education institutions (HEIs) were most often referred to and the most significant information flows took place between them and the deans. Similarly, the strategic apex used other HEIs as a source for this information type, as did those responsible for IM. The government and the ministries were used by the strategic apex and the middle level; regional councils, cities and municipalities were referred to by the strategic apex. The middle level also had contacts with firms, the Academy of Finland, organizations providing funding and centres for the development of industry.

Strikingly, the external boundaries were most frequently crossed informally by those responsible for IM. The network of academic libraries in general, the library's gatekeeper role and the social, external activities of the main librarian partly explain this phenomenon. However, this might also indicate that external, informal contacts may be used to their full extent because of problems with internal communications and potential lack of trust (Huotari and Iivonen, 2005). Also, rapid developments in the information field have created information needs in the computer centre, which needs to keep up with developments by using external informal contacts. Similarly, the strategic apex and the middle level used external informal contacts to some extent to obtain vital information. The nature of the University as a loosely-coupled, knowledge-intensive organization might also have a role in the use of external contacts as a part of its total information system.

Information sources and channels used

Electronic IS, both internal and internet, were the most frequently used sources for external information. Problems experienced in their use could be overcome through collaboration with the operative core to improve systems. E-mail and face-to-face contact were the most often used channels to obtain internal information. The telephone was used most for seeking external information and printed sources (publications, newsletters, scientific journals and reports); organizations, consultants and statistical services were also used.

Reports, including print outputs from the management information system, were the most frequently consulted internal information sources, though the MIS was harshly criticized. Magazines, newsletters, plans, journals, minutes of meetings, books, statistics, notice-boards and information services provided by other service units were also used.

Common problems and issues

Applying the SIM methodology was slow and time-consuming. The entire analysis was carried out in three phases of which the first phase was the most difficult. This first phase involved coding the interview transcripts to find the CSFs, define their individual areas, and to discover the primary activity of the value chain for whose performance an individual area of a critical factor was the most significant. Interpretation was strongly involved. However, the strength of the method lies in the grounding (in the extensive reporting of the participants) of a conceptual framework for analysis, which was consistently applied. Problems related to interpretation were most severe in analysis of the interviews carried out in the pharmaceutical sector, while the process became much easier in the publishing sector, and slowed down the process in the education sector.

Lessons learned

When analysing executives' perceptions of the factors critical to success, defining them through analysis of the material is critically important. The sub-groups of the CSFs should be substantial enough to enable the major organizational information needs to be smoothly mapped. If the number of sub-groups is high a very fragmented map of needs will result. Such a map, as a component of an advisory information audit, will not serve as a solid base to provide recommendations for the design of appropriate strategic information systems.

Because the CSFs overlap, some critical areas emerge as belonging to more than one main group. Therefore, the second level analysis tends to change the substance of the CSFs, resulting in a reduction in the number of themes. Thus, in the pharmaceutical case, the 129 areas referred to by 14 executives as critical to the achievement of the strategic goals of the R&D division fell into ten main themes; for the pharmaceutical company as a whole 95 references from 14 senior executives fell into eight main themes; in the publishing company the 113 critical issues put forward by 15 executives at the level of the publishing company as a whole fell into eight main themes and, at the level of marketing and sales, nine main themes emerged from 106 critical issues referred to by 13 executives; finally, at the

University of Tampere the new conceptual framework applied to the second level of analysis altered the classification and reduced the number of CSFs from 11 to eight.

It is evident that to gain and provide a comprehensive map or 'picture', organizational information needs should be analysed, e.g., by classifying them according to the most appropriate criteria for the organization in question. One way to conduct the analysis is to look at the needs for factual or qualitative internal and external information. However, the operating business environment of the organization determines the nature of needs for more specific types of information. Therefore, one should decide how detailed the level of analysis should be. For instance, in the private sector the needs for marketing and financial information are more central, more specific and more easily defined than in the educational sector in Finland. Therefore, analysis of these information needs requires more specialized knowledge of the nature of the industrial or service sector the organization is in.

The pilot study carried out at the University of Tampere tested the elaborated SIM methodology and demonstrated the process of mapping the CSFs and related information needs by figure or table displays (Huotari, 1999). This way of displaying organizational information needs assists in the comprehensive analysis required to fulfil the advisory role of an information audit. The figures can be further elaborated, e.g., to display problems in the information flows or with the use of IS to access essential information. It gives an overview of the critical issues and problems and provides the auditor with a solid base for recommendations for different units or organizational levels.

The studies testing the SIM methodology in the private sector demonstrated that the CSFs and related information needs cluster according to the primary activities of the value chain, and this clustering is determined by the industrial sector that the organization belongs to. Interaction between the first primary activity, at which stage product ideas are created, evaluated and product development decisions taken, and the primary activity of marketing, where products are launched and marketing activities carried out, was emphasized in both cases. It was also shown that the information management function is the most critical for the performance of all primary activities. The difference in the significance of the information management function, when compared with individual primary activities, is substantial. This finding adds knowledge to Porter's value chain analysis: Porter and Millar (1985, 152) indicate the importance of information technology to an organization's performance through its relationship to all value activities. We may argue, therefore, that IM is a significant support activity for an organization and should be included in the design and development of the overall infrastructure to enable organizational performance.

Conclusion

The series of studies reported here confirms the value of the CSF approach in iden-tifying organizational objectives (whether or not these are well defined in advance) and in relating the information needs of personnel in various positions to those objectives. In this way, organizational information needs emerge that corporate information management systems must support, if the organization is to remain com-petitive. The CSF approach can be used as one of the methods in determining the strategic information management needs of the organization and in contributing to the design of systems that aid competitive advantage.

5

Critical success factors and information needs in industry: an Estonian study

Aiki Tibar

Introduction

Estonia's economy has undergone very rapid and extensive development since the restoration of independence in 1991. There is still a very long way to go in order to catch up with the more successful and wealthy Western countries. At the end of the 1990s policymakers and other stakeholders began to realize that longer-term growth prospects were dependent on fostering 'knowledge-based Estonia'. As a result, the Estonian Parliament approved the innovation policy document *'Knowledge-based Estonia' – The research and development strategy of Estonia for 2002–2006* (Kurik et al., 2002). The wide objectives of the strategy are to update the overall knowledge pool and increase the competitiveness of local enterprises.

Innovative activities have an essential role in aligning business development priorities with new opportunities resulting from the EU's large internal market and innovation policy, in order to gain and retain competitiveness at the global marketplace. A comprehensive survey (Kurik et al., 2002) was conducted to collect in-depth statistical information about the innovativeness of more than 400 Estonian enterprises during 1998–2000. The survey aimed to find out how innovative Estonian enterprises were compared with their EU competitors, what the main barriers were to innovation, which sources of information for innovation were used, etc.

This survey treated innovativeness as implementing technologically new products, processes or services and significant technological improvements in products, processes or services. The results of the survey show that 36% of all observed enterprises were innovative enterprises.

The biggest factors hampering innovation were economic: shortage of money and high innovation costs. The most important internal factor was the shortage of competent personnel. Nearly half of the enterprises which did not implement new innovations in 1998–2000 claimed that their earlier innovations meet their requirements and/or that there is no market demand for innovation (Kurik et al., 2002).

In 1999 a study was conducted to identify the critical success factors (CSFs) and related information needs in successful Estonian enterprises (Tibar, 2000, 2002). This study focused on the need for and acquisition of information external to the enterprises, and problems in accessing the needed information. This chapter presents the findings of this study. The findings are discussed in relation to previous and more recent research on CSFs, environmental scanning and technological innovation in organizations.

Theoretical framework

The acquisition and use of external information (environmental scanning) in industry has been investigated in a number of studies (Choo and Auster, 1993). Roberts and Clifford (1986) found that the main areas where external information was needed were marketing, products, exporting, finance, competitors and patents. White and Wilson (1988) identified four main types of external information needed: information about customers, about competition, on statutory regulations and the problems of export. Auster and Choo (1993a, 1994b) focused on environmental scanning in organizations and revealed that the chief executives concentrate their scanning on the competition, customer, regulatory and technological sectors of the environment.

Several studies suggest that environmental scanning improves organizational performance and is an important factor in organizational decision-making (Choo, 2001).

Correia and Wilson (2001) identify and analyse the factors internal to the organization which affect the activity of environmental scanning. These factors include individual factors, such as information consciousness and exposure to information, and organizational factors such as information climate and 'outwardness'. The authors define the information climate as the conditions that determine access to and use of information in an organization (collecting, organizing and making information available, and disseminating it).

Huotari and Wilson (2001) state that an open, informal organizational climate that is favourable to the exchange of information and innovation clearly and significantly affects the chances of success. Therefore, the creation of conditions that facilitate the informal exchange of information not only among different departments and teams but also among innovation managers, partners, customers and suppliers can be recommended. Finally, it is recommended strongly that companies stimulate and facilitate the further education of staff involved in innovation (expansion and maintenance of organizational knowledge).

The Estonian innovation survey (Kurik et al., 2002) indicates that the three most important sources for innovation information were sources within the enterprise, suppliers, and customers. Competitors and sources of public information (fairs, exhibitions and professional conferences) were information sources with medium importance. After the survey some recommendations were made to entrepreneurs on the basis of discussions with experts. Many areas were seen to be very important for the competitiveness of enterprises, such as monitoring different information sources, conducting market surveys and developing the marketing plan, linking personnel policy to the firm's strategy, using the services of specialists and consultants in obtaining information or new methods introduction process, etc.

Souder and Moenaert (1992) state that technological innovation within the firm can be modelled as a process of uncertainty reduction or, alternatively, as a process of information collecting and processing. The four major sources of uncertainty are user needs, technological environments, competitive environments and organizational resources. They claim that the two most important uncertainties relate to consumer uncertainty and technological uncertainty, as these components have a positive effect on the other two components. Besides, organizational climate – i.e., the organization's internal nature including factors such as openness, harmony and trust between marketing and R&D – as perceived by its members, influences interfunctional integration, information exchange and innovative success.

Ottum and Moore (1997) demonstrated a very strong relationship between market information processing and new product success, with success most closely linked to information use. They conclude that innovation success is related to the successful integration of the marketing and R&D departments, because reducing uncertainties is the responsibility of the marketing and R&D functions within the firm.

An empirical study was conducted to explore internal innovation success factors (Van Riel et al., 2004). The findings suggest that innovation success is associated with the systematic reduction of decision-making uncertainty as a result of organizational information gathering, diffusion and processing activities. Furthermore, the study provides evidence that a market orientation contributes as an internal success factor. An organizational climate favourable to information sharing powerfully mediates the positive effects of intelligence gathering with respect to customers and technology. Another internal factor is the effectiveness of organizational decision-making. The study's authors stress the importance of internal success factors in dealing with rapid technological change and turbulence in the marketplace.

Van Riel et al. (2004) conclude that intelligence gathering generally takes place in three domains of the external environment: technological intelligence, competitive intelligence, and customer intelligence. These are environments where considerable uncertainty exists. Furthermore, efficiency and effectiveness of communication influence how well and how fast information is transferred and diffused throughout the organization. This survey found that the acquisition of technological and customer information strongly and positively affects the internal innovation climate. However, the acquisition of competitive information has a significant negative effect on the likelihood of short-term innovation success. It also does not stimulate the formation of an innovative climate. The study data confirmed that factors facilitating a free flow of information (informal communication) and an open culture increase the likelihood of innovation success. Thus, the quality of organizational communication affects the availability of information to the decision-makers and their decision quality.

The critical success factors approach

The critical success factors approach was developed by Daniel (1961) and refined by Rockart (1979). According to Rockart (1979, 85), critical success factors support the attainment of organizational goals, and if results in these areas are satisfactory, the organization is competitive. The CSF method focuses on individual managers and on each manager's current information needs. Rockart (1979) states that some CSFs may be related to the structure of the particular industry, the others are caused by environmental factors, and there are also temporal factors for a particular period of time.

The potential of CSF methodology was explored in an assessment of the information requirements of heads of university departments (Greene et al., 1999; Pellow and Wilson, 1993). Pellow and Wilson (1993, 429) conclude that the main strengths of the method are: acceptance by senior managers; consideration of all the information needed, not only that which is easy to collect; and the fact that critical success factors point to priorities for development.

Case studies carried out in two Finnish companies (Huotari, 1997, 2001; Huotari and Wilson, 1996) indicate the value of the CSF approach in identifying corporate information needs. Wilson's (1994c) proposition, to combine CSFs with the concept of value chain (Porter, 1985), was tested to identify information intensive areas in the pharmaceutical and the publishing company.

Huotari and Wilson in Chapter 4 report the series of studies conducted in the UK and Finland, in both academic and business institutions, and confirm the value of the CSF approach in identifying organizational objectives and in relating the information needs of personnel to those objectives.

Data collection and analysis

Data collection

Letters were sent to 25 successful manufacturing companies, the winners of the *Estonian Industry TOP 50* contest in 1998, from Tallinn, the capital of Estonia, and the surrounding area. Altogether, 27 managers and engineers from 16 companies agreed to take part in the study. Data were collected during the period May–November 1999.

In all, 19 managers and eight engineers participated in the study. Respondents came from the following industries: food industry (eight respondents); chemical industry (five respondents); transportation vehicles and devices industry (four respondents); energy (four respondents); furniture industry (three respondents); electrotechnical and electronics industry (two respondents); and textile manufacturing (one respondent).

The data collection was based on semi-structured interviews. The CSF approach (Daniel, 1961; Rockart, 1979) was used to identify the information needs of managers and engineers in various industries. Respondents were asked to specify the critical success factors for their organizational level, which support the achievement of company's goals. When the CSFs had been identified it was possible to specify related information needs.

Categories of critical success factors

The interview data indicate CSFs on different organizational levels in various companies. Using the CSF approach it was possible to focus on those areas of activity that needed careful attention from managers and engineers to support the attainment of company goals.

The statements of the respondents regarding CSFs were analysed and aggregated into ten broader subject categories that were close to some activity area. These categories are as follows: information management; marketing; product development; quality management and quality assurance; technological innovations; personnel; finance; general management; pollution-free technology and environmental management; and efficiency.

Information management

Information management as a CSF was mentioned the most frequently. Information management was mostly defined on the basis of statements by the respondents that expressed a need to develop their company's information systems and improve access to internal and external information.

Information systems in the enterprises studied, during the data collection period, mostly were not on the desired level. Lack of hardware and appropriate software was, in many cases, seen as a major barrier to disseminating internal information and accessing external information. In order to keep up with the most recent developments in knowledge and make relevant decisions it was considered critical to have fast access to important sources of information.

Reliable information systems were needed to gather, organize and disseminate internal information and documentation, including marketing information for reporting and analysing statistical data on sales.

Marketing

Marketing as a CSF was also mentioned by the respondents from all enterprises. Managers and engineers stressed that it was vital to analyse the market environment, be aware of competitors and their products and look for ways to meet consumer preferences. Being informed of the market's demands and of the target market's purchasing power was seen as a CSF.

Managers from the food industry regarded active selling and awareness of marketing techniques as CSFs. It was essential to carry out market analysis in order to be aware and respond quickly to market demands.

Product development

Respondents from the food industry, furniture industry, and transportation vehicles and devices industry regarded production development as a CSF. The reason behind this is high competition in these branches of industry between Estonian producers and with external producers. Product development was closely related to marketing and quality assurance.

The launching of new products and the use of cheaper and healthier materials in products was regarded as a CSF. The development of products with an excellent quality:price ratio was also mentioned as a CSF.

Quality management and quality assurance

Another major group of success factors was related to quality issues. The CSFs mentioned were as follows: implementation and development of quality control systems; ensuring stable quality and product safety; strict quality control of raw materials; and ensuring the quality of production processes and services.

Technological innovations

This category includes factors related to the flexibility and safety of production processes, and new technology implementation and equipment. It was viewed as important to introduce material- and labour-saving technologies. One firm was going to build up a laboratory for technological innovations, and the creation of a strong infrastructure in manufacturing was regarded as a critical factor.

Personnel

Several managers saw employees' qualifications as a CSF. It was stressed that a qualified labour force and training on an ongoing basis was needed to raise the level of productivity. Increased quality requirements and new technologies required new knowledge and skills.

Finance

Investment in the development of products, technologies and information systems was regarded as very important. Also the company's fixed costs, the cost per unit and low production costs were mentioned as a CSF.

General management

Several managers saw rational job management and planning processes as critical success factors. The managers from energy production stated that during company restructuring it was important to build up a competitive organization for the free market for energy. The quality manager from textile manufacturing also mentioned that the company was going through reorganization, improving its structure, and that that was a CSF.

Pollution-free technology and environmental management

This was mentioned as a CSF by the respondents from energy production, the food industry and the chemical industry.

Efficiency

Efficiency as a CSF was essential, to make processes more effective in order to achieve better results and cost savings. The efficiency of production and business processes, with relevant systems for information management, was also mentioned as a CSF.

Types of information need

When the CSFs had been identified it was possible to specify the information needed by managers and engineers in order to manage these factors. Interview results indicate that the main areas in which information was needed were:

- competitors, customers, suppliers and other market information
- products and technologies

- resources: information on finance, workforce and raw materials
- legislation and regulations: legal acts, directives, standards and norms
- economic and political trends.

Competitors, customers, suppliers and other market information

Market information was needed for scanning the business environment and improving the competitiveness of the company. In relation to several CSFs managers and engineers stated that information is needed on competitor products, its prices, the experience of other companies and new trends.

A study by White and Wilson (1988) indicated that external information on competitor activity was regularly cited as being the most important and the most difficult to obtain. Respondents in the Estonian study also claimed that they have had difficulties obtaining information on competitors and their products.

Managers needed information to organize marketing activity and define the place of the firm in its industrial sector. For this purpose statistical data were needed about their industrial sector as a whole. Information about the firm's finances, distribution and income was also needed. In order to consider the demands of customers, target market research was carried out. Customer complaints were analysed and data about the target group's purchase power were needed.

Market information was needed for product development, working out a price strategy and managing the processes more effectively. Managers said that accurate and timely statistical data, both internal and external, were needed to make relevant decisions.

Products and technologies

Technological information was necessary for the development of products and materials, and innovation in manufacturing technology. Information was needed on material processing technologies and effective and environment-friendly production methods. Regarding product innovation, attention was drawn to the quality and safety of manufacturing processes, reducing the costs of production, raising the efficiency of production and making it more flexible.

In relation to technological innovations, information was needed about the firm's operation: the manufacturing process; the balance between investments, accidents and working security; and effective instructions for the introduction of a new production process.

Resources: information on finance, workforce and raw materials

Internal financial data and information on investment possibilities were regarded as necessary for marketing and product development, modernization of technologies and equipment, safety and effectiveness of production processes, staff training, development of information systems and the acquisition of information and information sources. Information on raw materials and their characteristics was also very important.

Staff competence and training was seen as very important. Training possibilities were sought for every organizational level in the workplace and outside the firm.

Legislation and regulations: legal acts, directives, standards and norms

In order to maintain their present market position or to enter a new market, managers had to be well informed of the legislation relating to the target market. In the organization of production processes and construction of products one needs information on standards and norms as well as on the laws which govern the field of health and safety, etc.

Economic and political trends

Managers needed information on the external political and economic environment in order to make the right decisions. Changes in the economy or politics may, in their turn, bring about changes in markets and in legislation. This information was necessary for keeping market share or expanding it.

Use of external sources of information

Information external to the company was acquired through personal contacts, printed and electronic sources and other services. Personal contacts were established with clients, suppliers or other firms in the same field. Visits to foreign firms were useful in order to get general information about the market and specific information about a new product or technology. Information was also obtained and exchanged through personal contacts while visiting exhibitions, fairs, conferences and seminars.

Personal contacts were used to gain access to information that could not be acquired through formal sources, and also when information was needed quickly. White and Wilson (1988) found that information users rely on personal contacts because they regard them as trusted sources of information. Choo and Auster (1993) state that informal sources, including personal contacts, are sometimes even more important than formal information sources.

Material resources such as newspapers, journals, handbooks, official statistics and legislation, standards and EU directives were followed regularly. These materials, if felt to be relevant, were commonly acquired by the firm. Two of the largest firms had in-house libraries. Two respondents said that they used a research library regularly in order to get updated external information.

The internet was regarded as a universal source of information. The problem for some respondents was lack of skills in searching for appropriate information on the internet, and lack of time to search for and select needed information. Thus, the use of external information sources was influenced by individual factors, such as educational background, previous habits and experience. Respondents from companies that had established good information systems for internal information organization and dissemination were mostly very active in environmental scanning.

Most enterprises co-operated successfully with professional associations and research and educational institutions in working out local legislation, as well as with the field of consultancy or training. Some managers established closer contacts with researchers and experts from universities for sharing knowledge and know-how.

Discussion and conclusion

The CSFs approach enabled a focus on priority areas for development and related information needs in successful Estonian enterprises. The CSFs taken up were aggregated into ten categories. The most critical areas according to the study were related to information management, marketing, quality management, product development, technological innovations, personnel and finance.

Information management appeared to be a highly critical factor: disseminating and managing the information within the company, and accessing internal and external information at the right time. This finding is supported by previous research (Huotari, 1997, 2001; Huotari and Wilson, 1996): information management was identified as a critical success factor in two Finnish companies – highly critical for a pharmaceutical company but less critical in publishing (see Chapter 4).

The second most frequently mentioned CSF was marketing. It was seen as very important to run a company on the basis of real knowledge of the market situation. Access to information on customers and their preferences, and competitors and their activity, was crucial for managers and engineers on different organizational levels. Product development was closely related to marketing. Ottum and Moore (1997) have emphasized the importance of market information processing to new product success. The survey findings of Kurik et al. (2002) suggest that one of the factors inhibiting innovation in Estonian enterprises may be insufficient customer and market orientation.

In the Estonian survey (Kurik et al., 2002) three types of innovation were investigated: product innovation, process innovation and organizational innovation. All these innovations were mentioned as CSFs in the present study of successful enterprises. High priority was given to the quality of products, as well as of manufacturing and management. Training of personnel was also seen as very important. Innovation depends largely on the qualifications of the personnel, on their knowledge and skills. Huotari and Wilson (2001) stress the importance of further education of staff involved in innovation.

Investment is crucial to the development of products, technologies and information systems. This category of CSF was labelled 'finance'. The Estonian innovation survey (Kurik et al., 2002) also revealed that shortage of money often impedes innovation.

The study identified five main areas in which companies needed information. These are: competitors, customers, suppliers and other market information; products and technologies; resources: information on finance, workforce, and raw materials; legislation and regulations; and economic and political trends. Other studies (Souder and Moenaert, 1992; Van Riel et al., 2004) have concluded that the reduction of uncertainty, regarding consumer needs, technological and competitive environment, and organizational resources, is crucial for innovation.

Close contacts with professional associations and universities for information sharing and staff training refer to the openness of the studied successful enterprises to the external environment (as discussed by Correia and Wilson, 2001). All respondents were interested in expanding their information networks, although some of them had problems with access to information systems. Personal contacts were seen as very important means of acquiring information in environmental scanning.

Further contacts and collaboration with universities and other research institutions, in transfer of knowledge and know-how to the enterprises, are crucial for the development of a knowledge-based industry and economy.

The interview data on CSFs and problems in accessing needed information revealed some favourable and some inhibiting factors in accessing information inside and outside the enterprise. In the companies where investments have been made into information systems development, high priority was given to effectiveness of communication and information transfer. Most respondents in this study referred to the importance of information in decision-making. Thus, innovation climate is strongly supported by the information climate and 'open systems' are more likely to be innovative.

These findings, and the results of the Estonian innovation survey, suggest that further investigations are needed regarding success factors for innovation, relevant information needs and the innovative climate in Estonian enterprises.

6

Experiencing information seeking and learning: research on patterns of variation

Louise Limberg

Introduction

This chapter presents doctoral research concluded in 1998 (Limberg, 1999), to which some comments are added derived from later research in the same area, that is, the interaction between information seeking and learning. The overall research interest is: 'What and how do students learn while engaged in information seeking and use for learning tasks?' My research has been conducted with the aim of identifying and describing patterns of variation in information seeking and use. This aim is different from the cognitive approach, prevailing in the early 1990s and endeavouring to create general models. Since the mid 1990s, the area of information needs, seeking and use research has witnessed a range of approaches challenging the cognitive viewpoint, such as ethnography (Chatman, 2000), discourse analysis (Talja, 1997), phenomenography (Kirk, 2002), a socio-cultural perspective (Sundin, 2002) and the sociology of knowledge (Seldén, 2001).

Research problem

My dissertation grew out of a need for better research-based understanding of information seeking and use in a formal learning context. It is worth underlining that this study was not limited to information *seeking* but took an equally great interest in information *use*, which was considered necessary for the focus on learning outcomes, an observation made by Wilson (1981). In an analysis of approaches to research on information use, Savolainen (2000, 48) claims that such research will be broadened to cover knowledge creation, a concept similar to learning, as I see it.

During the last two decades we have experienced a shift at all levels of education from a teacher-centred to a student-centred view of learning. This entails an increased use of libraries and a wide variety of information tools, paths and sources. Although there is a substantial body of research on students' information seeking for learning, there is a lack of research-based knowledge on the interaction between how students seek and use information for learning assignments and what they actually learn about the subject matter. Pitts's (1994) study on (16–17-year-old) students' use of information for a science assignment is an early and rare example. Pitts found that various dimensions of a learning assignment such as information seeking, subject content and forms of presentation were constantly intertwined. These findings contradict the view of information seeking as a general process, disregarding the meaning of content, as often claimed in LIS (e.g., Ingwersen, 1996a and b). Pitts' findings raise further questions about the character of the relationship between task requirements, knowledge content and information seeking and use.

The aim of my dissertation was to study information seeking through an explorative investigation of the interaction between information seeking and use and learning outcome. The work was conducted along two interacting strands:

- an analysis of research and theory found relevant to the problem
- an empirical study of how senior secondary school students seek and use information to learn about the subject content of an assignment.

Theoretical framework

Phenomenography

As one aspect of my research problem was concerned with students' learning from the information they used I decided to use phenomenography, a research approach developed by Marton and colleagues at Gothenburg University during the 1970s (Marton, 1994; Marton and Booth, 1997). Since then, phenomenography has spread to other disciplines and other countries (Limberg, 2000). The approach may be described as a set of theoretical assumptions and a methodology. The main reason for choosing phenomenography was the need to study variation in students' learning outcomes and to compare this with variation in students' information seeking and use.

Phenomenography aims to explore people's different ways of experiencing phenomena. The core concept of conception, or way of experiencing, is not a mental representation or a cognitive structure. It is a way of being aware of something; that is, a relation between person and world (Marton, 1994, 1). A basic assumption in phenomenography is that it is possible to identify the various ways in which people experience or conceptualize phenomena and to present these in a limited number of categories. Another, empirically grounded, assumption is that people's ways of experiencing a problem or a situation reflect their ways of acting in relation to that particular problem or situation.

Frameworks from information seeking research

Kuhlthau's (1993, 2004) model of the information search process, developed in a learning context, was of particular relevance. Kuhlthau views information seeking as a process of construction embedded in the process of learning. The study design was influenced by Kuhlthau's model, as regards exploring information seeking during the entire learning process, the timing of the interviews with students and, to some extent, the formulation of interview questions. Kuhlthau (1991, 1993) emphasizes that her model describes the information search process as understood by users, which was consistent with my own intention of adopting a user perspective. However, the phenomenographic approach implies important differences from Kuhlthau's constructivist view of learning. According to a constructivist view, learning is a process of individual, subjective construction of meaning through human information processing.

At the time of the research, the cognitive viewpoint was predominant as a framework for information science, and particularly for information needs, seeking and use studies (Julien, 1996). User studies were focused on internal cognitive processes rather than on external behaviour. One purpose of the cognitive approach was to design adaptive interfaces for information systems through building valid models of users' cognitive processes (Hewins, 1990, 164). My aim was to find and try a research approach different from the constructivist and cognitive views, since many researchers felt discontent with the state-of-the-art of user studies in the 1990s (Ellis, 1992; Wilson, 1994a).

Comparison between theoretical approaches

The review of theory just outlined shows differences between cognitive or constructivist approaches in user studies and phenomenography in three important respects.

Content: general models vs. patterns of variation

Phenomenography views the content of learning as central to understanding learning processes. A cognitive approach in user studies tends to focus not on how users experience or understand the content of information, but on users' cognitive structures or mental models. Kuhlthau underlines that 'focusing the topic' is the pivotal point in her constructivist model of the search process. This implies that a topic (content) interacts with information seeking, but she has not investigated the character of this interaction.

Epistemology

The view of the relationship between information or learning content (the object) and the user or the learner (the subject) differs between constructivist and cognitive user studies and phenomenography. The cognitive viewpoint is explicitly dualistic in placing information (the object) outside the user (the subject). Information is said to be 'transmitted via a channel' (Ingwersen, 1996b, 101). The metaphors of conduit or gap-bridging illustrate the same idea of separation between subject and object, as discussed by Savolainen (2000). This dualistic view is in obvious contrast to the non-dualistic stance of phenomenography, which considers person and world to be internally related (Marton and Booth, 1997, 108). Therefore, to learn does not mean to receive knowledge or information, it means changing the relationship between a person and the world. Use of the terms 'receiver' or 'recipient' for 'user' was still common in LIS at the time of this research and indicated epistemological differences between the two research approaches.

Individual and group

Person-centred user studies as well as phenomenographic studies build on individuals' behaviour or understanding. While the aim of such studies in cognitive research is to try to identify different individual characteristics, for instance learning styles (cf. Heinström, 2002), phenomenographers focus on differences between people's experiences of a specific phenomenon or situation. Although empirical data in phenomenographic research originates from interviews with individuals, the analysis of data focuses on differences between conceptions of phenomena on a collective level, not on differences between individuals. This has consequences for the design of the study and for the interpretation of results. This research was not designed to study the differences between individual students but the differences between their experiences of information seeking and use.

Research questions

In accordance with Kuhlthau's and Pitts's view of the information search process as distinguishable but integrated in the larger learning process, my research object was to study how these two processes interact with one another from the perspective of the learner and user. Consistent with my choice of phenomenographic theory and method, the following four questions were formulated for the empirical study:

1 How do the students experience the information seeking process?
2 How do the students think about various information sources and their use of them?
3 How do the students understand or think about subject matter during and after the learning process?
4 How do students' conceptions of information seeking and use interact with their conceptions of subject matter?

The empirical study

Description of empirical case

Some prerequisites directed the case selection: a group of students engaged in a learning assignment requiring the independent seeking and use of information had to be found. The teacher and the students would have to tolerate my presence in the classroom many times during the process. They must grant time for interviews in their leisure time. There should be a reasonably well-equipped library in the school. The group selected included 25 students (18–19 years old) in their last year of secondary school in the science stream.

The topic of the students' assignment was: 'What will be the positive or negative consequences of a possible Swedish membership of the European Union?' The study took place in the academic year 1993–4, and was concluded six months before the Swedish referendum on EU membership. The students worked co-operatively in five groups, each group choosing a subtopic: the consequences for defence and security, education and research, environment, industry and competition, and the labour market. The students worked on the assignment for four months. Assessment of the assignment was based mainly on a written report of some 20 pages from each group.

Data collection

The main data collection method was interviews, with observational sessions in the classroom at the early and concluding stages of the assignment, and in the library during the phase of intense information seeking. The empirical material included students' written reports, and the teacher's detailed written assessment of each report.

The students were interviewed three times: at the beginning of their work, in a phase of intense information seeking and after presentation and conclusion of the assignment. Interviews were structured and contained questions on the goal of the assignment, subject content, information seeking tools, information sources, use of different materials and interventions by a teacher and a librarian. Questions were asked about how students thought, felt and acted in relation to their experiences. The interviews lasted 15–30 minutes in the first round, and 30–45 minutes on the second and third occasions.

Complementary interviews were conducted with the teacher and the school librarian before and after the assignment, to capture various conditions of students' work. The collected material comprised 80 interviews from 27 people. The total interview time was about 42 hours. All interviews were tape-recorded and transcribed.

My role was one of interviewer and observer and there is some evidence in the interview protocols that I may have influenced the students' ways of thinking about information seeking and use during their work process. However, I never actively intervened in their work. The design of the course unit was usual for the teacher, who had given identical assignments in other classes and who was familiar with having visitors in the classroom.

Data analysis

Throughout the analysis, two main foci were maintained: analysing the students' information seeking and use, and discovering their understanding of subject matter. Each implied several rounds of reading, re-reading and reflection to discern patterns and develop categories of conceptions of these phenomena. The next step was to compare the two sets of categories of description, i.e. students' conceptions of information seeking and use and their conceptions of subject matter grounded in variation in learning outcomes. The concluding step focused on the interaction between information seeking and use and learning outcomes.

Analyses focused on five dimensions of information seeking as expressed by the students: their relevance criteria, their experiences of information overload, their criteria for judging when they had enough information, their criteria for assessing the cognitive authority (cf. Wilson, 1983) of information sources, and their experience of bias in information sources. These aspects emerged from the manifest content of the interviews.

Figure 6.1 (overleaf) illustrates information seeking and use as embedded in the learning task. It is worth underlining that the three major categories of conceptions of information seeking and use are based on analyses of the five dimensions of information seeking, constituting altogether 13 categories and the relationship between them.

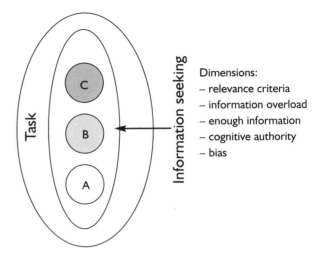

Figure 6.1   Three categories of conceptions of information seeking based on five dimensions

Findings

The most conclusive finding was that the quality of students' information seeking and use closely interacted with the quality of their learning outcomes.

Information seeking and use

A detailed categorization of students' conceptions of each of the dimensions of information seeking on an aggregated level is presented in Table 6.1.[1]

Table 6.1   Overview of distribution of students' conceptions of the five aspects of information seeking on an aggregated level

Student	Relevance criteria	Overload	Enough	Cognitive authority	Bias	Aggregated level
Agneta	A	A	A	A	A	A
Alex	A	A	A	A	A	A
Anders	A	A	A	A	A?	A

Continued on next page

---

[1] The names of students are fictitious and indicate (in Swedish) the subtopic that each student worked with (e.g., names starting with an M indicate 'miljö' = 'environment'). Table 6.1 therefore shows the strong impact of group patterns, where students working in the same group with the same subtopic expressed similar conceptions of information seeking and use. A detailed analysis of the interaction between group patterns and ways of experiencing information seeking and learning is presented in the dissertation, but has not been published in English.

Table 6.1 *Continued*

Student	Relevance criteria	Overload	Enough	Cognitive authority	Bias	Aggregated level
Annika	A	–	–	A	A	A
Anton	–	A	A	A	B?	A
Fanny	C	B	C?	A	C	C
Felix	C	B	C	A	B/C?	C
Filip	C	B	C	B	C	C
Fredrik	C	B	C	B	C	C
Frida	B/C	B	B	–	B	B
Madeleine	C	B	C	B	C	C
Maja	C	B	C	B	C	C
Marianne	C	–	C	A	C?	C
Matilda	C	B	C	B	C	C
Mona	C	B	C?	B	C	C
Nadja	B	–	B	A?	B	B
Niklas	B	A	–	A	B	B
Nils	B	B	B	B?	B?	B
Nina	B	B	B	A	B	B
Nora	B?	A	B	A?	B	B
Ulla	B	?	B	A	B	B
Ulla-Karin	B	B	B	A	B	B
Ulrika	B	–	B	A	B	B
Urban	B	B	B	A	B	B
Ursula	B	B	B	A	B	B

The aggregated categories are described in more detail below.

A. Information seeking as fact-finding

Students were looking for discrete facts or the right answer to a specific question. Ease of access, physical and intellectual, was an important criterion of relevance. Information overload was solved through avoiding information. Biased material was considered not useful because of a lack of facts.

B. Information seeking as balancing information to choose the right side

Students were looking for enough information to form a personal standpoint on the issue of Swedish EU membership. The most important relevance criteria were that information should allow students to cover their subtopic, and that information should be retrieved from both sides, i.e. in favour of and opposing EU membership. The approach to bias implied efforts to strike a balance between sources from opposing sides, then allowing one view to prevail.

C. Information seeking as scrutinizing and analysing

Information seeking was experienced as seeking and using information to understand a topic. In this case, the topic being a controversial issue, the students thought of information seeking as critically evaluating and discovering relations between various information sources. The most important relevance criterion was that information should provide different perspectives on the topic. Biased material was used to disclose the values and motives underlying various sources and to structure ways of argumentation for different standpoints in the sources.

The most important difference between the categories is related to the students' various approaches or intentions. The intention of category A was to lay hands on a ready-made answer. Category B focused on choosing the right side based on the relative quantity and availability of information from opposing sides, and category C aimed at creating an answer based on thorough scrutiny and analysis of a variety of information sources, and the relationship between these sources. Approaches to and experiences of information seeking reflect each other.

A comparison of the categories referring to these various aspects made it possible to discern an overall pattern. Often the same student held A-conceptions of relevance criteria, information overload, enough information and bias. There were similar patterns of coherence between B-categories and C-categories. Consistent with this overall pattern, three categories of conceptions of information seeking and use were developed on an aggregated level.

Learning outcomes

A second main theme for analysis was the students' understandings of the content of the assignment. Qualitative differences between students' learning outcomes were identified and described in three categories, grounded in students' understandings of the subject matter of the task as expressed in the final interview. A check between these categories and the teacher's assessment of the students' written reports indicated strong consistency.

A comparison between the three ways of experiencing information seeking and use and the three ways of understanding subject content shows great coherence. Those students who experienced information seeking as fact-finding according to category A also achieved a learning outcome described in the A category; the same is valid for categories B and C. The coherent pattern of students' experiences is presented in Table 6.2.

Table 6.2 Conceptions of information seeking and use, and of subject content

Category	Information seeking and use	Learning outcome
A	Fact-finding: finding the right answer, concrete evidence.	Consequences of EU membership could not be assessed because of lack of facts. Only fragmentary knowledge was gained about the EU.
B	Balancing information in order to choose the right side: finding enough information to form a personal standpoint on the issue.	Possible consequences of membership were related to the subtopic. The EU was understood as mainly economic co-operation.
C	Scrutinizing and analysing: critically analysing information sources; finding different perspectives; trying to reveal values in information.	EU membership was considered as a matter of ethical or political decision or commitment. The EU was seen as a power block.

These findings indicate a relationship between students' ways of experiencing information seeking and use and ways of understanding the subject content. An understanding of information seeking as fact-finding was not suited to such a complex learning issue. However, there is no simple cause–effect relationship but more of an interactive relationship. The findings show that students' different ways of understanding the subject matter of the task influenced the ways they sought for and used information. Likewise, students' different understandings of information seeking and use influenced their learning of subject content. Students' various approaches to information seeking influenced both information seeking and use and learning outcomes. This finding correlates with the findings of earlier phenomenographic research, into the close relationship between students' approaches to an assignment and learning outcomes (Marton and Booth, 1997). The findings point to variation in approaches to information seeking as a decisive dimension of the task with implications for learning outcomes.

Recent research on learning through the school library

In a more recent research project, *Learning through the school library* (LearnLib), we concentrated on how students use the library as well as other information paths and sources to seek and use information for their school assignments

(Alexandersson and Limberg, 2003). We were interested in the library as a means of acquiring information for learning tasks. The main research questions were: 'How is the school library used as a cultural tool and how do students learn subject matter through interaction with the school library?' The theoretical framework for LearnLib was a socio-cultural perspective on learning. The empirical material covers observations and field-notes from 11 classes in seven schools, with the youngest participants in year 2 (8-year-olds) and the oldest in year 12 (18–19-year-olds). Students were observed in the classroom and the library during the entire process of a learning task, from introduction to presentation.

Results indicate that information seeking in 11 classes is characterized by procedure rather than content and that information seeking is commonly understood as fact-finding, similar to category A described above. This fact-finding approach was prevalent regardless of the type of source used by the student – books, the web, multimedia, film, etc. There are surprisingly small differences in approaches to information between various age levels.

Major conclusions from the LearnLib project are that students' interaction with artefacts in the library and their communication with fellow students or adults are determined by the school context. Students define their task according to the school's discursive practice – and the school is a non-research environment, based not on genuine research questions but on the understanding that there are right answers to find, compile and re-present. This forms the basis for information seeking as fact-finding and for research as transport and transformation of text. To support more genuine research-based learning, the school's discursive practice needs to be dramatically challenged through conscious and systematic intervention from teachers and librarians.

Concluding discussion

The conclusions drawn from this research are in three areas, which have implications for theory development and professional practice.

The role of content

An important finding was the identification and description of the close interrelation between students' experiences of information seeking and use and their understandings of topic content. This indicates that information is given meaning linked to users' prior knowledge of the topic content and that information seeking is dependent on this interplay. It also indicates that students' various approaches to information seeking and use will impact knowledge formation. These results support those of Pitts (1994) and may be considered an elaboration of the role of topic in Kuhlthau's model with its emphasis on focus formulation. This opens up an area for further investigation into the interaction between users' understanding of information seeking and the content of information, which in turn points to the need for further studies of information use. Patterns of variation may be different for a task with content from natural sciences or humanities, as compared with my study where the topic concerned a controversial political issue. Comparisons between and across various contexts are equally important, for instance in workplace or everyday-life settings.

In LearnLib, we found that content was often disregarded by students and teachers, in favour of technicalities and procedure, resulting in trivial learning outcomes. This confirms the relationship between the quality of information seeking and learning outcomes. The shift from teacher-centred to student-centred learning, made possible partly through information and communication technologies, seems to have contributed to a trend toward individualistic rather than collective learning in class, as well as a procedural approach to learning, *to do the right things in the right order, with a view to presenting a product (report, web-page, etc.).* One conclusion from both projects is that adults, teachers and librarians should direct their interaction with students towards the knowledge content of tasks, challenge their students' understandings and perceive themselves as co-creators of student's knowledge. In the dissertation, the collective dimensions of learning were strong, both with regard to the interaction among students in the five groups and between the teacher and the students. There is reason to believe that this contributed to high-quality learning outcomes for the majority of students in that class. We also see a need to emphasize dimensions other than technology and procedure when teaching information seeking and use.

Critical features of variation

Findings showed that most important for the distinctions between categories of information seeking were conceptions of relevance criteria, assessment of enough and experience of bias. This emphasis on the evaluation and use of information as critical features of qualitative differences in variation of information seeking has been supported by subsequent research on information literacy (e.g., Bruce, 1997). Bruce (1997) identified and described seven categories of educators' conceptions of information literacy, three of which focused on the use of information. Most curricula for information literacy concentrate on finding information paths and sources as well as search techniques such as Boolean operators (Bruce, 1997, 172; Sundin, 2005). The LearnLib findings confirm the focus on procedure and technology.

These findings should have implications for information literacy education, where normative models of information seeking are abundant and based on the views of information experts. Researchers have attributed users' lack of abilities in information seeking to misconceptions or insufficient mental models (cf. Pitts, 1994), since they do not comply with ideal models such as 'the big six' (Eisenberg and Berkowitz,

2000) or Kuhlthau's process model. Researchers have shown less interest in describing how users who do not follow the models actually think or act. Many previous user studies have emphasized that information seeking is a complex process, but these results contribute to a better understanding of what is complicated and why this is so, from the users' perspective. There are similarities between the three conceptions of information seeking and use and Perry's scheme of the intellectual and ethical development of college students (Perry, 1970).

The implication is that the goals of information literacy education should be re-examined in comparison to typical standards of assessment, for instance those of various associations of librarians and teachers (e.g., Association of College and Research Libraries, 2000). Instead of listing a great number of skills, the goals of education should be for students to develop a repertoire of various ways of understanding information seeking and use and to be able to adopt an approach that is adequate for a particular situation or task. The phenomenographic description of variation offers such a repertoire. A substantial body of research emphasizes the importance of variation for purposeful learning, according to which it is essential for students to experience various perspectives on the same knowledge content in order to apply their knowledge to new situations. Encountering variation when learning at school prepares students for participating in the social practices of future communities of learning (Marton and Trigwell, 2000).

Theoretical implications

Identification of the pattern of variation in information seeking implies new ways of conceptualizing this phenomenon, and is a contribution to our theoretical understanding. Together, the three major ways of experiencing information seeking constitute the phenomenon of information seeking, as experienced by users. The consistent user perspective disclosed that common models of information seeking are normative, rather than neutral to information seeking. According to previous phenomenographic research the various conceptions are not tied to specific persons but instead may be encountered in other people in similar or different situations. This also implies that the various conceptions are dynamic; the relation between person and world (information seeking and use) can change. Information seeking, constituted in this way, is broader and more multifaceted than in more general models. The rich description of the various experiences of information seeking and the underlying dimensions provide new and detailed features of the phenomenon of information seeking. The identified conceptions call for further research to confirm and develop the pattern of variation found in my research. The research interest in understanding information seeking and use on a collective level rather than through individual differences between users was well served by the phenomenographic approach.

Part C
Environmental scanning and decision making

Introduction

The information content with which information management is concerned may be produced inside the organization, and intended predominantly for internal use by management, or it may be produced outside the organization by a multitude of organizations, from central government to market research companies and from business information services to newspapers and trade journals. Increasingly, of course, much of the external information of relevance to companies is found on the world wide web.

Environmental scanning is the process whereby organizational management make themselves aware of the conditions under which the company (or public sector agency) functions – the market, the competition, the state of the economy, legislative developments, etc. There is a degree of overlap here with the idea of competitive intelligence, since the scanning process is intended, in part, to reveal such intelligence.

The purpose of environmental scanning is to provide an information base relevant to the decisions the organization must take in its interaction with the environment, and the concept of decision-making is picked up by two of the authors in this section: one dealing with external information, the other with performance-related information from inside the organization.

First, however, Chun Wei Choo has revised and updated his paper on environmental scanning, relating it to the concept of the organization as a learning system. To some extent this chapter can serve as a bridge between Part B and Part C of this reader, as he treats environmental scanning as a part of organizational information behaviour. He explores four different modes of environmental scanning in relation to the perceived uncertainty of the environment, the organization's intrusion into it for collecting information, and the decision- and sense-making style of organizations. He employs the concepts of information needs, seeking and use and relates those to organizational strategies and managerial traits.

Zita Correia and T. D. Wilson investigate how managers in the Portuguese chemical industry scan their environments for information and, particularly, how managers' perceptions of environmental change affect the strategic change they implement. Their chapter explores the effectiveness of a grounded theory approach to discovering these perceptions.

'Gina' de Alwis and Susan Higgins's chapter reviews the literature on managerial decision-making and describes a study in Singapore, undertaken to identify the external information used by managers, and the sources of that information. As with other studies in other countries, a strong reliance upon trusted personal sources of information was found.

Finally, Judith Broady-Preston considers the role of performance data, gathered in accord with the balanced scorecard technique, in helping organizations to maintain a focus on customer needs and customer relationships, thereby to aid the process of strategy formulation. The context is the financial services sector, where this technique has been widely adopted.

All four chapters offer ideas and findings that may be of benefit to the practising information manager, especially in business and industry. Of course, the intention here is to provide an introduction to concepts, rather than to treat the field in detail, and to pursue the ideas further readers should consult part of the wealth of literature that now exists on this subject, from the classic *Scanning the Business Environment* (Aguilar, 1967) to more recent works such as Choo (1998b) and McGonagle and Vella (2003).

7

Environmental scanning as information seeking and organizational learning

Chun Wei Choo

Introduction

Environmental scanning is the acquisition and use of information about events, trends and relationships in an organization's external environment. It assists management plan future courses of action (Aguilar, 1967; Choo and Auster, 1993). Organizations scan the environment to understand the external forces of change and develop effective responses that secure or improve their future position. They scan to avoid surprises, identify threats and opportunities, gain competitive advantage, and improve long- and short-term planning. Environmental scanning constitutes a primary mode of organizational learning because an organization's ability to adapt to its outside environment depends on knowing and interpreting external changes. Environmental scanning includes both looking at information (viewing) and looking for information (searching). It could range from a casual conversation at the lunch table or a chance observation of an angry customer, to a formal market research programme or a scenario planning exercise. The aim of this chapter is to review the literature on environmental scanning and develop a model of the information needs, information seeking and information use patterns that characterize scanning; and then to elaborate the model by describing the sense-making, knowledge-creation and decision-making processes that constitute scanning.

Research into scanning

External factors (environmental turbulence and resource dependence), organizational factors (nature and strategy of the business), information factors (availability and quality of information) and personal factors (scanner's knowledge or cognitive style) influence scanning or browsing behaviour. Thus, many research studies into scanning investigate the effect of situational dimensions, organizational strategies, information needs and personal traits on scanning (see Figure 7.1).

Situational dimensions are studied by measuring the perceived uncertainty of the external environment. Organizational strategies refer to the position of the organization vis-à-vis the outside environment, and two examples of strategy typologies are those of Miles and Snow (1978) and Porter (1985). Studies of managerial traits include the managers' functional specialty, hierarchical level and cognitive style. Scanning as a form of information behaviour comprises information needs, information seeking and information use. In the context of environmental scanning, information needs are often studied with respect to the focus and scope of scanning. Information seeking is examined in terms of the sources used to scan the environment and the organizational methods and systems deployed to monitor it. Finally, information use is usually examined in relation to decision-making, strategic planning or equivocality reduction.

A summary of previous research leads to the following observations (Choo, 2002, 119–20):

1   Situational dimensions: the effect of perceived environmental uncertainty. Managers who perceive the environment as more uncertain will tend to scan more. Perceived environmental uncertainty is indicated by complexity, pace of change and the importance of the sectors comprising the external environment.
2   Organizational strategy and scanning strategy. An organization's overall strategy is related to the sophistication and scope of its scanning activities. Scanning

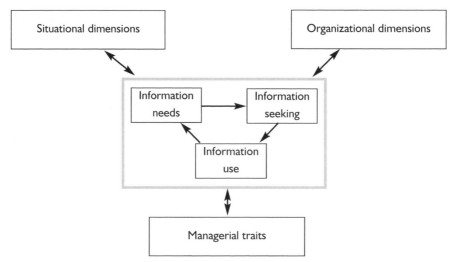

Figure 7.1   A conceptual framework for environmental scanning

must provide the information and information processing needed to develop and pursue the elected strategy.

3   Managerial traits: unanswered questions. The effect of the manager's job-related and cognitive traits on scanning is known. Upper-level managers seem to scan more than lower-level managers. Functional managers scan beyond the limits of their specializations.

4   Information needs: the focus of environmental scanning. Most studies look at scanning in various environmental sectors: customers, competitors, suppliers, etc. Business organizations focus their scanning on market-related sectors.

5   Information seeking: source usage and preferences. Although managers scan a wide range of sources, they prefer personal sources to formal, impersonal sources, especially when seeking information about fluid market-related sectors.

6   Information seeking: scanning methods. Organizations scan in a variety of modes, depending on their size, their dependence on and perception of the environment, their experience with scanning and planning and their industry.

7   Information use: strategic planning and enhanced organizational learning. Information from scanning is used to drive the strategic planning process. Research suggests that effective scanning and planning is linked to improved organizational learning and performance.

Figure 7.2 (overleaf) outlines these principal findings, using the conceptual framework of Figure 7.1.

Scanning and performance

Several studies suggest that scanning improves organizational performance. Miller and Friesen (1977) found that an intelligence-rationality factor, comprising environmental scanning, controls, communication, adaptiveness, analysis, integration, multiplexity and industry experience, was most important in separating successful companies from the unsuccessful, accounting for more than half the observed variance. Newgren et al. (1984) concluded that environmental scanning has a positive influence on corporate performance. Scanning also benefits small businesses. Dollinger (1984) concluded that intensive boundary spanning activity was strongly related to an organization's financial performance. West (1988) found that strategy and environmental scanning had a substantial influence on a firm's returns on assets and on sales.

Daft et al. (1988) studied scanning by chief executives and found that executives of high-performing firms increased the frequency, intensity and breadth of their scanning as external uncertainty rose. Subramanian et al. (1993, 1994) discovered that organizations with more sophisticated scanning functions performed significantly better. Ahituv et al. (1998) revealed that more successful firms showed a larger

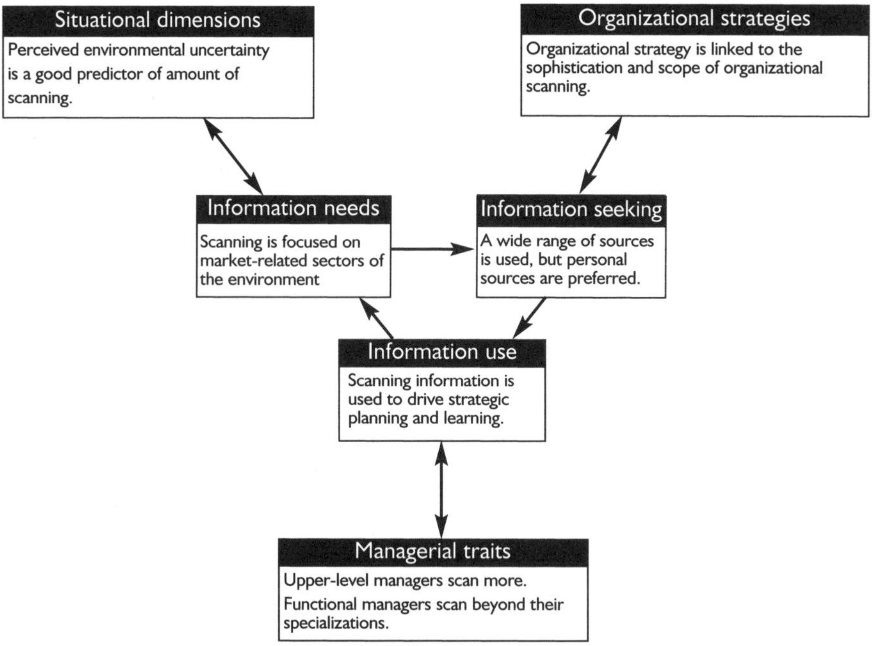

Figure 7.2   Summary of principal findings from research on environmental scanning (adapted from Choo, 2001, 120, Figure 4.4)

correlation between strategic uncertainty and scanning frequency in the technology, economic and socio-cultural sectors compared with the less successful firms.

The benefits of scanning were not solely economic or financial. In an in-depth case study, Murphy (1987) concluded that scanning is an important component of an organization's strategic planning process, and also contributes to increased communication among staff and greater employee involvement in the decision-making process. Ptaszynski (1989) found scanning had a positive effect on an educational organization in these areas: communication, shared vision, strategic planning and management and future orientation.

There is research evidence to show that environmental scanning is linked to improved organizational performance. However, the practice of scanning by itself is insufficient to assure performance – scanning must be aligned with strategy, and information must be effectively utilized in the strategic planning process. Coupled with the availability of information on external change, scanning can induce strategic, generative organizational learning. For a more complete review see Choo (2001).

Towards a model of organizational scanning

Theoretical understanding of organizational scanning is limited. Although all forms of scanning involve the seeking and use of information about the environment, different organizations operating in different environments may scan quite differently. Aguilar (1967) identified four modes and Daft and Weick (1984) build on Aguilar's work to develop a general model of organizational scanning based on two dimensions: environmental analysability ('Can we analyse what is happening in the environment?') and organizational intrusiveness ('Do we intrude actively into the environment to collect information?'). The objective of this chapter is to expand the Aguilar and Daft and Weick model in two ways. First, we elaborate the model by detailing the information needs, information seeking and information use patterns that characterize organizational scanning. Second, since the goal of scanning is the gaining of new knowledge that enables action, we elaborate the model by detailing the sense-making, knowledge-creation and decision-making processes that constitute scanning.

Environmental analysability and organizational intrusiveness

Daft and Weick (1984) suggest that organizations use different modes of scanning depending on management's beliefs about the analysability of the external environment, and the extent of organizational intrusion into the environment for understanding it. If an organization believes the environment is analysable, its events and processes determinable and measurable, it might seek to discover the 'correct' interpretation through systematic information gathering and analysis. An organization that perceives the environment as un-analysable might create or enact what it believes to be a reasonable interpretation that explains past behaviour and suggests future actions.

Daft and Weick (1984) hypothesize that differences in perceptions of environmental analysability are due to characteristics of the environment combined with management's previous interpretation experience. We may postulate that analysability could be related to perceived environmental uncertainty. Perceived environmental uncertainty measures the totality of the scanner's perception of the external environment's complexity and changeability. Duncan (1972) identified dimensions of the environment that determine its perceived uncertainty: the simple–complex dimension (the number of environmental factors considered in decision-making) and the static–dynamic dimension (the degree to which these factors change over time). Decision-makers in environments that are dynamic and complex experience the greatest perceived environmental uncertainty, as is determined by the perceived complexity (number of factors, opacity of causal relationships) and dynamism (rate of change) of the external environment. The combined effect of complexity and dynamism is the perception that the environment is un-analysable. Empirical research on scanning suggests that managers who experience higher levels of perceived environmental uncertainty tend to do a larger amount of environmental scanning (Choo, 2002).

The level of information about the environment may also be an important factor. Some industries regularly collect and analyse data about products, markets and competitors. Automation and information technology make it possible to amass and analyse data and trends efficiently. Affordably available, sufficiently detailed and timely information supporting decision-making may lead to the perception that the environment is analysable.

An organization that intrudes actively into the environment allocates substantial resources for information search and for testing or manipulating the environment. A passive organization takes whatever environmental information comes its way, and interprets the environment with the given information.

Daft and Weick (1984) hypothesize that differences in organizational intrusiveness depend on the degree of conflict between the organization and its environment. According to Wilensky (1967), when the environment is seen as hostile or threatening, or when the organization depends on it heavily, more resources are allocated to the scanning function. A hostile environment increases scanning because of new problems and the need to identify new opportunities and niches. Organizations in benevolent environments have weaker incentives to be intrusive. This line of reasoning is congruous with resource-dependency theory and institutional theory.

In resource-dependency theory (Pfeffer and Salancik, 1978), the environment is seen as a source of resources upon which the organization depends. Resource dependence is affected by the abundance of resources, concentration (the extent to which power and authority in the environment is dispersed) and interconnectedness (the number and pattern of linkages among organizations). The degree of dependence would be great when resources are scarce, and when entities in the environment are highly concentrated or interconnected. An organization can manage increasing dependence by adapting to or avoiding external demands; changing the patterns of interdependence through growth, merger and diversification; establishing collective structures to form a 'negotiated environment'; and using legal, political or social action to form a 'created environment'.

Institutional theory (Powell and DiMaggio, 1991) regards organizations as being 'forced to respond to, adapt to, or imitate the ebb and flow of normative and regulatory currents in their environments' (Aldrich, 1999, 49). Environments dominate or overpower organizations: change is imposed, authorized, induced, imprinted and incorporated (Scott, 1987).

In addition, the organization's overall business strategy may be related to the sophistication, scope and intensity of its intrusiveness. An organization that follows a particular strategy, such as product differentiation, cost leadership or focus strategy (Porter, 1985), or adopts a certain strategic stance, such as prospector, analyser or defender (Miles and Snow, 1978), is likely to adopt a scanning mode that provides the required information and information-gathering capabilities.

Intrusiveness may also be affected by: organizational size and inertia; slack or the availability of resources; past experience with scanning and interpreting the environment; and the availability of action or communication channels allowing the organization to influence the environment.

Environmental scanning as information seeking and organizational learning

An organization processes information to make sense of its environment, to create new knowledge and to make decisions (Choo, 1998a). Sense-making is induced by changes in the environment that create discontinuity in the flow of experience engaging the people and activities of an organization. People enact or actively construct the environment by bracketing experience and creating new features in the environment. Organizational sense-making can be driven by beliefs or by actions (Weick, 1995). In belief-driven processes, people start from an initial set of sufficiently clear and plausible beliefs, and use them as nodes to connect more information into larger structures of meaning. People may use beliefs to guide their choice of plausible interpretations, or may argue about beliefs and their relevance when these conflict with current information. In action-driven processes, people start from actions and grow structures of meaning around them. People may create meaning to justify actions that they are already committed to, or they may create meaning to explain actions taken to manipulate the environment.

An organization possesses three kinds of knowledge: tacit knowledge, explicit knowledge and cultural knowledge (Choo and Bontis, 2002). Tacit knowledge is learned through extended periods of experiencing and doing a task, during which the individual develops a capacity to make intuitive judgements about successful execution of the activity. Explicit knowledge is expressed formally using a code, and may be object-based or rule-based. Object-based knowledge is represented using strings of symbols (documents, software code), or is embodied in physical entities (equipment, substances). Explicit rule-based knowledge is codified into rules, routines or operating procedures. Cultural knowledge consists of the organization's beliefs based on experience, observation and reflection about itself and its environment. Over time, an organization develops shared beliefs about the nature of its business, core capabilities, markets, competitors, etc. These beliefs form the criteria for evaluating information and allocating attention. Nonaka and Takeuchi (1995) argue that organizations create innovations and capabilities by continuously converting and combining tacit and explicit knowledge.

Completely rational decision-making requires information gathering and processing beyond the capabilities of any organization. In practice, organizational decision-making departs from the rational ideal because of:

- lack of clarity of organizational goals that impinge on preferences and choices (goal ambiguity or conflict)
- too much, too little, or uncertain information about the methods and processes for the attainment of goals (technical or procedural uncertainty).

This can lead to four different decision-making modes. In the boundedly rational mode, when goal and procedural clarity are both high, choice is guided by performance programmes (March and Simon, 1993). Thus, decision makers 'simplify' their representation of the problem situation; 'satisfice' rather than maximize their searches; and follow 'action programmes' or routine procedures. In the process mode (Mintzberg et al., 1976), when strategic goals are clear but attainment methods are not, decision-making becomes a highly dynamic process; many internal and external factors interrupt and change its tempo and direction. In the political mode (Allison and Zelikow, 1999), groups pursue divergent goals, each believing that their preferred alternatives are best for the organization. Decisions and actions are then the results of bargaining among players pursuing their own interests and manipulating available instruments of influence. In the anarchic mode (garbage can model; Cohen et al., 1972), when goal and procedural uncertainty are both high, decision situations consist of independent streams of problems, solutions, participants and choice opportunities arriving and leaving. A decision then happens when problems, solutions, participants and choices coincide. Then, solutions are attached to problems, and problems to choices, by participants who are present and have the interest, time and energy to do so.

Modes of environmental scanning

Depending on the organization's beliefs about the environment's analysability, and whether the organization intrudes into it actively or passively, four modes of scanning may be differentiated: undirected viewing, conditioned viewing, enacting and searching (Figure 7.3).

Undirected viewing

Undirected viewing (Aguilar, 1967) takes place when the organization perceives the environment as un-analysable and does not intrude to understand it. Information needs are ill-defined. Much of the information obtained is non-routine or informal, usually gained through chance encounters. As the environment is assumed to be un-analysable, organizations are satisfied with limited, soft information, and do

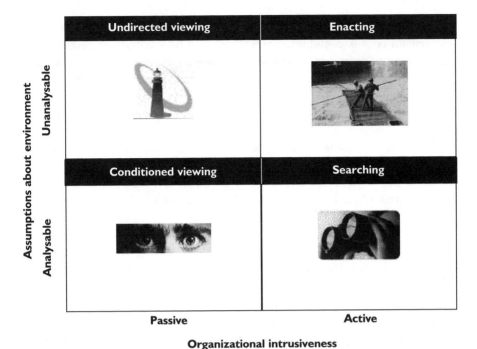

Figure 7.3   Modes of environmental scanning

not seek comprehensive, hard data. Information seeking is casual and opportunistic, relying on irregular contacts and casual information from external, people sources. Because the information received is ambiguous and supports multiple interpretations, information use is concerned primarily with reducing high levels of equivocality. Weick (1979) suggests that to reduce equivocality, organizations use assembly rules to shape data into a collective interpretation. The greater the equivocality, the fewer the number of rules activated because of uncertainty about information meaning. Arriving at a common interpretation requires many cycles of information sharing.

The advantage of undirected viewing is that the organization does not need to expend resources on formalized scanning, but this saving incurs the risk of being caught off-guard.

During undirected viewing, sense-making is characterized by informal bracketing, i.e., the organization brackets external signals informally, depending on which subjective cues observers attend to at the time. Partly because multiple observers with different frames of reference may be involved, many cycles of sense-making are required to reduce equivocality about what is happening. This may require many episodes of face-to-face dialogue, negotiation and persuasion. Undirected viewing is based on tacit beliefs that the complexity, opacity and dynamism of the environment render it un-analysable. These beliefs, shared by the organization's members, can remain unspoken and unexamined. There is little stable knowledge to help interpret and make sense of environmental changes. Decision-making has to deal with high levels of uncertainty and ambiguity. Daft and Weick (1984) suggested that coalition building may be necessary for management to achieve a particular interpretation and a single course of action. Alternatively, a strong, powerful leader may choose the course of action.

The mode of learning in undirected viewing is one of stimulus and response: the organization maintains its status quo until a strong stimulus is recognized and necessitates a response. A summary of the information seeking and organizational learning in undirected viewing is shown in Figures 7.4 and 7.5.

Conditioned viewing

Conditioned viewing (Aguilar, 1967) occurs when the organization perceives the environment to be analysable but passively gathers information and influences the environment (see Figures 7.4 and 7.5). Information needs focus on a small number of relatively well-defined issues or areas. These are often based on widely-accepted industry assumptions and norms. Information is sought using standard procedures, typically employing internal and non-people sources. A significant

		Undirected viewing		Enacting
	Information needs	General areas of interest	Information needs	Specific areas of exploration
Unanalysable	Information seeking	Informal	Information seeking	Testing
	Information use	Noticing	Information use	Experimenting
		Conditioned viewing		Searching
	Information needs	Sensitized areas of concerns	Information needs	Detailed search goals
Analysable	Information seeking	Routinized	Information seeking	Formal
	Information use	Watching	Information use	Discovering

Assumptions about environment

Passive   **Active**

Organizational intrusiveness

Figure 7.4   Environmental scanning as information seeking

Undirected viewing		Enacting	
Sense-making	Waiting for important change	Sense-making	Create features in environment
Knowledge creation	Little pre-existing knowledge	Knowledge creation	Tacit knowledge: learn by doing
Decision making	Coalition/political mode	Decision making	Anarchic/process mode
Conditioned viewing		**Searching**	
Sense-making	Driven by norms and beliefs	Sense-making	Determine objective reality
Knowledge creation	Cultural knowledge: expectations, frames	Knowledge creation	Explicit knowledge: hard data, formal models
Decision making	Programmed/rational mode	Decision making	Process mode

Environmental analysability — Unanalysable / Analysable

Passive — **Active**

Organizational intrusiveness

Figure 7.5   Environmental scanning as organizational learning

amount of data comes from external reports, databases and respected sources widely used in the industry. Thus, viewing is conditioned in the sense that 'it is limited to the routine documents, reports, publications, and information systems that have grown up through the years' (Daft and Weick, 1984, 289). Because the environment is perceived as knowable, there is less need for equivocality reduction. A greater number of rules can be applied to construct a plausible interpretation.

During conditioned viewing, sense-making is belief-driven, and there are fewer cycles of equivocality reduction. Over time, the organization (or the industry it is in) develops a set of assumptions and beliefs and uses them to define areas of particular interest to structure or 'condition' the scanning activity. Fewer cycles of sense-making are required to reduce equivocality because the organization starts from an initial set of accepted beliefs, and already knows its critical issues. Cultural knowledge plays an important role, supplying assumptions and beliefs about the business and the environment: who the customers, competitors and stakeholders are; which environmental sectors to watch; and which information sources to use. These assumptions and beliefs may be shared by firms in the same industry. They draw a frame of reference within which knowledge about the environment is created. Decisions tend to be programmed (March and Simon, 1993) by standard procedures and premises derived from past experience. Representation of the decision situation is simplified, search is 'satisficing' and procedures are structured by rules and routines adopted from standard industry practice or from the firm's own experience. The mode of learning steers the organization to use existing knowledge to focus scanning and action taking.

An illustration of conditioned viewing gone awry is provided by Christensen (1997). Several generations of disk-drive manufacturers were highly focused on listening carefully to their largest customers, and failed to see that new technologies rejected by them did appeal to new customer groups which expanded into new market segments. Thus, the advantage of conditioned viewing (procedures and mental model established to structure the scanning process) becomes a disadvantage, as these rules and routines might miss the emergence of new, possibly disruptive developments.

Enacting

Enacting takes place when the organization perceives the environment to be unanalysable but intrudes actively into it to influence events and outcomes (see Figures 7.4 and 7.5). Information is required for experimentation and for testing the environment. This involves identifying areas for fruitful intervention. Information is sought from external sources and channels created by the organization through intervention, and may include collecting feedback about the organization's actions. Enacting organizations 'construct their own environments. They gather information by trying new behaviour and seeing what happens. They experiment, test, and stimulate, and they ignore precedent, rules, and traditional expectations' (Daft and Weick, 1984, 288). Information use focuses on the actions that have been taken, and aims to reduce equivocality as well as to test existing rules and precedents.

An example of enacting would be introducing a new product based on what the firm thinks it can sell, rather than waiting for an assessment of market demand. An organization may also actively influence and shape attitudes: 'manipulate shareholder perceptions toward itself, environmental issues, or political candidates by sending information to shareholders through various media' (Daft and Weick, 1984, 290). In today's network society, organizations are increasingly using the world wide web as a channel for enacting their environment innovatively.

During enacting, sense-making is action-driven. The organization intrudes actively into the environment to construct new features and concentrate sense-making on them, e.g., by test-marketing a new product, organizing a seminar or publishing a document. The information generated from enactments constitutes new raw material for sense-making. Thus, equivocality is reduced by testing the environment. Tacit knowledge is important since the pursued enactments and the interpretation of information depend on individual intuition and creativity. Through reflecting on signals returned by enactments, organizations acquire new ways of seeing the environment. Daft and Weick (1984) suggest that decision-making in enacting follows the process model of Mintzberg et al. (1976): the organization decides on a course of action, designs a custom solution, tries it then recycles the process if the solution does not work. Decision-making may also resemble the anarchic mode. Here, actions are not goal-driven but are taken in order to discover goals. Decisions happen when solutions (enactments) appear to work and become attached to problems. The mode of learning is to learn by doing – trying out new actions to reveal new goals and methods.

Searching

Searching takes place when the organization perceives the environment to be analysable and actively intrudes to collect accurate facts about it (see Figures 7.4 and 7.5). Information needs are based on well-defined, broad, detailed, open-ended search goals. The organization is prepared for unexpected findings revealing new information needs. It seeks hard, formal, often quantitative data, typically from rigorous surveys or market research. The organization is likely to have its own scanning unit systematically analysing data to produce market forecasts, trend analyses and intelligence reports. There are important differences between conditioned viewing and searching. Information seeking and use in conditioned viewing is restricted to a few issues; routinized, and based on received knowledge. In contrast, searching is broad, open, and based on a willingness to revise or update existing knowledge.

An example of formalized searching would be Motorola's strategic intelligence system. Its corporate intelligence office maintained a central database, co-ordinated the collection of data and strategic intelligence reporting, led corporate-wide analysis projects and supported operational divisions' intelligence. The divisions ran their own intelligence collection, performed division-level analysis and supported corporate intelligence efforts. A high-level policy committee assigned intelligence priorities to the unit (Gilad, 1994; Penenberg and Barry, 2000).

During searching, sense-making is based on formal, systematic scanning to determine the verifiable facts in the environment. This systematic scanning can be both action- and belief-driven. Data gathering about the environment is intense and involves intrusive actions, e.g., polls, surveys, focus groups, etc. Interpretation is likely to be belief-driven: the organization extrapolates from past experience and constructs meanings from current beliefs. Developing and working with explicit knowledge is the essence of searching. Measurement, modelling, forecasting, trends analysis and other formal, quantitative methods are utilized to discover the true condition of the environment. The organization believes that there is a stock of knowledge about the environment that it can draw upon for analysis and planning. Because the organization is actively searching for information about a knowable environment, decision-making is likely to follow the process mode in which the organization takes the time and resources to look for or develop alternatives. Choosing a course of action is based on a diagnosis of the situation. Decision-making is based on logical, rational procedures, often involving the use of analytical, quantitative techniques.

The mode of learning is to invest resources in collecting information and analysing the environment, and then to adjust the organization's actions according to this new knowledge. The main difference between searching and conditioned viewing is that searching requires significant resources for entering the environment to create new features and/or collect information. Another difference is that searching scans broadly and comprehensively, whereas conditioned viewing concentrates on selected areas or issues.

The different modes of scanning are compared in Figures 7.4 and 7.5. Research suggests that the model proposed by Daft and Weick is consistent with empirical knowledge about organizational scanning (Choo, 2002). This action-learning perspective is increasingly evident in the strategy literature, which emphasizes improvisation, discovery-based planning and emergent strategy-making (Mintzberg et al., 1998). In summary, the scanning model appears to be a viable framework for analysing the primary environmental and organizational contingencies that influence environmental scanning as cycles of information seeking and information use.

Implications for practice and research

Implications for practice

In today's highly volatile environment, organizations face a dilemma. On the one hand, the environment appears un-analysable because of its complexity and rate of change. On the other hand, organizations recognize that they must be proactive in scanning and shaping their environments. Some organizations believe that precisely because the environment is in flux, there is an opportunity (or a necessity) to intervene and influence developments to their advantage. The model implies that to encourage proactive scanning organizations must raise levels of environmental analysability and organizational intrusiveness. To increase environmental analysability, the organization might keep in touch with important actors; make information about customers, competitors and industry widely available to employees; and encourage staff to take part in collective discussions and sense-making of external developments. To increase organizational intrusiveness, the organization might create channels to communicate with and influence stakeholders; encourage managers and employees to test environments by allocating resources or providing organizational slack; and tolerate innovative enactment experiments that do not 'succeed' but increase understanding of a difficult problem.

Implications for research

The model suggests hypotheses that may be tested empirically. The variable of perceived environmental uncertainty could be studied as a metric of environmental analysability. Several scanning studies have operationalized perceived environmental uncertainty by measuring subjects' responses to questions about perceived complexity, rate of change, and importance of environmental sectors (e.g., Choo, 2001; Daft et al., 1988). Organizational intrusiveness can be measured by the amount of scanning, particularly the frequency and extent of use of external sources, or the size of the budget for acquiring external information and building information resources. Other indicators might include the frequency and quality of communications with external stakeholders, and the use of enactments such as surveys, seminars or web-based interventions. The characteristics of information seeking and use could guide analysis to identify modes of scanning. Studying the scanning modes in terms of sense-, knowledge- and decision-making might call for a more narrative, ethnographic approach.

In summary, the model of environmental scanning presented here offers plausible explanations for the different levels and patterns of scanning that are observed in practice.

Acknowledgements

The author is grateful for comments from Professor Pierrette Bergeron of EBSI, Université de Montreal, and from participants in the 2001 Summer School on Information Management at the Department of Information Studies, University of Tampere, led by Professor Maija-Leena Huotari.

8

Scanning the business environment: from perceived environmental change to strategic change

Zita Correia and T. D. Wilson

Introduction

This chapter reports part of the findings of research that sought to provide a comprehensive understanding of the environmental scanning process. The purpose of this research was to investigate how managers in the Portuguese chemical industry scan their environments for information, the contextual factors that affect their scanning, and how managers' perceptions of environmental change affect the strategic change they implement. This chapter addresses this last issue in particular.

The conceptualization of organizations as open systems implies that the environment is regarded as a source of resources and a source of information. The notion of an environment external to the organization, affecting its actions as well as its outcomes, raises the question of how the organizations actually come to know their environments.

The history of research on the organizational environment revolves around two main approaches: one advocates objective measures of the environment and the other takes a subjective approach to describing organizational environments. The complexity of the relations between the organization and its environment, and the ambiguity of organizational boundaries, provide fertile ground for disagreement about what constitutes dimensions of the organization or its entities and what constitutes dimensions of the environment.

Bourgeois (1980) argues that the cause of contradictory results in empirical research lies with an unresolved issue in the literature: that of objective versus perceived environment. Bourgeois distinguished three categories of definition currently used to describe the environment: objects, attributes and perceptions. The first category refers to entities or objects external to the organizations. The most influential contribution to this category was that of Dill (1958; 1971) who distinguished between general and task environments, the latter including customers, suppliers, competitors and regulatory groups. The category of attributes focuses on the complexity and turbulence of the task environment. The category of perceptions refers to managers' perceptions of environmental uncertainty. Sutcliffe (1991) found that a number of mismatches may occur between managerial perceptions of environmental attributes and actual environmental attributes.

Weick proposed the concept of enacted environment as a substitute for external environment, since 'The human actor does not react to an environment, he enacts it' (Weick, 1979, 64). The process of enactment itself is the result of attentional processes that are retrospective and selective, and it is described as the 'sequence whereby some portions of the elapsed experience are made meaningful' (Weick, 1979, 64). Weick's concept of enacted environment is of great importance to understanding the subjective approach to organizational interactions with the environment. Since the enactment process relies upon specific individuals in focal organizations, objective measures of the environment become irrelevant. This means that different organizations and different individuals will react differently to the same context. Because individuals are subject to innumerable constraints, their perceptions and understanding of reality are necessarily limited, and their representation of the world is shaped by their own experience.

However, Pfeffer and Salancik (1978, 74) note that the enactment process is to a large extent determined by the organizational and informational structure of the organization, thus introducing an important nuance to more radical approaches to individual differences as the only determinants in the process.

Methodology

Research design

In the context of this research, the case study approach was considered appropriate for providing a holistic approach to the study of environmental scanning in industrial organizations operating in the chemical industry. Strauss (1987) emphasizes the usefulness of the case study approach when used in conjunction with the grounded theory method of qualitative analysis. Grounded theory seeks to generate theoretical statements and, ultimately, complex theories based on empirical evidence. The research design adopted can be described as a multiple case study, composed according to the theory-building structure described by Yin (1989), where the sequence of chapters follows a theory-building logic, and using the grounded theory method of qualitative analysis to develop the theory.

Information about the companies was obtained from business databases, publicly available data conveyed by the annual reports of the companies, promotional material and newsletters, and also historical and cultural information provided by the managers interviewed – either orally, as an introductory part of the interview, or in printed form, when available. All this information was of great importance to contextualize and illuminate the core information regarding the environmental scanning phenomenon in the companies analysed. Not all cases, however, provided equally rich frameworks.

In the end, 19 companies were studied: five small companies (with more than ten and fewer than 99 workers), ten medium-size companies (with up to 399 workers) and four large companies (with more than 400 workers).[1] These 19 companies cover several sub-sectors of the chemical industry, and are listed in Table 8.1 according to their respective standard industrial classification codes (SIC).

Table 8.1 Number of companies by SIC, and number of interviewees by company

SIC	Production	Firms	%	Interviews	%
2812	Alkalies and chlorine	1	5.3	2	5.0
2821	Plastics materials	4	21.0	8	20.0
2823	Man-made fibres	1	5.3	3	7.5
2833	Medicine/botanical chemicals	1	5.3	1	2.5
2834	Pharmaceutical preparations	5	26.3	11	27.5
2844	Cosmetics/toilet preparations	2	10.5	5	12.5
2851	Paints and allied products	2	10.5	5	12.5
2861	Gum and wood chemicals	2	10.5	4	10.0
2879	Farm chemicals	1	5.3	1	2.5
	Total	19	100	40	100

The sample used did not obey the principles of statistical sampling (see footnote for the characteristics of Portuguese industry), but did adhere to the principles of maximum variation sampling, as defined by Patton (1990), and those of theoretical sampling, as defined by Strauss and Corbin (1990), i.e. sampling on the basis of concepts that have proven theoretical relevance to evolving theory. Grounded theory strives towards verification through the process of category saturation. This involves staying in the field until no further evidence emerges from which the researcher can develop properties of the theoretical category. This explains the high number of cases studied and the number of managers interviewed.

---

[1] This classification was adapted from that used by IAPMEI (Instituto de Apoio às Pequenas e Médias Empresas e ao Investimento, or, Institute for the Assistance of Small- and Medium-size Businesses and on Investment) and reflects the characteristics of Portuguese industry, where very small (up to ten workers), small and medium-size companies make up more than 90% of the total number of companies.

The main tool used for collecting the core information was the semi-structured interview, a tool flexible enough to favour adaptation to each context, organization or individual, and to pursue unexpected paths and clues suggested by the theoretical sensitivity (Glaser, 1978) developed by the researcher throughout the research process. In all, 47 interviews were carried out, although seven played a complementary role: these seven interviewees were not questioned about the issues approached in the main interview guide, but about related issues that needed to be clarified. The 40 main interviewees had the following job titles: managing directors (19 top managers performing the roles of chief executive or managing partner), marketing and commercial directors (14), deputy directors (two, one with planning functions and the other with commercial functions) and financial directors (two).

Observation played a minor, but non-negligible role. Visits to the premises, including the factory plants in some cases, meals in the canteens of some of the companies, attention paid to the way-of-doing-things in all the companies – how visitors were announced, how meetings were scheduled and cancelled, absence or frequency and type of interruptions in the course of the interviews, degree of formality or informality in interpersonal relations – contributed to consolidate impressions or confirm information based on documentary evidence or on the interview contents.

Conceptual framework: the categories and the model

The interviews provided an empirical basis for the articulation of a grounded theory of environmental scanning. The articulation of the theory implies the identification and description of a set of categories and the relationships among them, which explain a significant part of the phenomenon under study. Those categories and relationships must be clearly defined, and the theory itself should be meaningful for both organizational theorists and information scientists.

The grounded theory proposed – generated in the context of a multiple case study, composed according to the theory-building structure, as explained before – comprises three main components: the categories, the principal relationships among them, and the contextual factors that shape the categories and their relationships. From an internal perspective, these contextual factors include corporate history and culture. From an external perspective, the contextual factors include the overall economic, social, cultural and political conditions that characterize a specific space–time reality (Portugal at the beginning of the 1990s) and that shape, to a certain extent, the organizations studied.

The model of organization implied by the theory is that of an open system. The phenomenon under study is that of environmental scanning, which refers to the exposure to and acquisition of 'information about events and relationships in a company's outside environment, the knowledge of which would assist top management in its task of charting the company's future course of action' (Aguilar, 1967, 1).

Figure 8.1 depicts the proposed model of the environmental scanning process, according to the paradigm model of the grounded theory (Strauss and Corbin, 1990).

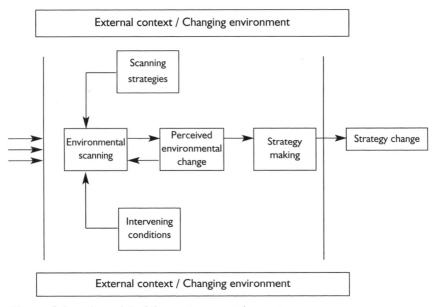

Figure 8.1   A model of the environmental scanning process

The intervening conditions refer to the internal factors that influence the scanning activity, which were found to be both of an individual nature (information consciousness and individual exposure to information) and of an organizational nature (organizational outwardness and information climate). The scanning strategies refer to the scanning focus, scanning mode and the use made of information sources. The intervening conditions are described and analysed elsewhere, as were the principal relationships identified among them: the information consciousness–information climate connection and the organizational outwardness–individual exposure to information connection (Correia and Wilson, 2001).

The following sections will therefore address the relationship identified between the environmental change perceived by managers and the strategic change they implement, based on their perceptions and through their strategy-making activity.

Research findings

Perceived environmental change

The category 'perceived environmental change' emerged from analysis of the managers' perceptions of the factors causing change to their companies' environment.

That main category was built upon two other categories – regulatory framework and business structure – each of these clustering a number of concepts corresponding to a number of events and factors affecting the business environment. The changes of a regulatory nature derived from joining the EU and from government intervention, while the changes of a business nature were linked to the trend for concentration in the chemical industry and the crisis of client industries.

The changes of a regulatory nature associated with joining the EU included the necessary adoption of new rules and procedures, such as regulations concerning the registration of medicines, the adoption of the patent regime in force in Europe and the demand for higher standards regarding product quality. It included also the progressive elimination of customs tariffs and its consequences upon the fragile competitiveness of Portuguese companies. Managers also feared that customs barriers might be replaced by technical barriers, but the enlargement of the market derived from joining the EU was evaluated as a positive issue.

As for government intervention, it was seen as excessive – especially concerning the regulation of the market, in particular in the health sector (approval or rejection of the production of new medicines, establishment of medicines' prices). The policy of high interest rates practised by the banking system was another negative issue, with responsibility being attributed to the government, as most of the banks were nationalized when the fieldwork was carried out and high interest rates were part of the government policy to keep inflation down. The government was also accused of lack of capacity to defend the national interests within the EU and of the mismanagement of development programmes such as PEDIP (Strategic Programme for the Development of Portuguese Industry).

Changes in the business structure were described as multiple, because of the acquisitions and mergers taking place, and the disappearance of smaller companies that sank under the pressure of competition. These changes were a result of the trend for concentration that prevails in the chemical industries at large, especially in the pharmaceutical and cosmetics sub-sectors, and also in the segments of resin-derived and synthetic fibre products. An important factor causing instability was said to be the crisis of the client industries, such as the shoe industry and the textile industry. Factors of a cultural nature were invoked to explain the reticence of Portuguese entrepreneurs to engage in strategic alliances.

The assessment of environmental attributes showed that the environment had become extremely hostile and rather complex, even though turbulence was thought to be relatively low. Comparative analysis of the results regarding environmental change, obtained both through the assessment of environmental attributes and through the analysis of perceptions of environmental change, evidenced compatible results. However, the use of the quantitative approach, based on the counting of responses to limited choices, as presented in the framework used in previous research, proved limiting. It was the use of the grounded theory method of analysis that provided data that was effectively grounded, corresponding to the managers' experiences and conceptualizations of their organizations' environment.

Table 8.2 displays the results of that comparative analysis. The table integrates the classic attributes of 'complexity' (number and diversity of external factors in the company's task environment) and 'turbulence' (degree of change of those factors) (Huber and Daft, 1987) with that of 'hostility', used by Miller and Friesen (1983). This third attribute was adopted as it makes an important contribution: the notion of threat caused by hostile competitor strategies, regulatory restrictions and shortage of resources. However, these attributes were used in previous research to assess the change occurring in the task environment. Their application to the analysis of perceptions of environmental change in the task as well as in the general environment had a remarkable revelatory effect.

The advent of the single market was seen as inevitable and was faced predominantly with moderate optimism; it was widely believed that the worst had passed, meaning that the adaptation process to the common market had been hard enough and that something positive could still be expected from the single market, like keeping market shares or conquering a niche market or realizing a successful alliance. Plans for internationalization did not go further than Spain in most cases.

The peripheral condition of Portugal was seen as a hindrance to penetration of other regions as well as a protection against competitors from central Europe, especially in industries producing low-value-added products with high transportation costs.

Strategy-making

Mintzberg (1994, 23–7) uncovers the multiple meanings attached to the term 'strategy', in its use by planners and managers, as well as in the management literature:

- strategy as plan – 'direction or guide into the future'
- strategy as pattern – 'consistency in behaviour over time'
- strategy as position – 'determination of particular products in particular markets'
- strategy as perspective – 'organization's way of doing things'.

Planners, Mintzberg argues, have favoured plan over pattern and position over perspective.

Strategy formulation is inseparable from planning and constitutes the first of the two stages of the planning process (the second being implementation). Ansoff (1987, 235) describes strategy formulation as 'the logic and techniques of strategy analysis' and warns that 'the flow of decisions leading to strategy formulation is

Table 8.2 Assessment vs. perception of change

	Turbulence (low)	Hostility (high)	Complexity (high)
Assessment of change in the task environment	Competitor activity (65% find it predictable or fairly predictable)	Market activity of competitors (90% think it has become more hostile)	Diversity of production methods and marketing tactics in the companies studied (70% think diversity has increased)
	Clients' preferences (67.5% find them predictable or fairly predictable)	Industry ups and downs (47% find them unpredictable)	
	Rate of innovation (48.7% think it has stabilized or decreased)		
Perception of change in the environment (task + general)		Global: Gulf War (affected oil prices and availability and cost of oil-derived raw materials)	
	Regional: EU and Single Market trend for concentration (mergers, acquisitions, strategic alliances and the disappearance of smaller companies)	Regional: EU and Single Market regulatory impact (abolition of tariff protections, replacement of customs barriers by technical barriers)	Fall of fibre consumption Unethical marketing tactics of multinational competitors Dramatic change in the distribution channels
		Local: Entry of new competitors and products Crisis/expansion of client industries Shortage of resources (difficulty of access to credit, shortage of qualified manpower, pressure to reduce energy consumption) Government role (intervention in setting prices and high interest rates)	Social pressure towards environment protection

complex, involves many contributing studies and can be very time consuming'
(Ansoff, 1987, 131–2).

Such characteristics – the segmentation of the process into two stages and the
assumption of stability in the firm's environment – were criticized by Mintzberg,
who argues that strategy itself is always associated with conditions of stability:

> Intended strategy refers to the effort to impose a *stable* course of action on the
> organization, while realized strategy refers to the achievement of a *stable* pat-
> tern in the behaviour of an organization. Thus, whether deliberate or emergent,
> strategy is always about stability in an organization's behaviour.
>
> (Mintzberg, 1994, 239)

In order to cover both possibilities – intended as well as emergent strategies, since
'effective strategies mix these characteristics in ways that reflect the conditions at
hand, notably the ability to predict as well as the need to react to unexpected
events' (1994, 25) – Mintzberg proposes the expression 'strategy formation' (or
strategy-making), to denote an eminently dynamic process of dealing with change.

The scenario emerging from the interview transcripts reveals the making of strategy as a rather hectic process, entirely dependent on environmental conditions in
the first place: availability and cost of manpower and raw materials, technological
developments, competitor strategies, client needs and government regulations,
sometimes dependent even on weather conditions. Companies have to scan the environment continuously in order to detect trends and spot opportunities and threats
as early as possible so that they can influence the course of events or, more commonly, adapt to the new conditions. Once an opportunity is spotted, or a threatening
circumstance is identified, the company engages in a *tour de force* in order to work
out a strategy to deal with it.

For small companies, the process of adaptation is a condition of survival and
the sales force plays an important role in the early detection of emerging needs and
alterations in the tastes of clients. Great flexibility is demanded from companies
in order to adapt to changes in the environment. However, Loasby (1991) reminds
us that 'flexibility is not the result of good early warning, it is an alternative to it'.

Strategic change

The category 'strategic change' emerged out of the analysis of the strategic initiatives undertaken by managers as a means of adapting to the changes occurring in
their business environment or as a means of trying to influence the course of
events.

Strategic change in the companies analysed revolved mainly around increasing
product quality, which involved in some cases improvement in the conditions of

production and was associated, in specific cases of highly pollutant industries, with measures of environment protection. Other important changes of a strategic nature were internationalization and diversification, pursued by dynamic companies enjoying steady growth. Companies targeting internationalization chose growth through acquisitions. Companies oriented to the internal market, needing to secure a position threatened by strong competitors, embraced strategic alliances. Companies with little scope for growth adopted specialization as a form of strategic change.

Increasing product quality was a generalized target. However, some companies made it clear that they had always pursued quality, while others admitted that they had to improve the quality of their products and the conditions of production in order to satisfy EU regulations. This concern was particularly acute among companies from the plastics sub-sector and the large manufacturers in declining industries, such as the chlorine producer and the synthetic fibre manufacturer. In this last case, fear was expressed that technical barriers could replace customs barriers. The companies that engaged in improving product quality as part of an adaptive process to cope with EU regulations are indicative of firms that are not well-prepared to face the single market, and present a typical reactive behaviour.

The companies that opted to specialize operate in the paints and in the pharmaceutical sub-sectors, where multinational companies have dominated for decades — hence the need to seek product and market niches not covered by the giant corporations; choosing this option in these conditions may be regarded as an adaptive behaviour, but is not necessarily a reactive behaviour. Growth, diversification and internationalization involve complex and risky processes and are more clearly associated with proactive behaviours. Table 8.3 (overleaf) displays the range of strategic choices made by the companies studied.

More than any other factor, the changeability of the environment proved to be a determinant in the rejection of tight planning schemes. The size of the company influences the adoption of planning (larger companies tend to engage in planning) but other factors interfere with that tendency, such as the form of the organization and the management style or the dominant culture. There emerged no indication that industrial segment or sub-sector might influence the adoption of planning as a management tool. On the other hand, planning offices are rare and their main role is to collect the hard data needed to support top managers' decision-making.

Ansoff (1987) considers acquisitions and mergers to be major instruments of strategic change, and that internationalization and domestic diversification are alternative routes to expanding a company's portfolio. Only three of the companies studied engaged in these actions: a pharmaceutical company which, when the study was carried out, ranked among the top ten companies operating in this country and in this sub-sector, a paints company ranking among the 300 major companies operating in Portugal in 1989, independently of sector; and a plastics company that had recorded fast and steady growth throughout the 1980s.

Table 8.3   Range of strategic choices made by the companies studied

Type of behaviour	Action taken	Goal
Reactive ————→	Increase of product quality (acquisition of new equipment, automation of production, building of new plants)	Quality certification
	Specialization (product or market differentiation)	Creation of a product or market niche
	Growth (acquisitions, mergers, strategic alliances, internal development)	Increase of business volume
	Diversification (new products and markets in the same geography)	Expansion
Proactive ————→	Internationalization (new geography)	Expansion

Theoretical statements

The perceived environmental change–strategic change connection

Perceived environmental change refers to the perceptions developed by managers concerning the alteration in the pattern of events and relationships occurring in the company's outside environment, which may lead the company to adjust to the new conditions. Strategic change refers to the alteration of the company's course of action in order to create new conditions or adapt to new conditions. The perceived environmental change–strategic change connection translates the decisive role of top managers' perceptions of environmental change in their decisions to change their companies' course of action.

It was found that managers perceive their business environment to be extremely hostile, very complex and rather turbulent. Change in the task environment was believed to be relatively predictable. The discontinuities identified originated outside the task or industry environment, and were caused mainly by regulatory actions. Under these conditions, the principal concern for most companies became their ability to respond flexibly to such changes as they arose. This was shown by managers' declarations concerning the inadequacy of tight planning schemes. The critical factor became the capability to respond, which is often dependent upon the availability of resources. Access to resources of critical importance, such as certain raw materials, credit and qualified manpower, was often mentioned as problematic.

The fact that for many of the companies increasing product quality was the main and, in some cases, the only strategic concern denotes behaviour of the reactive type. Few companies had clearly proactive behaviour, engaging in actions such as diversification and internationalization. Building on previous research on managerial interpretations of the environment (Daft and Weick, 1984; Miles and Snow, 1978; Sutcliffe, 1991) and on the impact of national culture on the interpretation of and response to strategic issues (Schneider, 1989; Schneider and de Meyer, 1991), it is possible to suggest that reactive behaviour is associated with perceptions of the environment as a source of threats and, therefore, as uncontrollable, while proactive behaviour is associated with perceptions of the environment as a source of opportunities and, therefore, controllable.

It was apparent that the regulatory activity of the national government and of the EU was at the centre of managers' preoccupations, as was the limited availability of certain resources. However, information acquisition and use patterns were not in accordance with these preoccupations; managers attribute much more importance to, and use much more frequently, market-related information (Correia, 1996). This means that managers continue to engage in scanning patterns that are appropriate to conditions of stability but are unsuitable in an environment where important discontinuities were identified.

Similarly, the predominant use of the surveillance or viewing scanning mode is appropriate for scanning the task environment but is not appropriate for scanning the general environment, and line managers usually lack the skills needed to search for information on the general environment, which is available from public sources. Interpretation of this type of information also requires analytical skills that most companies do not have. Specialized staff would be needed for this task. In fact, Ansoff (1987, 108) noticed that not only do organizations generally lack information about themselves and their respective environments, they also lack 'the managerial talents capable of formulating and implementing strategy'.

The model revised

The model of organization adopted is that of an open system that interacts with its environment and is made up of several interdependent sub-systems. This research focused mainly on the interaction of the informational and functional sub-systems, and in particular on the impact of managerial perceptions of environmental change (based on information that represents or recreates the external environment) on managerial strategy-making that leads to strategic change. The initial proposal (see Figure 8.1) of a model of the environmental scanning process proved to be inaccurate. Part of that model, corresponding to the informational sub-system, is now revised according to our research findings, and is illustrated in Figure 8.2.

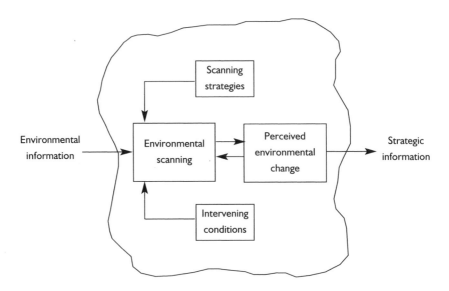

Figure 8.2   The informational sub-system at work

The environmental information collected by managers provides a representation of the external environment. By shaping managerial perceptions of the environment, some of that information becomes of strategic importance for driving the company's future. It was found that most managers do not adapt their scanning strategies to their perceptions of environmental change, either because they perceive their environments as uncontrollable or because they lack the information skills necessary to search for information and their companies lack the analytical skills necessary to interpret certain types of information. The loop linking perceived environmental change to the environmental scanning activity is, at best, tenuous.

9

Managerial information seeking and use behaviour: a case study of Singapore

Shrianjani M. (Gina) de Alwis and Susan Higgins

Introduction

The last two to three decades have seen countries, companies and employees grappling with new forces within a turbulent and uncertain state resulting from the collapse of economic boundaries, increasing globalization, the information, communication and telecommunications (ICT) revolution, an emphasis on intellectual over resource power, and increasing buyer sophistication (Kanter, 1991; Thurow, 1996). These upheavals challenge traditional business models, requiring companies to embrace continuous change to maintain competitive advantage. Companies become more knowledge-driven and managers build new core competencies in their employees (Hamel and Prahalad, 2000; Schein, 1994).

Singapore has followed an investment-driven strategy of economic development and achieved an extraordinary level of prosperity. But external volatility has affected the country and exposed weaknesses in the business environment that need to be addressed if the country is to move to the next level of competitiveness (Porter, 2002). The Singapore Economic Review Committee's (2003) report recommends changing Singapore into a more creative and entrepreneurial nation with a diversified economy. The next few years will be critical as Singapore attempts to activate an entrepreneurial culture in its people and transform itself into a knowledge-based economy. This transition requires Singapore to enhance its capabilities in the production, distribution and use of information as it previously did with goods and services. Toh et al. (2002) recently compared Singapore's capabilities with those of OECD countries to gauge the level of its development. They found that Singapore's knowledge-based economy (KBE) capabilities are generally competitive with those of the OECD countries (OECD average = 1):

- Knowledge creation index   1.03
- Knowledge acquisition index   1.49
- Knowledge dissemination index   1.05
- Knowledge application index   0.93

The study reveals that Singapore is strongest in the knowledge acquisition index, which is attributable to its reliance on multinational companies and foreign talent for knowledge transfer. However, the acquisition of foreign talent alone does not necessarily represent organizational learning, because companies need to ensure knowledge becomes embedded across the organization. Managers need not only to identify information which can add value to the business but also to integrate new knowledge into the company's existing store of knowledge. Given that intellectual capital is the differentiating source of competitive advantage for companies today, Singapore companies need to maintain and tap dynamic knowledge bases (Poh, 2001). Managers, therefore, are challenged to adopt new ways of working and management styles to ensure internal diffusion of information throughout the organization, since a culture of sharing is essential for organizational learning.

Scope of study

Our objective was to provide an insight into the information behaviour of Singapore's managers as they contribute to the company's knowledge base and link these patterns to the role of dissemination of information in Singapore's business environment. The study sought to establish what information managers need regularly, why they need it, how the information is sought and used, their preference for sources and issues faced in the process of seeking and using information. Such knowledge would enable information providers to improve existing services and to develop more relevant services and products.

Characteristics of the Asian and Singaporean manager

Management practices and styles are a reflection of the socio-cultural milieu (Tan, 1996) and studies confirm that Asia uses different forms of managing and organizing to those found in the West (Redding, 1996).

According to Min (1995), the world's most inspiring management experiments are taking place in the east Asian and south-east Asian regions. Min identifies four predominant management systems: Japanese, mainland Chinese, overseas Chinese and Korean, all considered to be heavily influenced by the Confucian tradition and following strong vertical information sharing and management control. Leadership styles and decision-making are highly authoritarian; the most authoritarian is found in Chinese family businesses. The participation of professionals in decision-making is lowest in this group.

Other characteristics of Asian management practices include paternalism, which incorporates loyalty, diligence and deference; emphasis on relationships or *guanxi*; and the concept of collectivism as opposed to the Western notion of individualism (Redding, 1996). Asian managers are perceived as individuals who limit their areas of involvement to their own community and the segment of society where they feel a sense of belonging (Mendoza, 1991).

Singapore follows a variety of management practices and styles. This is attributed to two factors: the multicultural origins of immigrants and the open, pragmatic and pro-business policies developed to attract foreign investors (Tan, 1996). A recent study (Straits Knowledge, 2002) concludes that Singapore is a special operating environment, and faces uncommon issues in management cultures, decision-making and power cultures. Ditzig and You (1988) reveal that 61.3% of managers are traditionalists, with visionaries a distant second. The traditionalists follow an authoritarian leadership style and exert tight control; they are logical, analytical, decisive, tough-minded and well-organized, and they plan well in advance. Their strengths are maintaining stability and setting up and maintaining routines, regulations and hierarchy, with great respect for policies, contracts and standard operating procedures. Possible weaknesses are impatience with delays, hastiness in decision-making in the interest of efficiency, and relative slowness and even reluctance to respond to the changing needs of the organization. The authors highlight that these characteristics hinder effective communication within organizations.

Why managers seek information

Managers need information at two levels: about the immediate business environment to guide them in tactical and operational decisions and about the broader business environment for long-term strategic planning (Ghoshal and Kim, 1986). The immediate business environment covers current competitors, existing technologies and product markets in which firms operate daily. As change agents, managers need constantly to review changes taking place internally and externally, to interpret these events and analyse how they affect the organization, its departments and individuals. The defining context of managerial work, therefore, is the need to solve problems immediately, as managers rarely have the luxury of extended contemplation.

Managerial information seeking for decision-making

Authors have repeatedly noted that one of the main reasons managers seek information is for decision-making. In fact, management comprises a series of decision-making processes and this process is at the heart of managerial activity (Cyert et al., 1956).

A decision is defined as a specific commitment to action and is described as a somewhat hesitant, cyclical process which usually begins with a little understanding of the decision situation (Langley et al., 1995; Mintzberg et al., 1976). The literature reveals that information seeking is central to decision-making and, therefore, it is not surprising that more has been written about this than any other information seeking situation (Allen, 1996; Katzer and Fletcher, 1992).

The decision-making model most frequently referred to in the literature is Simon's (1960). The three-phase model identifies an 'administrative man' who 'satisfices' (Simon, 1957) rather than maximizes, as the real world is too complex for all alternatives to be known and understood and all consequences to be considered. It is argued that the manager seeks a result that is good enough, although not necessarily the best. 'Satisficing' is considered to be mainly due to a lack of information, the cost of additional information in terms of time, frustration or money, or the inability of the decision maker to process, analyse and use the information.

Studies identify many contextual, social and individual variables that affect the extent to which decision-makers seek and use information. These include managers' positions in the hierarchy, which provide the power and control to act as boundary spanners and information gatekeepers. This also influences how much information they can acquire, how it is shared in the workplace, and the roles and tasks that managers perform. Managers' information behaviour may also be conditioned by personality preferences, measured according to Jungian constructs. Therefore, information seeking for decision-making is dependent on the individual's preferred and most developed mental function which provides overall direction and consistent focus to their personality, and the individual's preferred way of perceiving the problem or situation with which they are faced. Kirk's (2002) analysis of interviews with managers showed that the five different ways of experiencing information use were related to three different views of information: as an object, a construct or a transformative force.

Information is more likely to be used by decision-makers if it is readily accessible, summarized and presented orally, and is from a source deemed to be credible and trustworthy (O'Reilly, 1983). Preferred information includes that which is supportive of outcomes favoured by decision-makers, does not lead to conflict among the relevant actors and cannot be attacked by those in opposition. Therefore, given the same information set, different decision-makers may use different parts of it in different ways by selecting and weighting the information differentially. But while some individuals seek information to make decisions and cope with crisis situations, others follow strong, agreed-upon, tightly-constructed sets of beliefs in order to reduce the amount of information sought in decision-making or to reduce negative decisions (Allen, 1996).

As highlighted above, managers may be categorized based on how they approach information seeking in decision-making. Some proceed to making decisions with only partial information which they may have had no time to process fully or analyse, while others obsessively collect information rather than make decisions (Radford, 1981). Some others rely on intuitive skills rather than information to make decisions (Agor, 1986). Using intuitive skills in decision-making is tied to the categorization of managerial decision-making styles based on the thinking styles of Jung and the personality types identified by the Myers-Briggs type indicators (MBTI).

These studies reveal that innate personality traits, and the context of the situation in which the decisions are made, impact upon managers' information seeking and rational decision-making. Therefore, it can be concluded that information seeking for decision-making is complex and has varied implications for managers.

Managerial information seeking behaviour

Managerial information behaviour has been written about extensively over many years from the perspective of business, management, psychology, public administration, etc. But research covering the information studies perspective on managerial information behaviour is of fairly recent origin beginning with Taylor (1986) and is limited to a few studies. Auster and Choo (1994a) concur that, relative to the large number of studies available on other professionals, only a few look at the information seeking behaviour of managers as a distinct group. In the context of Singapore, the studies available are limited to De Alwis (1997), De Alwis and Higgins (2001) and Cheuk (1998a and b).

The first noteworthy study on managerial information behaviour is Aguilar's pioneering work which conceptualizes environmental scanning as 'scanning for information about events and relationships in a company's outside environment, the knowledge of which would assist top management in its task of charting the company's future course of action' (Aguilar, 1967, 1). Subsequently, studies of managers' information seeking have focused mainly on environmental scanning in large companies and multinationals in the USA, relying chiefly on data collection techniques such as mail surveys and interviews (e.g., Culnan, 1983; Daft et al., 1988; Keegan, 1974; Miller, 1994; O'Reilly, 1980, 1982).

Studies in other countries include one of large companies based in Korea (Ghoshal, 1988; Ghoshal and Kim, 1986),one of the first covering environmental scanning in the UK from an information studies perspective (Lester and Walters, 1989), and Auster and Choo's (1993a and b; 1994a and b) studies on environmental scanning in Canada. Other themes identified in the literature, again originating mainly in the USA and the UK, include the relationships between managers' functional specialities and their information needs, uses and preferences

(White, 1986; White and Wilson, 1988), information use and information overload (O'Reilly, 1980), source use and accessibility (O'Reilly, 1982), accessibility of sources and task environment in source selection (Culnan, 1983) and source preference across management levels.

The period beginning 1990 reflects a change of direction in research – a decline in studies on environmental scanning and a wider thematic and geographic coverage. Topics covered include relationships between source use and work complexity in Nigeria (Tiamiyu, 1992), source preference and information use in Canada (McKinnon and Bruns, 1992), New Zealand (Chalmers, 1995; Keane, 1999), six nations (Oppenheim, 1997; Reuters Business Information, 1994), Portugal (Correia and Wilson, 1997; 2001) and Singapore (De Alwis, 1997; De Alwis and Higgins, 2001), and information seeking in organizational settings (Rosenbaum, 1996).

The literature was fully reviewed in our original *Information Research* paper (de Alwis and Higgins, 2001) and the key points to emerge, which have not been challenged by later research, are:

1   Managers have access to a wide range of information sources, which may be categorized as internal or external to the organization and as personal or impersonal.
2   Managers need to be competent in the acquisition and use of information to improve the competitiveness and profitability of the firm.

The Singapore case study

The study population was selected from the membership of a professional management body using purposeful sampling to enable the selection of information-rich cases (Patton, 1990). The questionnaire was developed and pre-tested on a sample of five respondents. The survey instrument comprised three parts. Part I focused on information resources and comprised a mix of quantitative and qualitative questions where respondents were also required to list services and products according to preference. Examples were provided to avoid confusion. Part II was on information use. The elements listed under types and sources of information and preference for sources were adapted from previous studies to suit local conditions. Part III of the questionnaire captured the demographic details of the respondents.

The questionnaire was mailed to a sample of 369 managers, accompanied by a cover letter describing the objectives of the survey and assuring confidentiality, and a self-addressed envelope. Follow-up included two reminder letters and telephone calls. The survey was conducted over a period of three months in 1996.

Response rate

A total of 20 responded to the survey, a response rate of 5.4%. Though the low response rate undermines the validity and reliability of the study, the paucity of previous research in the Singapore context makes the findings of this study usable as indicative information. Owing to the low response rate a careful reliability check was carried out and findings compared and contrasted with previous research of a similar nature (Glazier and Powell, 1992). The results of the survey were more or less consistent with those of similar studies in Canada, the USA and New Zealand. It is postulated that significant differences might have been evident with a qualitative survey. However, the depth of the information retrieved is considered indicative of the wider information needs and information seeking behaviour of Singaporean managers.

Use of information resources

Part I of the survey covered use of resources such as libraries, information suppliers, CD-ROMs, online databases and the internet. More than half the respondents indicated that their companies maintain libraries, but that many of these are confined to minuscule document collections housed in small rooms with no professional supervision. Reasons given for not setting up a library include high overheads and the need to assess its value to the company. However, it is known that even an extensive library forms only a small part of a company's information system (Keegan, 1974) and planners often find these tedious, time-consuming and frustrating to use as they have difficulty locating what is available (Lester and Walters, 1989). These could also be reasons that affect policy-makers' decisions against allowing the establishment and expansion of libraries. Findings also confirmed that libraries outside the company are used on a regular basis, corroborating the idea that users are fully aware of where relevant sources can be found (Chalmers, 1995). Use of foreign libraries and information suppliers drew a zero response and is attributed to the high costs of doing so.

Use of CD-ROM and online services drew a low response and is comparable to the findings of similar studies conducted around the same time period. The main reason for low usage in Singapore and the region is attributed to high costs. Results reveal that respondents were not only fully aware of the usefulness of these as sources of information, but that they were also aware of the range of titles available. The use of the internet is primarily for e-mail and searching. Over half the respondents used personal and company accounts for this purpose.

Use of information

Types of information used for decision-making

The types of information considered 'very important' for decision-making included competitor trends followed by economic and industry/market information. Types of information considered 'important' included business news followed by political, social and supplier trends, regulatory information, use of information technology, demographic trends and new management methods. Low importance was given to political, social and stock market trends and best practices.

One finding of the local survey not generally consistent with previous studies is the importance given to suppliers. Singapore companies place ISO certification and quality high on their agendas and, therefore, it is not surprising that they consider supplier trends important. The importance of suppliers as a source of information is corroborated by Auster and Choo (1993a and b). It is surprising that this category has been given little emphasis in previous studies considering the focus companies place on quality.

Other findings not consistent with previous results include the high importance given to economic, political and social trends. This can be attributed to the entrepreneurial skills inherent in the Chinese culture and the spill-over effect of the Singapore government's *Strategic Economic Plan* (Singapore Ministry of Trade and Industry, 1991) which outlines a vision for the country to reach the top league. The top priority given to competitor trends may be attributed to Singapore's business being driven at a regional and global level. The high use of regulatory information is consistent with the reviewed literature.

Preference for sources of information

Respondents were asked to rate their preference for a series of sources of information such as personal contacts, subordinate managers, company library, radio/TV, newspapers and internal computer printouts to acquire information on political, economic, social, consumer, supplier, competitor and industry/market trends, regulatory information, use of IT, forecasts, stock market, business news, company performance, demographics and new management methods.

Personal sources such as personal contacts, subordinate managers and colleagues were given a 'very high' preference for information on political trends, competitor trends, use of IT, forecasts and company performances. A 'high' preference rating was given to personal sources to obtain information on industry/market, supplier and competitor trends and company performance. Printed sources such as government publications, newspapers, internal reports, and materials available in the company library as well as other libraries were given 'very high' preference for obtaining information on political, economic, social and competitor trends, regulatory information, business news and forecasts. A 'high' preference was indicated for printed sources such as newspapers, government publications and internal computer printouts to obtain information on political, economic, social, consumer, supplier, demographic and competitor trends, industry/market trends, regulatory information, forecasts, business news and company performance.

In the final analysis it is seen that managers use different sources of information to fulfil their different information needs.

Reasons for preference

A summary of the results, given in Table 9.1, includes only sources rated as 'very high' preference and 'high' preference by five or more respondents. Survey findings reveal that personal contacts are rated 'very high', and preference for subordinate managers and colleagues within the organization is 'high'.

Previous studies reveal that the important factor to note when using personal sources is the need to know who to consult to avoid being overwhelmed by lots of information. It is interesting to note that the Reuters study (Reuters Business Information, 1994) offers the contradictory finding that although word of mouth is an important source, word of mouth, meetings and personal contact are considered the least accurate or reliable sources of information. This finding has to be seen in the light of Reuters' business interests in electronic information and news products. The study also reveals that Singaporean managers' *high* use of personal sources is attributed mainly to prior experience and easy access because of recommendations or referrals.

Table 9.1 Summary of preference for sources of information and reasons for preference (N = 20)

Source	Preference rating		Reasons for preference		
	Very high	High	Prior experience	Easy access	Recommended or referred
Personal contacts	7	–	10	8	–
Subordinate managers	–	7	7	9	–
Company library	–	–	–	7	–
Radio and TV	–	–	–	7	–
Newspapers	–	–	–	9	5
Internal computer printouts	–	–	–	5	–

One other finding of the study is that newspapers are placed second as a source of 'very high' preference. Newspapers are voted as a popular source owing to their easy access and because they are recommended or referred. One reason for 'high' preference is the availability of a wide range of foreign newspapers in the local market.

While use of the company library received a middle ranking ('very high'), use of the broadcast media such as radio and TV received a 'high' rating which may be attributed to the choices available.

Internal computer printouts received a middle ranking under both 'very high' preference and 'high' preference, mainly owing to ease of access.

The literature on managerial information seeking refers to a complex set of inter-actions between information and its source which influences the way information is perceived and acted upon by managers (Ghoshal and Kim, 1986). The same piece of information is seen differently when received from a favourite and trusted sub-ordinate than when received from the manager of the intelligence unit. The local study concurs that users base their selection of information on the effort required to gain access to the source (Miller, 1994). Accessibility not only determines the overall frequency of the use of the source, but also the choice to use it as the first source.

Preference for using information

The three most important types of information usage relate to use of information for personal purposes. Collection of information to pass on to other persons was not considered important. Further research needs to be carried out in this area to determine whether Singapore managers are protective of information to the point of withholding it from others and are similar in their behaviour to Britain's man-agers (Reuters Business Information, 1994) who were found to keep information to themselves as a competitive advantage, or whether they are operating under an essentially dissimilar mandate. This finding also leads to speculation about the extent to which Singapore companies may be defined and considered as knowledge-based where information sharing and the free flow of information are a given.

Information challenges managers face in the 21st century

As early as 1960, Simon referred to a revolution taking place in decision-making which he attributed to computers. He conceived that computers would offer speed and new techniques for decision-making. This was confirmed by Marchionini (1995) who stated that the technology-driven work environment affects personal information infrastructures at all levels. The digital environment has generated stud-ies on information seeking on the web (Choo et al., 1998, 2000a and b; Choo and

Marton, 2003), the use of corporate portals (Detlor, 2000; Stenmark, 2003) and the internet as an information source (Teo, 2000; White and Jacobs, 1998). We might say that a change in information gathering has occurred with technology, which has also changed personal information infrastructures, but that the information seeking behaviour of managers remains essentially unchanged in its preference for readily accessible sources, primarily human.

Therefore, the importance of face-to-face communication and network building (Luthans et al., 1988) persists as acquiring information useful for achieving managerial agendas is a high priority. This importance has given rise to a new body of literature which signifies the value of social capital, social networks, social relations at work and communities of practice (e.g., Cohen and Prusak, 2001; Cronin and Davenport, 1993; Cross et al., 2001; Cross and Parker, 2004; Wenger, 2002).

Conclusion

Although the response rate to the survey was low, the findings, with a few exceptions, can be considered more or less consistent with previous studies. Singapore managers use a range of sources, print and personal as well as sources which are internal and external to the organization, to obtain information. The preference for sources or source selection is influenced by the users' perception of or attitudes to the accessibility of sources. But it is doubtful if the mix of sources Singapore managers use is the right balance to produce the required information with 'appropriate richness'. The local managers do not exploit the wide range of sources easily available to them, mainly because of a lack of awareness of their availability and usefulness and also because of a lack of skills in the use of such sources. Drucker's proclamation that 'few executives yet know how to ask, What information do I need to do my job? When do I need it? In what form? And from whom should I be getting it?' (Drucker, 1995, 109) may be considered universally applicable.

The future

The *Library 2000* report (1994) highlighted that information plays an important role in Singapore's emerging knowledge economy. Looking at the bigger picture, managing businesses in the 21st century is also predicted to be a great challenge to the Asian manager. Somewhat ironically, in order to maintain a competitive edge managers must share information and value employees. According to Jones, 'Managerial concerns with the "bottom line" may subvert broader conceptions of company "competitiveness" which include improving the skills, knowledge and commitment of shop-floor employees' (Jones, O., 2003, 245). To improve these skills will take a commitment from management to the development of employees. Common sense tells us that managers need to be up to date with information on market trends, benchmark data and productivity indicators to stay competitive, but, in order to enable them to assess their business performance and to strengthen the longer-term strategic position of stakeholders, knowledge and skills must be disseminated throughout the company. Information professionals in Singapore have a role to play here, a more proactive, intermediary role, not only to connect managers with relevant and timely information, but to support them with ideas for continuing education for their employees. In this way, their service will be value-added. Organizations that can take a lead here are the National Library Board, the Singapore Institute of Management and the two schools of information studies. They can be the main leaders supporting the creation of an organizational and 'marketplace of ideas' culture which is the cradle of progress for creative decision-making.

10

The balanced scorecard, strategy, information and intellectual capital

Judith Broady-Preston

Introduction

In the contemporary competitive economic climate, companies must harness information effectively to ensure optimum performance in the market. This chapter reviews the use of the 'balanced scorecard' technique as a means of identifying a range of performance measures that can guide strategic development. It also considers the implications for information management of the balanced scorecard technique. As McAdam and Bailie (2002, 972) state:

> Businesses today require better information across a wider scope than that of the traditional, often linear, financial measure, to achieve understanding of the factors that create the foundations of future success. . . . It is important to establish a comprehensive view of performance measures that indicate the overall health of a business, which can then be more fully aligned with business strategy.

In a recent survey of information value in the legal sector, Broady-Preston and Williams concluded:

> Information was viewed as adding value to the business via its role in enhancing overall business performance, improving service delivery and customer service. It also assisted in increasing the profitability of the firms, helping organizations to achieve and sustain competitive advantage.

Moreover, there was also recognition that 'Information had a significant impact on organizational performance, as an integral element of an overall strategy' (Broady-Preston and Williams, 2004, 8).

Traditionally, companies achieved competitive advantage from their management of, and investment in, tangible assets such as property, equipment, stock and so forth. This was held to be true for the 19th and much of the 20th century (Chandler, 1990). However, as several commentators have observed (e.g., Blair, 1995; Webber, 2000), by the end of the 20th century, intangible assets became the major source of competitive advantage. This coincided with what Tyson (1998) has described as the move from an information age to an intelligence age. In this new age, companies were required to build both a knowledge base of their competitive environment and a perpetual strategy process to ensure its continual renewal. Hence:

> Strategies for creating value shifted from managing tangible assets to knowledge-based strategies that create and deploy an organization's intangible assets. These include customer relationships, innovative products and services, high-quality and responsive operating processes, skills and knowledge of the workforce, the information technology that supports the work force and links the firm to customers and suppliers, and the organizational climate that encourages innovation, problem-solving, and improvement.   (Kaplan and Norton, 2001b, 88)

It is possible to appreciate the scale of this seismic shift by comparing the tangible book values as percentages of organizations' market values. Blair (1995) states that in 1982 tangible book values formed 62% of organizations' market value. In contrast, by 1999, less than 20% of companies' market value was accounted for by their tangible assets (Webber, 2000). Thus:

> Increasingly intellectual capital, synonymously used to refer to intangible assets and to knowledge capital, is becoming the driver of value in an organization. It is an important economic resource for many organizations and directly affects competition in markets. . . . There is also an indication of the growing importance corporate executives place on non-financial measurements and value drivers in communicating how value is created for shareholders.
> (Lim and Dallimore, 2004, 181–2)

In addition to this recognition of the role of intellectual capital in achieving competitive advantage, there are problems associated with measuring its worth or demonstrating its value. Indeed, it could be said that the drive to represent these intangible assets on the balance sheet of organizations has become the holy grail for accountants in the 21st century. However:

> . . . [the] attempts to 'value' individual intangible assets [are] almost surely . . . a quixotic search. . . . Companies achieved breakthrough performance with

essentially the same people, services, and technology that previously delivered dismal performance. . . . Value creation came not from any individual asset – tangible or intangible. It came from the coherent combination and alignment of existing organizational resources.   (Kaplan and Norton, 2001a, 102)

Methods for measuring intellectual capital and intangible assets have been investigated and/or proposed by, among others, Kaplan and Norton (1992, 2001b, 2004), Sveiby (1997) and Oppenheim et al. (2001). Indeed, *The Journal of Intellectual Capital* is devoted to investigating and building theory in this area. Some companies are employing Sveiby's intangible assets monitor (1997), and although the balanced scorecard (BSC) did not emerge until the early 1990s, statistics quoted in Drury (2004) show that this is arguably the predominant model employed by organizations both to measure and to manage intellectual capital. Indeed, the authors of this model, seemingly in contradiction to their views expressed above, stated recently that:

The balanced scorecard tool and strategy map offer a framework to measure intangible assets, and to describe strategies as a series of cause-and-effect linkages among objectives. They provide a language that executive teams can use to discuss the direction and priorities of their enterprises.

(Kaplan and Norton, 2004, 10)

Scorecard models

The balanced scorecard (BSC) was devised by Kaplan and Norton in 1992, and subsequently modified and enhanced (1993, 1996a and b; 2001a, b and c). A key assumption of the BSC, and similar models such as that of the European Foundation for Quality Management (2001), is that measures of performance are an integral component of a cause-and-effect relationship, linking strategy formulation to financial outcomes. The use of scorecard models, in particular, entails a reconsideration of the traditional corporate management style, and a move away from reliance on purely financial measures as a basis for strategy development. The assumption of a causal relationship is crucial as it then allows non-financial measures to be used in predicting future financial performance. However, as can be seen below, there have been some difficulties in successfully demonstrating this basic assumption.

What is a balanced scorecard?

Interestingly, Kaplan and Norton do not appear to provide a clear definition of a scorecard in any of their writings to date (January 2005). Indeed, one of the most frequently reported questions posed by managers is: 'What is a Balanced Scorecard?'

(Lawrie and Cobbold, 2004, 612). However, it has been described as a performance measurement framework with two key objectives: converting strategy into specific goals for different sections of the organization and communicating that strategy to all parts of the organization (Migliorato et al., 1996).

The original design of the scorecard (Kaplan and Norton, 1992), which was categorized as 'first-generation' by Lawrie and Cobbold (2004), clustered a mixture of financial and non-financial measures into four different perspectives:

- financial (how do we look to our shareholders?)
- customer (how do our customers see us?)
- internal business (what must we excel at?)
- innovation and learning (can we continue to improve and create value?).

Each perspective required the definition of relevant objectives, measures, targets and initiatives, and scorecards operate by specifying a limited number of goals and measures. Thus, a financial goal may be mere survival, measured by cash flow, whereas a customer goal may relate to new product developments, measured by the percentage of sales from new products. Many companies already use these types of financial and non-financial measures as key information components in their strategic decision-making process. However, the contribution of the balanced scorecard is to ensure that these measures become an integral part of the information system for employees at all levels of the organization. Thus, while the financial and non-financial measures are derived from a top-down process driven by vision, they also provide bottom-up feedback to strategic decision makers.

The 1992 design and its subsequent modifications has been the subject of frequent criticisms (cf. Eagleson and Waldersee, 2000; Kennerley and Neely, 2000; Norreklit, 2000, 2003). Seemingly in response to such criticisms, especially with regard to the perceived vagueness of definition, and the subsequent practical difficulties experienced by managers in designing successful scorecards, the original design underwent significant changes in the mid-to-late 1990s (Kaplan and Norton, 1996a and b). The burgeoning number of books, articles and websites offering advice and guidance on successful scorecard design and implementation may be viewed as evidence of such practical difficulties (cf. Niven, 2002; Olve et al., 1999; Parmenter, 2002; Radnor and Lovell, 2003). Interestingly, one of the original authors, David Norton, is the founder and chair of the Balanced Scorecard Collaborative, a company offering practical seminars on scorecard usage and design.

These second-generation scorecards (Lawrie and Cobbold, 2004) enabled the balanced scorecard to evolve from 'an improved measurement system to a core management system' and become a central component of 'a strategic management system' (Kaplan and Norton, 1996b). The two major innovations in design from the 1992 scheme are:

- the identification of 20–25 strategic objectives, each of which is associated with one or more measures and assigned to one of the four perspectives
- documentation of the major causal relationships between strategic objectives visually in a 'strategy map' (Kaplan and Norton, 2004).

This latter innovation was made seemingly in response to severe criticisms as to the lack of empirical evidence to support the assumption of a cause-and-effect relationship between non-financial and financial measures, as indicated above (cf. American Accounting Association, 2002; Norreklit, 2000). Speckbacher et al. (2003), in a survey of 38 companies, found that only half were able to formulate cause-and-effect relationships among the different objectives and measures.

Third-generation scorecards

Third-generation scorecards are now proposed (cf. Andersen et al., 2004; Lawrie and Cobbold, 2004). These offer the following enhancements on second-generation models:

- a 'destination statement' describing the appearance of the organization at an agreed future date, including quantitative details
- the financial and customer perspectives are replaced with a single 'outcome' perspective, and the internal business process and learning and growth perspectives with a single 'activity' perspective (Barney et al., 2004).

The first of these enhancements would appear to address concerns expressed by Norreklit: 'Because . . . [a scorecard] measures cause and effect at the same time without considering any time lag, it has no time dimension' (Norreklit, 2000, 71).

Originally, although providing senior managers with information from four differing perspectives, the balanced scorecard was believed to minimize information overload by limiting the number of measures used: 'Companies rarely suffer from having too few measures. More commonly, they keep adding new measures whenever an employee or a consultant makes a worthwhile suggestion' (Kaplan and Norton, 1992, 71–3).

The use of so few measures has been criticized, primarily in relation to the omission of important perspectives, notably that of environmental impact (Drury, 2004). Nonetheless, as Drury observes in commenting on such criticisms:

Kaplan and Norton presented the four perspectives as a suggested framework rather than a constraining straitjacket. There is nothing to prevent companies adding additional perspectives but they must avoid the temptation of creating too many perspectives and performance measures since one of the major benefits of the balanced scorecard is its conciseness and clarity of presentation.

(Drury, 2004, 1004)

Moreover, the 'third-generation' scorecards,

with just two perspectives, [eliminate] debate about 'missing' perspectives . . . the issue is simply whether the right activities are represented, and whether the correct consequent outcomes from these activities also are shown.

(Lawrie and Cobbold, 2004, 618)

Arguably, with third-generation models information overload is reduced still further, while at the same time optimum flexibility is provided for managers by allowing them to select perspectives of relevance to their organizations. This latter point is of special concern within the public sector. As the scorecard concept matured, more and more public sector organizations began to produce their own scorecards (e.g., Chan, 2004; Johnsen, 2001). Chan states: 'With growing interest in improving performance management in the government sector, the balanced scorecard can be a valuable management tool that meets the need for improvement and change' (Chan, 2004, 208).

Public sector scorecards

Echoing the concerns identified by Drury (2004), it could be argued that many public sector managers found the apparent rigidity of definition of the four perspective labels problematic, as typified by the large number of suggestions proffered for alternative labels (cf. Elefalke, 2001; Irwin, 2002). However, while Lawrie and Cobbold (2004) argue that this is a key driver towards a third-generation model, there is evidence from the public sector managers themselves that this is neither a widespread nor a universal phenomenon. Ceynowa (2000), for example, reporting on the pilot scheme to implement BSCs in a range of state and university libraries in Germany, concluded:

The balanced scorecard compels the library management to concentrate on evaluations critical to success in the quality, cost efficiency and promptness of university information provision. . . . The development of a scorecard requires the clear definition and formulation of strategic objectives . . . [and] can thus make an essential contribution to strategy-based academic controlling.

(Ceynowa, 2000, 163–4)

While accepting that some modifications may have to be made to the original model, Ceynowa, like Self (2004), believes these to be within a public sector manager's competence, with the necessity for such modifications not detracting from the overall efficacy of the model. Both authors contend that the financial perspective is of lesser significance in public sector scorecards than in those of private sector organizations, but that this does not constitute a problem *per se*. Self observes:

> The BSC has its limitations. It gives us a snapshot of organizational health; it does not give a three dimensional picture. It can point out problems, but does not reveal the solutions. . . . On the positive side, the scorecard has clarified and focused our thinking. It has made us figure out what areas are important, and what constitutes success in those areas. We now look beyond customer service, realizing that success in the other categories . . . ultimately improves service to our customers. (Self, 2004, 104)

From measurement to management

Kaplan and Norton noted:

> [T]he Balanced Scorecard evolved from a performance measurement system to becoming the organizing framework, the operating system for a new strategic management system . . . using this new strategic management system, we observed several organizations achieve performance breakthrough within two to three years of implementation. . . . The magnitude of the results achieved . . . reveals the power of the Balanced Scorecard management system to focus the entire organization on strategy. (Kaplan and Norton, 2001a, 102)

Thus, the designers of this system note the symbiotic relationship between measurement and strategic management, which becomes possible with a system linking market performance and information to strategic decision-making. In other words, it requires the 'outside-in' thinking necessary for a customer-focused organization (cf. Zeithaml and Bitner, 2003).

The system involves four management processes:

- translating the vision
- communicating and linking
- business planning
- feedback and learning.

The process of translating the vision attempts to achieve consensus for the organization's vision and strategy:

> By clearly defining the strategy, communicating it consistently, and linking it to the drivers of change, a performance-based culture emerges to link everyone and every unit to the unique features of the strategy. The simple act of describing strategy via strategy maps and scorecards makes a major contribution to the success of the transformation program.   (Kaplan and Norton, 2001a, 102)

The communication and linking process is divided into three sub-phases:

* communication and education plays an important role in bottom-up strategic input by communicating to the board that long-term strategies to ensure competitive success are in place
* setting goals ensures that the vision and objectives designed by the corporate centre have relevance to business units and individuals
* employee rewards linked to performance measures.

Malmi (2001) and Palmer (2005) contend that few organizations have made such a link successfully, albeit that one of the assumed strengths of the BSC is its link with an organization's reward system. Speckbacher et al. (2003) note that from a sample of 38 companies, 27 had linked incentives to the BSC. However, fewer than 25% of these were able to link incentives to BSC measures. The German Direkt Anlage Bank AG (DAB) resolved this issue by using the BSC to record information at the level of the individual employee. Thus, each employee has a personal BSC, derived from the company BSC, with the bank devising a system to capture data monthly, thereby facilitating the development of employee payment systems rewarding good performance (Kudernatsch, 2000). Similarly, Widmier (2002) reports the results of studies demonstrating the positive effects of incorporating non-financial measures into employee reward schemes.

The first three management processes play a vital role in implementing strategy but do not require a re-examination of the strategic process. The final process, feedback and learning, identifies three ways in which the balanced scorecard aids strategic learning by

* linking the work of individuals to business unit objectives
* providing a strategic feedback system
* enabling a strategic review as part of strategic learning.

Thus, this final process of the BSC links the work of Kaplan and Norton to that of such key theorists as Porter (1980, 1985, 1990, 1996) in respect of competition,

Argyris and Schoen (1978; Argyris et al., 1996) with regard to organizational learning, and Boisot (1998) with regard to charting learning and knowledge flows in organizations. Arguably, this may also lead us into a consideration of theories of knowledge management, but such a wide-ranging review is beyond the scope of the current chapter. However, Marti neatly summarizes current thinking: '[S]ustainable competitive advantages are mainly due to core knowledge that, together with tangible and (especially) intangible resources, develops competitive products and services' (Marti, 2004, 31). The contribution of the BSC is to 'ensure that the strategy gets implemented and to enable an organization to continuously learn from its performance and adapt its strategy accordingly' (Marti, 2004, 40).

Such necessity to ensure continuous organizational learning is of key concern in the service sector. In many national economies, this sector has become the dominant force, accounting for 68% of GDP in the European Union in 2000 (Euromonitor, 2001, quoted in Palmer, 2005, 4). Arguably, therefore, it is of vital importance to managers in this sector to develop both a 'marketing orientation' (Narver and Slater, 1990), and to ensure that their strategic thinking remains customer-focused, i.e. outside-in rather than inside-out (cf. Zeithaml and Bitner, 2003).

UK financial services sector research project

A research project in the late 1990s investigated the role of information in strategy formulation and strategic management in UK retail banks. The survey reviewed the roles and responsibilities of strategic and information managers with regard to information processing in the leading 20 UK retail banks, measured by business performance (cf. Broady-Preston and Hayward, 1999, 2000, 2001).

Obviously, the results in themselves are now somewhat dated. However, as the views of those involved in rolling-out first-generation BSC models were examined, a selection of the results has been reassessed for its contemporary relevance, in the light of developments to the BSC and in strategic thinking, as outlined above. The data from this project are robust; the response rates for the survey were:

- 70% of strategic managers in the sample completed the questionnaire, with 50% interviewed subsequently
- 85% of all information managers returned questionnaires, with 76% participating in subsequent interviews (Broady-Preston and Hayward, 1999).

The financial services sector was surveyed for several reasons. From the 1980s onwards, the sector experienced extensive and dynamic changes. The driving forces for change included deregulation and privatization; the introduction of new products and services; and new players entering the market, offering increasing levels of competition, being unwilling or unable to play the game by the existing rules (Broady-Preston and Hayward, 1999). Subsequently, the industry has had to cope with the demands of providing new delivery channels to customers, such as telephone and internet banking (Sievewright, 2001). Furthermore, the recession of the 1990s led to pressures on profit margins, resulting in reductions in staff numbers and a narrower range of services and products (O'Brien and Meadows, 2003). Thus, this sector is still categorized as 'turbulent', arguably to an even greater degree than during our investigation of the late 1990s, and has been the subject of subsequent investigations (e.g., Kim and Davidson, 2004; O'Brien and Meadows, 2003).

Scorecard models in retail banks

In our survey of scorecard usage by banks we found:

* 43% used the balanced scorecard
* 29% had a business excellence model
* 29% devised a scorecard specific to the organization
* 21% referred to the use of other paradigms such as value-based management
* 21% used none of the models identified.

As revealed by the above percentages, some companies used a scorecard together with a business excellence model (Broady-Preston and Hayward, 1999). These results correlate well both with later, general surveys, as outlined in Drury (2004), and those specific to the financial sector, (cf. Kim and Davidson, 2004; O'Brien and Meadows, 2003). A general UK-wide survey in 2001, for example, found that 43% of companies surveyed were using BSCs (cited in Drury, 2004, 1006).

Top-down versus bottom-up information flow

As indicated earlier, identifying and communicating an organization's vision or strategy throughout the organization is a key component in achieving competitive advantage. In our survey, 86% of managers believed a bottom-up, participative informational input existed in their organizations and, normally, business units were responsible for their own strategic direction within a framework set by the group. Nonetheless, as one manager observed:

> Strategic planning would certainly be top-down. It's what we describe as 'what-down', 'how-up'. So these are the goals, these are the initiatives, these are the objectives, how are we going to achieve it. That would be the bottom up part of the process.   (Broady-Preston and Hayward, 2001, 9)

Therefore, while business units had a degree of autonomy, they had to comply with the framework or vision set by the centre. In a more recent survey of 'visioning' in the financial services sector (O'Brien and Meadows, 2003), directional flow was predominantly top-down, while informational flow remained bottom-up – this despite the BSC being employed to monitor progress towards the organizational vision by all but one of the organizations surveyed. Furthermore:

> [T]he people who are asked to 'live' the vision 'at the coalface' are typically not involved in creating or generating it; if at all, they are involved in (what often appears to be) a token gesture. It hardly seems surprising that many staff admit to cynicism or scepticism about their organization's vision, if they have been excluded from a process in which someone else makes statements about how they will do their work. . . . Staff may observe a sharp contrast between the organization's public image, as described in 'warm' vision statements . . . and what they observe to be the true business drivers (such as shareholder value and profitability).
>
> (O'Brien and Meadows, 2003, 496)

Information flow and formalized information gathering

Whilst writers such as Mintzberg (1998) have identified a key role for strategists in monitoring information flows, clearly this is difficult to manage successfully. In summary, we found that:

- there were blockages in information flow within the majority of banks surveyed
- while information was believed to flow more readily within the smaller banks, nonetheless blockages in the flow of customer information were acknowledged
- problems in sharing information across the organization were acknowledged to exist
- information was dispersed throughout the organization
- the development of corporate intranets was believed to be of potential use in resolving problems in information sharing and flow
- blockages in information flow existed, arising from a 'squirrel like mentality; people running round grabbing information, taking it back and sitting on it because information is power and we've got to get away from that' (Broady-Preston and Hayward, 2001, 13)
- problems were discernible in merging internal operational data with market data (Broady-Preston and Hayward, 2001).

It was often difficult to identify a particular area or department within retail banks with responsibility for formalized information gathering; however, 71% of strategists surveyed viewed information as a distinct source of competitive advantage, with it being recognized as such by their organizations (Broady-Preston and Hayward, 1999). Again, this resonates with current thinking. The requirement to ensure efficient information sharing, and the pivotal role it plays in achieving competitive advantage, has been recognized subsequently by a number of commentators (cf. Barney et al., 2004; Marr et al., 2003; Marti, 2004). In a recent survey of the legal sector (Broady-Preston and Williams, 2004), lawyers within the larger organizations were required to contribute legal opinions to the corporate intranet, or 'know-how' system. Contributions brought tangible rewards to individuals, in the form of financial incentives and promotion. Thus, not only was information being routinely captured, codified and, more importantly, shared within the organization, but it was becoming institutionalized within the processes of the firm; arguably a trend of greater significance in this context.

Role of information professionals

In our survey, strategic managers were largely unaware of the role and function of information professionals in strategy formulation. Only two of the information professionals surveyed were involved actively in the development of scorecard models (Broady-Preston and Hayward, 2001). However, there are indications of changing perceptions. Abels et al., in their review of competencies for information professionals, define an information professional as one who 'strategically uses information in his/her job to advance the mission of the organization' (Abels et al., 2003, 1).

Moreover, specialists in information management

provide the competitive edge for the knowledge-based organization.... Information ... is the lifeblood of the knowledge-based organization and essential for innovation and continuing learning. Information sharing is also essential for any organization that is attempting to understand and manage its intellectual capital, often in a global context.   (Abels et al., 2003, 2)

Interestingly, this listing of competencies was derived partly from a review of training and education needs for information specialists, a further outcome of the research project outlined earlier (cf. Broady-Preston and Hayward, 2000).

Subsequently, little empirical evidence has been found indicating any increase in the degree to which information professionals participate in strategic management and measurement within the corporate sector. Participation in scorecard use and design in this sector has resulted largely from information managers devising scorecards as a means of demonstrating the value of their service to the parent organization, rather than participating actively in scorecard development for the organization as a whole (cf. Jones, R., 2003; Matthews, 2002). Nevertheless, as reported earlier, with the increase in the use of scorecards within the public sector, there is evidence of information managers implementing scorecards within library and information organizations (e.g., Barrionuevo, 2000; Ceynowa, 2000; Self, 2004).

Conclusion

Since the original research results from the project were published, evidence suggests that the balanced scorecard has been widely adopted across a range of sectors. The rise in popularity of this model is perhaps unsurprising, given its flexibility as a suggested framework, rather than a recipe. While criticisms are acknowledged, all the empirical evidence suggests that with the modifications made to the 1992 design, no other models or frameworks offer a similar ability to align organizational strategy with key business drivers. Furthermore, as the successful implementation of a scorecard necessitates the acquisition of reliable, robust customer information, it enables organizations to ensure that their strategic thinking is always customer-focused. This latter requirement is of vital importance in the service sector, especially in knowledge-based organizations. In linking measurement, customer information and management in an ongoing cycle of review, use of the BSC prevents strategy formulation becoming divorced from operational realities.

Part D
Knowledge management

Introduction

Perhaps no topic in the overall area of information management has caused as much uproar as 'knowledge management' and views on the subject range from totally uncritical acceptance of the concept to highly critical denial of the possibility of ever managing knowledge.

The subject has a curious history: it seems, originally, to have arisen in the field of expert systems, sometimes described as 'knowledge-based systems', from which the transition to knowledge management was relatively easy. Ford's (1989) paper on the subject was typical of this period. From about 1997, however, the term became associated with the consultancy companies, following the publication of Nonaka and Takeuchi's *The Knowledge Creating Company* (1995). From this point three streams appear to diverge. In one, the IT-focused consultancy companies began to promote knowledge management as something to be accomplished through the technology and many kinds of software packages re-branded as knowledge management products (an article describing the integration of a number of databases as a 'knowledge management system' is fairly typical of this stream – Newcombe, 1999). In the second stream, those who had previously worked in organization development, who had seized upon the 'learning organization' as a vehicle for promoting the effective sharing of information in organizations, turned to the new buzz-word to continue their efforts under this umbrella (see Senge, 1990, which is used as a starting point for much writing in this area). Finally, the nature of intangible assets and intellectual capital in companies and the need to account for them in the balance sheet had emerged as a subject of concern to corporations, and knowledge management was used as an alternative way of speaking about this phenomenon (Karl-Erik Sveiby is strongly associated with this strand – see, e.g., Sveiby, 1998).

There is, therefore, a degree of confusion over what the term 'knowledge management' actually means, and various discussion lists continue to pursue it 'with forks and hope' like a snark that has 'softly and suddenly vanished away', presumably to dance with the other angels on the head of a pin.

We have two chapters on this topic: in the first, France Bouthillier and Kathleen Shearer update their original research with new work carried out in 2004, choosing five companies and five public sector organizations for review. Their focus is, broadly, on the second stream of activity noted above – the sharing of information in organizations. They conclude that knowledge management, defined in these terms, does constitute a separate field of activity from information management, although closely entwined with that field.

In the second chapter, T. D. Wilson reviews his 2001 paper, revisiting the literature and the consultancy websites, and adding a new visualization tool to the armoury of analysis. The tool, RefViz, suggests that the main focus of the literature remains in the field of information systems development, where the term is used largely as a synonym for information management. His conclusion, to a degree, supports the approach taken by Bouthillier and Shearer, since he suggests that the second stream of work, referred to earlier, is an extension of the information life-cycle into the domain of information use, sharing and application.

For further work on the topic, examining the concept from a variety of viewpoints, the reader is referred to the papers that appeared in the issue of *Information Research* devoted to knowledge management – volume 8, issue. 1, which can be found at http://informationr. net/ir/8-1/infres81.html.

11

Knowledge management and information management: review of empirical evidence

France Bouthillier and Kathleen Shearer

Introduction

This chapter, which is a revision of a previously published paper (Bouthillier and Shearer, 2002), summarizes a review of the 'knowledge management' (KM) practices of several organizations conducted in 2004. The typology of KM methodologies, previously proposed, is revisited and used to illustrate the particular nature of KM. A description of the conceptual framework used for the study is provided as well as a presentation and discussion of recent outcomes. Our hope is that the KM practices that are identified will contribute to a greater understanding of the particular nature of the emerging field of KM and to a constructive debate about the distinctions between KM and IM.

For several years now, there has been an ongoing debate on whether KM is a distinct activity from information management (IM) and it seems the discussion is far from over. Indeed, it is still unclear whether KM and IM involve different goals, processes and methodologies, or whether IM is part of KM or vice-versa.

At the heart of this debate is a question about the distinction between the concepts of knowledge (tacit and explicit) and information. That is, if tacit knowledge, or the knowledge that is contained in a person's head, cannot be managed, then KM is really no different to IM and refers to the management of information. Critics of KM, such as Wilson (2002), Gorman (2004) and others, describe 'the nonsense of KM'. In their opinion KM is, at best, just another management fad, which is being promoted by consulting companies to generate new revenue streams. At worst, it is seen as the prelude to an Orwellian world where organizations seek to capture and store individual thoughts and ideas in enormous databases for the sake of organizations (Gorman, 2004). Meanwhile, other authors have argued that managing knowledge is not only possible, but is a new field which promises to improve the productivity of organizations (Hobohm, 2004).

There have been many attempts to define these concepts and there exists no real consensus on definitions. And, although this is not the topic of this chapter, it is instructive to examine briefly some of the definitions found in the literature. Meadow et al. describe knowledge as involving 'a higher degree of certainty or validity than information' (Meadow et al., 2000, 38), while Wiig (1999) defines information as facts and data organized to characterize a particular situation and knowledge as a set of truths and beliefs, perspectives and concepts, judgements and expectations, methodologies and know-how. For Mitchell (2000), information is data made meaningful by being put into a context and knowledge is data made meaningful through a set of beliefs about the causal relationships between actions and their probable consequences, gained through either inference or experience. It is generally understood that knowledge is predictive, subjective and can be used to guide action, while information is merely contextualized data.

The discussions about the difference between information and knowledge are remarkably similar to the distinction made in the KM literature between tacit and explicit knowledge. Tacit knowledge is defined as action-based and entrained in practice, and it therefore cannot be easily explained or described, but is considered to be the fundamental type of knowledge on which organizational knowledge is built (Choo, 2002; Nonaka and Takeuchi, 1995). Explicit knowledge, unlike tacit knowledge, is defined as knowledge that can be codified and therefore more easily communicated and shared. KM writers view explicit knowledge as structured and conscious and therefore it can be stored in information technology (Martensson, 2000). Explicit knowledge is often equated with information, providing the argument that KM is simply another terminology for IM. Whether tacit knowledge can be converted to explicit knowledge remains a point of contention (Tsoukas and Vladimirou, 2000).

After reviewing the literature, it still remains unclear what knowledge is and whether it can be managed. The KM literature subscribes to fairly inclusive definitions of knowledge and, in practice, concepts of knowledge and information are often used interchangeably (Kakabadse et al., 2001). Considering that the concepts of both information and knowledge are unsatisfactorily defined and that the notion that tacit knowledge can be transformed into explicit knowledge is troublesome, some authors have suggested that the expression 'knowledge management' is perhaps misleading. Gourlay (2000), for instance, argues that knowledge itself cannot be managed and it is 'knowledge representations' that are the actually focus of KM. And, Abram (1997) wrote that the knowledge environment, or the conditions of its use, are the only dimensions that are manageable. Hlupic et al. (2002), citing Marshall and Brady, mention that given the complexity of knowledge, the depiction of types of knowledge, such as tacit and explicit, as mutually exclusive categories might be also misleading and prevent researchers from seeing the interrelated dimensions involved in the process of knowing.

Despite these ongoing theoretical problems, KM continues to be a topic of interest in the literature of library and information studies, management and even information technology (Ferguson, 2004). Although too little attention has been devoted to delineating the differences between IM and KM, Gorman (2004) and Ferguson (2004), using our conceptual framework of KM and typology of KM methodologies (Bouthillier and Shearer, 2002), have argued that the tasks of KM managers seem to be very close to those of information managers. For Gorman (2004), information managers are engaged in discovery, acquisition, storage, organization, use and sharing of information. Gorman concludes that the processes involved in KM are not significantly different from those involved in IM. Ferguson (2004) concurs with this and suggests that the tasks of information managers as presented by the British government over a decade ago look very similar to those of knowledge managers: for example, the idea of information audit is very close to the one of knowledge mapping.

It is our hypothesis that the practice of KM differs significantly from IM and, therefore, does constitute a separate organizational function, although there are overlaps. In particular, KM initiatives focus on tacit knowledge rather than explicit knowledge.

Managing knowledge: a conceptual framework

One way to gain a better understanding of the differences between KM and IM is to identify the processes or steps involved in each field. Certainly, the concept of IM is far from simple, since it has evolved and is linked with various disciplines. For example, discussing the evolution of information resource management (IRM), Trauth (1988) suggests that IM can be seen as equivalent to IRM and is closely related to database management, record management and data processing management. Today, distinguishing database management, rooted in computer science, from data processing management rooted in the management of information systems, may seem odd but this distinction reflects the shifts that were made in those years in computing. According to Trauth (1988, 101), IM is 'primarily concerned with effective storage and retrieval of documents', translated to mean the management of documents. However, it can also have a much broader interpretation and encompass disparate information-handling activities. The definitions of IM and IRM are indeed numerous, and there are many conceptual overlaps between these types of concept.

At the end of the 1990s, Choo (1998a) proposed a process model of information management. Presented as a cycle, IM entails five basic steps: identification of information needs, information acquisition, information organization and storage, information distribution and information use. Each step requires the planning, organization, coordination and control of a number of activities supported by information technology. According to Choo (1998a), IM is key to sustaining the creation and application of knowledge in organizations and should lead to an 'intelligent organization'.

Several authors have applied a process model to KM. Nonaka and Takeuchi (1995) describe four knowledge conversion processes: socialization, externalization, combination and internalization. Each process involves converting one form of knowledge (tacit or explicit) to another form of knowledge (tacit or explicit). This model focuses on the important issue of how knowledge may be created through organizational sharing and is useful for identifying and evaluating certain key activities in the management of knowledge. This model is not broad enough to allow for a complete analysis of organizational knowledge flow. It doesn't include all possible steps in the knowledge chain that need to be managed, such as acquiring knowledge or storing knowledge. Another, more complete model (Oluic-Vukovic, 2001) outlines five steps in the knowledge processing chain: gathering, organizing, refining, representing and disseminating. This model more comprehensively covers the length of organizational knowledge flow.

Based on the IM process model, we have developed a conceptual framework for knowledge management (see Figure 11.1). This model has been slightly altered from

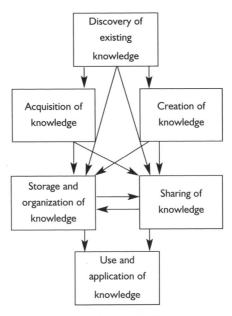

Figure 11.1 Conceptual framework: knowledge management processes

the model presented in our previous study (Bouthillier and Shearer, 2002), and consists of five basic knowledge processes involved in knowledge management.

The knowledge processes

1 Knowledge discovery involves locating internal knowledge within the organization and addresses the oft-quoted phrase, 'if only we knew what we know'. Large, non-hierarchical or geographically dispersed organizations find this knowledge gathering process especially helpful, as one part of the organization may not be aware of the knowledge existing in other departments.
2 Knowledge acquisition involves bringing knowledge into an organization from external sources, and also coordinating employees' efforts to gain new knowledge through formal activities (training, continuing education, etc.).
3 The creation of new knowledge may be accomplished in several ways. First, internal knowledge may be combined with other internal knowledge to create new knowledge. Second, information may be analysed to create new knowledge. One such example of this is competitive intelligence, where value is added to information in order to produce action.
4 Organization and storage: once knowledge is recorded and codified it becomes amenable to the processes involved in the organization and storage of information.
5 Knowledge sharing involves the transfer of knowledge from one (or more) person to another one (or more). Knowledge sharing is often a main preoccupation for knowledge management and is frequently addressed in the literature. Not only must organizations abandon the idea that all knowledge can be reified or documented, but they should also be ready to implement different methods for the sharing of different types of knowledge.

One way of examining the theoretical issues is by comparing KM and IM practices. It was our assumption at the outset of this study that, unlike IM, the focus of KM initiatives was not the acquisition, dissemination, organization or storage of knowledge or information (as is the case with information management), but rather the sharing of tacit knowledge, as the overwhelming emphasis in the KM literature is on knowledge sharing. The next section will describe the methodology and results of a review of knowledge management practices in order to test this assumption.

The study

In line with our previous review (Bouthillier and Shearer, 2002), the purpose of this study was to identify general trends in KM practices across several organizational types in order to gain insight into why and how organizations are practising the management of knowledge. In particular, the goal was to determine five specific dimensions of KM initiatives:

- stated goals and objectives
- methodologies employed
- knowledge processes involved
- types of knowledge being managed
- technologies used.

The research questions are:

1 What are the particular methodologies that characterized KM projects?
2 What are the predominant knowledge processes involved in KM?
3 Is there a difference between KM activities and what we traditionally perceive as IM activities?

The methodology consisted of conducting a small number of case studies using published materials on various organizations that undertook KM projects. Ten cases were identified through a literature search of ABI Inform and LISA as well as an internet search using the key phrase 'knowledge management': five private sector organizations and five public sector organizations. The public sector organizations include both governmental and intergovernmental institutions.

Three selection criteria were used:

1 Only the cases for which sufficient descriptive information was available were included.
2 Only cases for which the information was published after 2000 were retained.
3 For the private sector, only cases that were not related to the consulting business were considered.

Each case was reviewed and details of each area of interest were extracted and recorded. The data were then compared and analysed. The case studies are not assumed to be an exhaustive examination of the KM activities of each organization. It is apparent that knowledge management practices are often performed under other designations and were therefore not identified in the literature review. And, presumably, many of these organizations practise KM in other areas not described in the publications used. A comprehensive study of KM practices within any organization would require collecting data from each organization, combined with observation and interviews, and ideally an ethnographic approach. However, organizations practising KM are, not surprisingly, prone to document and share their experience: this seems to be consistent with the philosophy underlying KM.

Therefore, in spite of the limitations of our methodology, it was possible to collect significant amount of information on each case.

The five organizations retained from the private sector were: British Telecom, Caterpillar, Novartis, Siemens and Xerox. (In the previous study we examined the following companies: Monsanto, Hoffmann-LaRoche, Hewlett-Packard, BP Amoco, Case Corporation and Buckman Laboratories.)

The five organizations retained from the public sector were: the Canadian International Development Agency (CIDA), the Kennedy Space Center (NASA), USAID, the US Army and the World Bank. (In the previous study we examined the following companies: CIDA, the US Army and the World Bank. Our previous group of public sector organizations included also Health Canada and the US Department of Navy.)

Research outcomes and discussion

Our analysis is entirely based on the terminology used in the documentation, terminology that is not always clear in terms of conceptual implications. For the most part, knowledge is not defined in any concrete way by these organizations. As such it is only through surveying each of the five dimensions that we were given an indication of the organizational conception of knowledge.

Goals and objectives

The goals of all of the KM initiatives were to improve the use and application of knowledge to further the objectives of the specific organization or department implementing KM. Since organizational goals differed tremendously among the organizations studied, especially between the public and private sector, it was expected that the specific objectives of KM initiatives would also vary significantly. In fact, this was not the case. The stated objectives were actually very similar across organizations. For the most part, the stated goals and objectives of the KM projects reviewed were 'knowledge sharing'. In the private sector, this mainly involved sharing existing internal organizational knowledge with employees. For example, the Xerox initiative aimed to improve service quality and productivity by converting local knowledge into forms that other members of the organization can understand and act on. The exception to this was British Telecom, which indicated that 'acquisition of information' was the aim of their KM initiative (Compton, 2001). In the non-profit sector, sharing existing organization knowledge internally was also a major objective, but the organizations also aimed to share internal organizational knowledge with external partners, such as clients and the general public (USAID, World Bank). For example, the objective of the KM initiative was to assist World

Bank staff, clients and partners in capturing and systematically organizing their wealth of knowledge and experience.

Several other processes were also mentioned in the objectives of KM initiatives. In the private sector, knowledge discovery was a commonly stated objective, with four out of five organizations identifying this as a goal of the KM initiative. Knowledge discovery has been the focus of a significant body of KM literature. It involves locating internal knowledge within the organization and is especially helpful for large non-centralized organizations, where one part of the organization may not be aware of the knowledge existing in its other parts.

Furthermore, several of the stated objectives specifically indicated that tacit knowledge was the target of the initiative. Caterpillar referred to 'lessons learned', CIDA talked about 'technical expertise' and 'learning from experience', the Kennedy Space Center aimed to 'transfer tacit knowledge', and the World Bank talked about 'capturing' knowledge and experience. All of these terms refer to tacit or experiential knowledge.

Methodologies

The methodologies used in the KM activities studied varied considerably between organizations. In some cases, organizations developed and employed a specific technology (British Telecom, Siemens, Xerox), encompassing their entire KM initiative. In other cases, organizations have employed a number of different methods and used several technologies under the KM banner.

In order to illustrate the nature of KM at these organizations, we propose a typology of 11 distinct methodologies that were identified in this study. These methodologies are categorized according to their particular knowledge processes.

Focus on discovery

1 Knowledge mapping – performing an audit to discover the knowledge resources within an organization, as well as developing a guide for employees describing and providing location information for these knowledge resources. This methodology involves the discovery of tacit knowledge in order to facilitate eventual sharing (three organizations).

Focus on acquisition

2 Organizational learning – acquisition of new knowledge by individuals through training and continuing education (two organizations).
3 News feeds – automatic importation of news stories or other content (one organization).

Focus on sharing

4 Communities of practice – bringing people together, often from different departments, to share ideas. This methodology involves the process of sharing tacit knowledge and development of informal networking (nine organizations).

5 Question and answer forums – bringing people together, often geographically dispersed but with similar jobs, usually through e-mail or chat rooms, to solve problems. This methodology involves the sharing of tacit knowledge and also storage of knowledge as the exchanges are usually archived for future use (three organizations).

6 Virtual collaboration – enabling people from various areas to work together (one organization).

7 Expert databases – similar to mapping of knowledge, this maps experts by identifying the knowledge of each expert and providing a guide map to help employees find those experts. This methodology may involve discovery if performed by others and may just facilitate the sharing of tacit knowledge if, as in many cases, it is up to each employee to provide his or her own expert profile (five organizations).

8 Information databases – explicit knowledge is stored in databases similar to standard document databases. This methodology facilitates the storage and sharing of explicit knowledge (ten organizations).

Focus on storage and retrieval

9 Information databases – explicit knowledge is stored in databases similar to standard document databases. This methodology facilitates the storage and sharing of explicit knowledge (ten organizations). This methodology has also been listed in the 'focus on sharing' category, since it facilitates both sharing of explicit knowledge and a storage and retrieval function.

10 Indexing and categorization initiatives – developing hierarchical subject categories for knowledge resources (two organizations).

Focus on creation

11 Research – creation of new knowledge through research (two organizations).

Focus on dissemination

12 News/information alerts – provide for the distribution of selected information and explicit knowledge (two organizations).

This typology serves to clarify the types of knowledge process being addressed within the various KM activities, rather than accurately define the various methodologies involved. The typology is rather crude and there are some obvious overlaps between many of the methodologies. That being said, some important insights can be gained from examining the KM methodologies according to their various typologies.

All organizations employed more than one methodology in their KM initiative, and several employed three or four. The most common methodology used was the information database. All of the organizations used some type of information database in their KM initiatives. This clearly indicates that the organizations consider the management of explicit knowledge to be within the scope of knowledge management. In some cases, the information targeted is actually tacit knowledge that has been codified.

The other commonly employed methodology was communities of practice (CoPs). CoPs aim to share tacit knowledge within an organization. In this methodology, the aim is to bring together people who have a common interest in some subject or problem, so they can collaborate to share ideas, find solutions and build innovations. CoPs are viewed as ways of creating new knowledge, as well as sharing existing tacit knowledge within an organization. In distributed organizations, an information database or intranet is often used to facilitate communities of practice.

The other methodologies listed above were not so widely used. Expert databases were used by half of the organizations studied. This methodology seeks to enhance tacit knowledge sharing, but without codification of the knowledge. In some cases, the experts are internal to the organizations; in others, the experts are external to the organization. At Novartis, for example, they have both 'yellow pages' for internal and 'blue pages' for external knowledge sharing. Question and answer forums and knowledge mapping were each employed by three of the ten organizations.

Knowledge processes

The KM initiatives examined here target two to three KM processes each. The most common knowledge process targeted in these initiatives is the knowledge sharing process. All of the case studies investigated facilitated at least one type of knowledge sharing and we identified five separate methodologies that addressed knowledge sharing (CoPs, question and answer forums, expert databases, virtual collaboration, and information databases). For the most part, these methodologies aim to share tacit rather than explicit knowledge. However, although they are rarely the focus of these KM initiatives, information databases were implemented in all cases. This suggests that the sharing of explicit knowledge is considered to be a fundamental aspect of knowledge management.

All other knowledge processes were addressed in at least one of the initiatives, but not with the same frequency as knowledge sharing or organization and storage. Knowledge discovery and knowledge acquisition were both addressed by three of the organizations, knowledge creation by two organizations, and knowledge dissemination by two organizations. This makes sense, in that other processes such as knowledge acquisition and creation might be considered to be part of other organizational areas such as training or research and development, and knowledge storage and organization is considered a part of information management.

Types of knowledge

All of the KM initiatives reviewed addressed both tacit and explicit knowledge within the organization. However, the primary target was tacit knowledge. That being said, the process of knowledge sharing often required the codification of tacit knowledge. A good example of this is Xerox's Eureka system. Eureka was designed to help its service engineers with hard-to-tackle repair problems. The system promotes knowledge sharing via 'tips' submitted by service technicians, who identify machine problems and propose solutions. The tips are stored and comprise a knowledge base that can be added to and accessed by all members of the community. This is one of the advantages to using information and communication technologies to facilitate KM: it helps to convert tacit knowledge to explicit and stores it so that it can be reused in the future (Eureka, 2004).

There were also a number of methodologies that targeted tacit knowledge in which the knowledge was not codified. This included in-person communities of practice, organizational learning and expert databases. All of these methods facilitate human-to-human contact where knowledge is acquired or shared without it being captured by the organization.

Technologies

All the case studies included the employment of information and communication technologies. In fact a wide variety of technologies were used in KM initiatives, including: RSS feeds, relational databases, web-based intranets, e-mail alerts, text messaging, discussion forums, collaborative tools, video-conferencing and satellite broadcasting. These technologies were used to aid in knowledge sharing, as well as in the discovery, acquisition, organization and storage of knowledge. All of the KM initiatives employed relational databases and web-based intranets. Several of the organizations designed systems for their unique purposes (British Telecom, Caterpillar and Xerox), and reliance on technologies was greater in organizations that are geographically distributed. (British Telecom, Caterpillar, Siemens, Xerox,

USAID, the US Army and the World Bank). On the other hand, more centralized organizations tended to rely less heavily on technology and employed more in-person interactions.

Conclusion

The results of this review support the conclusions arrived at in our previous study – despite the many similarities between KM and IM, there are enough substantial differences between the two to make a distinction. The notion of IM is far from simple and it has evolved over time. One accepted definition, outlined by Trauth, is that IM is 'primarily concerned with effective storage and retrieval of documents', which can be translated as the management of documents (1988, 101). However, IM can also have a broader interpretation and can encompass disparate information-handling activities. Generally speaking, IM involves the integration of a variety of activities designed to manage information and information resources throughout their life-cycle.

Although all of the KM activities reviewed here incorporated information management activities, they also employed methodologies that are not considered to be under the purview of information management. Sharing knowledge was the primary aim of all of the case studies. And it is the use of knowledge-sharing methodologies such as communities of practice, virtual collaboration and expert databases that distinguishes these KM initiatives from IM. The nuances between different types of knowledge were rarely addressed. The stated objectives of these initiatives were often to share tacit knowledge; however, in practice, most KM initiatives addressed the sharing of both: tacit knowledge through bringing people together, and explicit knowledge through the use of information databases.

This study does not solve any of the ontological and epistemological problems associated with KM. KM initiatives still reflect an incredible diversity of methodologies. One can see, however, a certain refinement of strategies, especially in relation to communities of practice, and an attempt in each organization to adapt basic KM approaches to particular organizational needs. Yet the overwhelming concern in all cases is to establish mechanisms to facilitate access to both information and knowledge. Does this mean that KM is seen as the solution to some of the access problems that were supposed to disappear in the digital age? This study of new KM initiatives suggests that the attraction of KM is still very strong in many organizations, and further studies are needed to explain such attraction.

12

'The nonsense of knowledge management' revisited

T. D. Wilson

Introduction

'Knowledge management' as a strategy of consultancy companies is one of a series dating from Taylor's (1911) 'scientific management'. 'Time and motion study' developed directly out of scientific management and continued into the 1970s as a widespread industrial engineering technique. In the late 1930s, the 'human relations school' emerged out of research between 1927 and 1932 at the Western Electric Hawthorne Works in Chicago (Mayo, 1933) and had a considerable influence in the consultancy companies emerging after the Second World War.

In the second half of the last century, the pace of new techniques quickened considerably: we have seen many consultancy strategies from 'management by objectives', 'the repertory grid' and 'T-groups' of the 1950s and 1960s to the more recent 'total quality management', 'organizational learning' and 'business process re-engineering'. And now we have 'knowledge management'.

These have sometimes been called management fads and some have been disastrous: Stephen Roach, Chief Economist at Morgan Stanley, was a strong protagonist of downsizing, arguing that it was the cure for any company's problems, but in 1997 he reversed that opinion, arguing that, on the contrary, it could be a recipe for industrial disaster. Jenkins (1997) reports Cameron, a researcher in organizational behaviour, as saying that, 'downsizing [is] the most pervasive yet unsuccessful change effort in the business world'.

Some techniques fail, or are dropped from the repertoire, because they are utopian in character: organizations are told that the technique must be applied throughout the organization for the full benefits to be achieved. This happened with business process re-engineering, but businesses quickly realized that the costs of implementing BPR throughout the organization would be crippling and, because they attempted to apply the technique only to part of the company, the results were less than satisfactory. Two-thirds of BPR efforts are said to have failed (Hall et al., 1994). Knowledge management (whatever it is) also shows signs of being offered as a utopian ideal and the results are likely to be similar.

My original paper 'The nonsense of "knowledge management"' (Wilson, 2002), caused active discussions on mailing lists and weblogs and continues to be the most frequently 'hit' paper in the journal with, at the time of writing, more than 74,000 hits – a rate of almost 2000 hits a month. It seems that the debate about the nature of knowledge management and the reality of its existence continues to attract interest and this chapter revisits the phenomenon to see what might be different, two years on.

The main arguments of the 2002 paper were:

1   The advocates of knowledge management make no clear, operational distinction between knowledge and information, and such a distinction is absolutely essential if 'knowledge managers' are to demonstrate that they are doing something that is a) different from information managers, and b) different from other organizational specializations such as organization development, change management and the management of organizational communication.
2   The knowledge management movement originates from artificial intelligence and expert systems, where the idea of knowledge-based systems emerged, but it has been adopted and distorted by information technology vendors and management consultancies to serve their marketing operations.
3   There is no 'core' to the literature of knowledge management; rather, it is scattered across a wide diversity of fields from artificial intelligence, through applications of information technology, to organization development.
4   The distinction made by Nonaka and Takeuchi (1995) between tacit and explicit knowledge is an illegitimate corruption of Polanyi's (1958) idea of tacit knowledge. For Polanyi, tacit knowledge is that part of what we know that we cannot tell, because it is inaccessible to our consciousness; for Nonaka and Takeuchi, it is what we know but have not previously told. The difference is crucial because it reveals their distinction as false.
5   Ideas of 'communities of practice' are unlikely to gain widespread adoption in business and industry because they are incompatible with the short-term, market-oriented, shareholder-value-driven management of such organizations.

Information and knowledge

The distinction proposed in the paper was:

> 'Knowledge' is defined as what we know: knowledge involves the mental processes of comprehension, understanding and learning that go on in the mind and only in the mind. . . . Whenever we wish to express what we know, we can only do so by uttering messages of one kind or another. . . . Such messages do not carry 'knowledge', they constitute 'information', which a knowing mind may assimilate, understand, comprehend and incorporate into its own knowledge structures. These structures are not identical for the person uttering the message and the receiver, because each person's knowledge structures are, as Schutz (1967) puts it, 'biographically determined'. Therefore, the knowledge built from the messages can never be exactly the same as the knowledge base from which the messages were uttered.   (Wilson, 2002)

The knowledge management community appears to treat knowledge as a 'thing' or commodity, but it is a complex, dynamic process. What we know is always changing as we acquire, or are exposed to, new information about the world. The associations among the elements of what we know are continually changing for the same reason; what we know about something appears to decay over time unless we put that knowledge repeatedly to use.

The corollary of this is that knowledge can never be captured, nor can it be shared: all that is captured or shared is information about what we know. And it is unlikely that we can ever report the totality of what we know because of the multitude of associations that anything we know has with everything else that we know.

Authors, however, continue to use the terms 'knowledge' and 'information' as though they are synonyms: it seems that they are incapable of describing what knowledge management may be other than in terms of information and information resources. However, describing a library as a knowledge repository, does not make it anything other than a library. Here is a description of a 'dynamic knowledge repository' (DKR):

> A DKR is a knowledge base that encompasses all of the relevant information of a particular project. It includes recorded dialog (i.e. internal knowledge), intelligence collection (i.e. external knowledge), and knowledge product (i.e. a snapshot of an organization's knowledge, with links into recorded dialog and intelligence collection).   (eekim.com at www.eekim.com/ohs/lc/dkr.html)

Here we have knowledge, information and intelligence all conflated into what is evidently a database – nothing more or less than an electronic filing system, with a classification scheme.

The scope of knowledge management

The 2002 paper showed the distribution of journals carrying papers on knowledge management (see Table 12.1).

For this chapter, I examined the journals in which papers using 'knowledge management' in the title were published in 2003 and 2004, using the Web of Science databases. The 223 papers were distributed over 89 journal titles and various compilations in the *Lecture Notes in Artificial Intelligence* and *Lecture Notes in Computer Science* series. In Table 12.2, the titles with more than two papers (i.e. an average of one a year) are shown; the first two items are the *Lecture Notes* series.

Of course, there are journals in the field of knowledge management that are not included in the ISI citation indexes, but this is often for the very good reason that they do not operate full peer review of submissions.

Table 12.1   Subject range of journals

Subject area	No. of titles
Computing and information systems	26
Information science, information management and librarianship	18
Management	13
Artificial intelligence	10
Engineering	8
Medicine	4

Table 12.2   Journal coverage of knowledge management in 2003 and 2004

Lecture Notes in Computer Science	48
Lecture Notes in Artificial Intelligence	39
International Journal of Technology Management	5
Journal of Computer Information Systems	5
Journal of the Operations Research Society	5
Information Research	4
International Journal of Information Management	4
Annals of Agricultural Economics	3
Automation in Construction	3
Decision Sciences	3
Industrial Management and Data Systems	3
Information and Management	3
Journal of the American Society for Information Science and Technology	3

The conclusion reached in the 2002 paper is supported here — the literature on knowledge management is fragmented over a variety of different subject areas, often having little in common, but with a strong focus on computer applications in business and industry.

This conclusion is also supported by using RefViz, an information vizualizer designed to work with EndNote. RefViz uses term–term association measures to group papers on the basis of their abstracts and keywords. From the initial set of references, the software automatically selected references with sufficient information and structured them into 14 groups, with varying numbers of documents — the term–term association measures determine how closely documents are located one to another. We can see from the diagram that there is a wide spread of topics through the available space and that the biggest cluster of documents (168, contained in six closely connected groups) is actually concerned with applications of information technology (shown as B in Figure 12.1).

We can also carry out a textual analysis of the abstracts, using a simple frequency counting program called TextStat, with the result (for the 2003 papers) shown in Table 12.3 (overleaf). When we removed the terms 'knowledge' and 'management' from the list, we are left with the inescapable conclusion that the papers were actually about the development of organizational information systems.

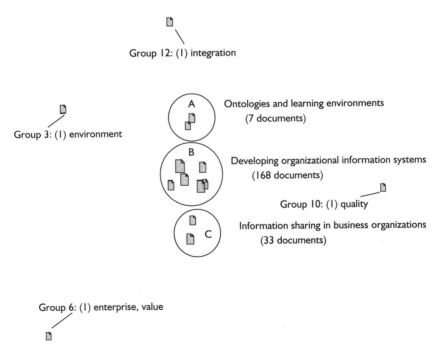

Figure 12.1   RefViz analysis of references on knowledge management

This analysis of the papers published in 2003 and 2004 appears to support the conclusion reached in the original paper: that there is no core to knowledge management, rather we have a series of disparate groups, all using the concept to deliver, essentially, papers in the field of information systems development.

Table 12.3 Frequency of terms used in abstracts

Term	Frequency
knowledge/km	274
management/km	175
organiz-ed-ing-ation-s-al	84
information	63
system-s	60
development	41
technology-ie-ies-ical	40
project-s	37
support	36
process	31
new-ly	25
tool-s	24
ontolog-y-ies-ists-ical	24
model	24
work-ing	22
user-s	21
require-s-ed-ments	21
decision	21
operat-ion-s-ing-ional-ors	20
design	19

Management consultancies and knowledge management

The websites of the following consultancies were reviewed in 2002 and have been re-examined: Accenture, Cap Gemini Ernst and Young, Deloitte and Touche, Ernst and Young, KPMG Consulting, McKinsey and Company and Pricewater-houseCoopers.

Accenture's position on knowledge management is not very obvious from its main website, but a search for 'knowledge management' revealed many links – mainly to various Accenture partners selling services. As suggested in the earlier paper, it uses the term 'knowledge management' as a synonym for 'information management', as the following quotation suggests:

Information can be the key to understanding customers, increasing internal efficiency, streamlining the supply chain and, ultimately, getting ahead of the
competition. We help companies make the best use of information, unlocking
its business value.
(www.accenture.com/xd/xd.asp?it=enweb&xd=services%5chp%5ccapabili-
ties%5cinformation_accessible.xml)

Cap Gemini Ernst and Young is now simply Capgemeni and its site features
mainly 'enterprise resource planning' and the integration of computer architectures.
Knowledge management does not feature in any of its drop-down menus on the
top page, and a search for 'knowledge management' revealed little of interest, since
the top search term appeared to be 'management'. A search for 'knowledge',
however, revealed some interest in the topic. It was principally a synonym for 'information', with expressions such as 'information and knowledge sources' being
used without explanation of what the difference might be. The term is used partly
to sell the development of portal software and services and partly to sell the company's own knowledge to clients.

Deloitte Touche Tohmatsu is another new name for the conglomerate.
Knowledge management is not featured on this company's main pages. As the search
engine was not functioning, I could not find any specific documents. However, a
new service for sale is on 'information dynamics':

The information your company creates is one of its most valuable assets. Our
Information Dynamics services can assist you in designing, developing and
implementing technology and processes which create efficient information
capture, archival [sic], analysis and distribution within and between organizations. This scope of services covers the areas of Enterprise Information Strategies
and Architectures, Data Warehousing, Business Intelligence, Enterprise Content
Management and Enterprise Portal.
(www.deloitte.com/dtt/section_node/0,2332,sid%253D27772,00.html)

which is amazingly reminiscent of what other firms are calling knowledge management!

Ernst and Young lacked information on the subject in 2002 and the same
applies today – a search for 'knowledge management' resulted in one revealing document on developing a corporate information strategy.

KPMG is no longer interested in knowledge management – its risk advisory services itemize 'information risk management' (which appears to be concerned
with business systems infrastructure) and 'intellectual property services', which are
concerned with 'better management of contracts and licences potentially leading
to improved business relationships; improved cash realisation and income generation

and stronger competitive position through better protection of IP' (www.kpmg.co.
uk/services/ras/ips/index.cfm)

McKinsey and Company – in 2002 this company used 'knowledge management'
as a synonym for 'information management' and the same applies today. No sector of the website is devoted specifically to knowledge management and a search
reveals mainly information on the company's own information management practices or papers in the company's house journal, *McKinsey Quarterly*.

PricewaterhouseCoopers is now owned by IBM and, given that company's
commitment to the idea (although it is concerned principally with selling hardware
and software for data and information handling), it is not surprising that there is
some attention to it on the PwC site. However, it is not obvious: the site map reveals
no major division of the company devoted to the subject and when a search for
'knowledge management' is carried out, many of the links refer to older material,
such as the 1999 publication *The Knowledge Management Fieldbook* and the joint
publication, in 2001, with the British Standards Institution, *The KM Guide to
Good Practice*. Most of the items appear to be rather elderly. However, a recent page
illustrates the confusion that persists: a very good start is made in establishing that
'knowledge' is a personal phenomenon:

> Knowledge is information that has been processed, interpreted and linked to other
> relevant pieces of information by a person based on his or her particular set of
> experiences. Even when two people with similar backgrounds access the same
> information, the knowledge each takes away is unique. When someone uses infor-
> mation to achieve a business goal, that person is creating value by putting his
> or her knowledge to work.   (Degagne et al., 2003, 16) •

This acknowledges the distinction made in the first part of this paper and, implic-
itly, recognizes the point made by Miller (2002) that 'information has no meaning'
until it is encountered by a knowing mind.

However, the piece then goes on to complicate the position by confusing information, data and knowledge – although the effort has been to distinguish these
concepts. Thus, having said that 'information is data placed in a meaningful context,'
the authors state, 'The root cause of information overload is that most of the information received in today's complex business environment is raw and unstructured'
– here, they are clearly talking about data, since how can information be raw and
unstructured when it is already data that has been placed in a meaningful context?

Overall, the impression is that knowledge management does not have a very high
profile at PwC.

For the consultancies as a whole, therefore, the early interest in knowledge management, dating from around 1997, appears to have faded or, at best, be fading.
Perhaps this is not surprising: the global economy appears to be coming out of the

post-dot-com recession and they can once again push for work in their core businesses.

The people perspective

The literature on knowledge management claims that the 'people' dimension is more important than the technological (in spite of the fact that most of the same literature is heavily oriented towards technology use). Sveiby (2001) holds that the management of people is one of the two tracks of knowledge management and it seemed useful to explore the literature to discover how this people dimension was represented. One can argue that the management of people is not a very useful concept, since people are extremely difficult to manage and self-management has been shown to be much more effective for organizations. What Sveiby is actually talking about is the way organizational processes, work practices and reward systems are devised to encourage information sharing, and, in the 2002 paper, this was referred to as the management of work practices.

One of the key concepts in this area is 'community of practice' and I searched the Web of Science to discover what had been published on this topic. The search resulted in 30 papers in English, published in 2003 and 2004. The journals are listed in Table 12.4.

Table 12.4 Journal coverage of communities of practice

Adult Education Quarterly	Journal of Business and Technical Communication
Ambulatory Pediatrics	
American Journal of Medical Quality	Journal of Computer Assisted Learning
ASIST 2002: Proceedings of the 65th ASIST Annual Meeting	Journal of Philosophy of Education
	Journal of Strategic Information Systems
British Journal of Educational Studies	Journal of Urology
Discourse & Society	Journal of the American Board of Family Practice
Educational Technology and Society	
Exceptional Children	Management Learning
General Hospital Psychiatry	Organization Studies
Health	Patient Education and Counseling
IEEE Intelligent Systems	Production Planning & Control
Information Society (2)	Public Administration
Journal of Architectural and Planning Research	Science Education
	Teaching and Teacher Education
Journal of Asthma	Women's Studies International Forum

In all, 30 papers were distributed over 27 journals (only *Information Society* included more than one paper), plus one series of *Lecture Notes in Computer Science*, suggesting, as with knowledge management, that there is no core journal covering this area.

It is also interesting to see that journals on education and medical sciences dominate in this area and useful to speculate why this might be the case. The answer, I believe, is fairly self-evident: both of these fields — notably involving public sector organizations rather than business (although this is not true in some countries that have no public medical care) — are fields in which there are 'natural' communities of practice. Organizations in both sectors are generally divided into discipline-based departments, e.g., departments of English, history and science in a school, and departments of cardiology, dermatology, diabetes, neurology, etc. in a hospital. Medical specialities also usually have national and even international associations of which doctors are members and, in the UK, there are Royal Colleges, professional bodies that set standards and hold examinations to establish that physicians and surgeons meet the required standards. Teams are also natural work groups in both schools and hospitals: people collaborate in devising syllabuses and teaching programmes in education, and in treating patients or running an operating theatre in hospitals.

It would be surprising if communities of practice did not arise in these organizations, but it is a very different matter to transplant this concept into organizations where the prevailing ethos encourages competition rather than collaboration.

There may be circumstances in organizations of all kinds that encourage the formation of communities of practice and the comments above, on the 'natural' conditions in schools and hospitals, may offer a clue as to what these conditions might be. One can imagine, for example, that the finance directors of member companies in a large multinational corporation would have a great deal in common in terms of financial management, and that a community of practice could be created involving these people in regular information exchange sessions (face-to-face or in electronic forums). Such people share common interests, operate according to commonly understood norms of financial practice and may have been trained in very similar ways, to the point where they share a common language. They are also at a level in the organization where they may derive more benefit from sharing information than from hoarding it.

Knowledge management as the management of intellectual assets

Finally, in this review of the state of knowledge management, I turned to another area to which the tag has been assigned: that is, intellectual capital or intangible assets. Sveiby now devotes much of his time to the development of ideas in this area, for example, the intangible assets monitor (Sveiby, 2003) and methods for measuring intangible assets (Sveiby, 2004). These are desirable developments, since they relate directly to obtaining a better estimate of the true worth of a company – whether they can be called 'knowledge management', however, is questionable.

Only 18 documents were found in a search for 'intellectual capital' or 'intangible asset(s)' in the title field. Table 12.5 shows the journals in which the papers appeared, again demonstrating the lack of any core journal devoted to reporting research in this area.

Table 12.5 Journals dealing with intellectual capital or intangible assets

American Journal of Agricultural Economics	*Journal of Education Policy*
American Journal of Roentgenology	*Journal of Management Studies*
CIM Bulletin	*Journal of Petroleum Technology*
Computers in Industry	*Journal of Strategic Information Systems*
Expert Systems with Applications	*Lecture Notes in Computer Science*
Harvard Business Review	*Management Learning*
IBM Systems Journal	*Organization Science*
Industrial Marketing Management	*Research Evaluation*
International Journal of Technology Management	*Stahl Und Eisen*

Remarkably, no journal contained more than one item and, once again, we have to conclude that these subjects do not possess a core journal – interest in the subject, expressed in different ways, is found in a variety of fields.

Conclusion

In 2002 I wrote:

> The inescapable conclusion of this analysis of the 'knowledge management' idea is that it is, in large part, a management fad, promulgated mainly by certain consultancy companies, and the probability is that it will fade away like previous fads. It rests on two foundations: the management of information – where a large part of the fad exists (and where the 'search and replace marketing' phenomenon is found), and the effective management of work practices.
>
> (Wilson, 2002).

Revisiting the literature of the field, as well as the consultancy websites, has simply confirmed that view. It is evident that, on one hand, the consultancies are losing interest in the concept and, on the other hand, that a core literature of the field has not developed.

It also remains clear that there is still a very strong focus in the literature on aspects of artificial intelligence and the development of information systems of various kinds. Nothing has emerged to convince me that knowledge management is anything more than a buzz-phrase, designed more than anything to sell hardware and software to an otherwise resisting corporate management.

This still leaves us with the question: Why has the concept been seized upon with enthusiasm by some in the fields of information management and information systems? Part of the answer, of course, is that these fields are not immune to fads of one kind or another, especially in management, but, as far as academia is concerned, one answer may be (as argued in Ellis et. al., 1999) that these topics are taught and researched by departments that have a rather weak position in their universities and, increasingly, are subsumed within larger groups, such as business studies or computer science. The need to establish academic 'respectability' may drive staff in these departments to seek novelty at all costs, secure in the knowledge that the fields they seek to colonize will not be sought after by the 'big beasts' of the academy.

However, from the point of view of practice, another part of the answer lies in the very weak position held by library and information services in business and industry. Those who run them rarely have access to the upper echelons of the business and most organizations consider them expendable when times are difficult. There is a long history of special libraries being closed down during economic recessions. Anything, therefore, that offers the possibility of establishing a stronger position in the organization is seized upon, pursued and promulgated – and when senior management has already been persuaded that knowledge management is the next big thing, the information officer who fails to take the opportunity presented would be lacking in common sense. Similarly, information systems departments have been under very great pressure as a result of downsizing, reduction in spend on information technology, and a perception that they have failed to deliver improvements to the bottom line of company accounts. Knowledge management acts, for a time, as a convenient new peg upon which to hang the IT director's hat, under the rubric of chief knowledge officer. That this is temporary is confirmed by a report by Michael Earl which notes that:

In a 1998 article in the Sloan Management Review, I reported on the work of 20 chief knowledge officers at large corporations. Sceptics may not be surprised to know that most of these CKO positions no longer exist. More than half had gone within two years of our study. In other words, knowledge management is tantalising. It still appeals to many, but success is elusive. Even defining it is not easy. Perhaps this is because knowledge management is concerned with an intangible and, in some ways, invisible asset.

(Earl, 2004)

Another observer, Larry Moyer, is reported (Davenport, 2005) as noting that knowledge management is 'generally considered a failed initiative'. He goes on to say '[W]e can no more manage knowledge than we can manage change. We can help people adapt to it, and we can help facilitate it, and help people recover from it, but we have great difficulty managing it' (Davenport, 2005, 22).

There are two problems for those who accept the rhetoric of knowledge management and seek to make it their own: one is that, eventually, it will be recognized that all that is available is 'old wine in new bottles' and support will ebb away. The second is that knowledge management under one definition refers to the implementation of organization development strategies to change work practices so that information sharing and the possible development of communities of practice become a reality. The difficulty here is that the library and information manager is not trained in organization development techniques and the control of the area of practice concerned, that is, organizational communication, is generally outside his or her remit – and the same applies to the IT director.

What appears to have happened is that the well known life-cycle of information has been extended to embrace an area outside the control of the information manager – the use of information. Figure 12.2 illustrates the situation.

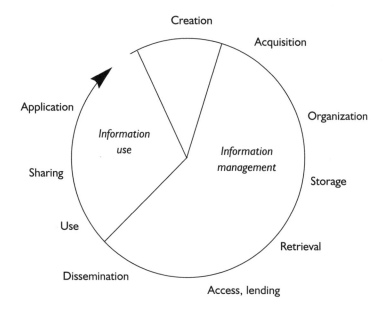

Figure 12.2 The extended life-cycle of information

Information management is the management of the life-cycle to the point of delivery to the information user: what happens after that depends upon many things, such as the organizational climate, reward systems, organizational culture, etc. — all of which are outside the control of the information manager. Where knowledge management has a focus, it is upon ensuring the effective application of what is known in the organization to secure the organization's development and survival — no management of knowledge takes place because the knowledge is embodied in people. All that can be done is to try to manage the organization in ways that ensure that learning and skills development are encouraged and that the culture supports information sharing. These are major tasks and they are certainly outside the scope of information management.

Acknowledgement

My thanks to Frank Miller for his usual perceptive observations on an earlier draft.

Part E
Information strategy

Introduction

With the emergence of information management in the 1970s, and especially in relation to the information as a commodity concept, there came the associated idea of *information strategy*. There was, and still is, a certain amount of ambiguity in the term: sometimes it has been interpreted as information technology strategy, particularly in the literature on information systems in business and industry. A consideration of the topic, therefore, must take into account both of these perceptions, since the effective delivery of information content to support the strategic direction of an organization – or of a country – depends today to a significant extent upon having an effective information technology strategy in place. Information strategy may be seen as aiding business strategy or as central and leading other types of strategy in the organization. In both cases its main goal is to equip the organization with appropriate information resources for effective performance in the knowledge society or provide a competitive advantage on the market. However, there are various components and factors (external and internal) that add or distract from the effectiveness of information strategy. Some relate to organizational structures and processes; others can be attributed to organizational cultures and climates. Internal organizational policies and the interests of various stakeholders also come into play when information strategies are discussed, adopted and implemented.

The topic is sufficiently mature for a range of texts to have appeared, presenting the different perspectives; for example Silk (1991) clearly takes a technological perspective, while Brindley (1989) presents the proceedings of a conference with a much wider remit and Orna (2004) presents a more integrated view. Another useful guide is that by Corrall (2001). Recently, as we might expect, the internet and intranets have begun to assume strategic significance in organizations, and this is dealt with by Griffiths (2004).

Our authors in this section present equally wide views on the subject: first, David Allen updates his paper on information systems strategy formation in higher education institutions. He presents some of the results of the work initially described, and explores the role of trust among academics and administrators in the development of information strategies.

Hugh Preston presents a complete rewrite of the paper he originally wrote with Les Smith under the new title 'Healthcare Information Management and Technology Strategy: the story so far', noting that in an organization the size of the National Health Service (the biggest single employer in the UK), national strategies cannot get very far without equal attention to local circumstances.

Finally, Cheryl Marie Cordeiro and Suliman Al-Hawamdeh revisit their paper 'National Information Infrastructure and the Realization of Singapore IT2000 Initiative', an example of information strategy at the national level. Although Singapore is a geographically small city-state, its development has been specifically technology-based and much larger nations might learn from its infrastructure strategy. The authors also employed an interesting research approach to check the validity of governmental information strategy.

13

Information systems strategy formation in higher education institutions: lateral trust

David Allen

Introduction

Allen (1995) described a research project on the formation of information strategies in UK higher education institutions, which, at the time, was an issue facing most UK universities. Ten years after its publication, this paper reflects on one aspect of the results of the research: organizational climate and 'lateral' trust among individuals in strategy formation.

Early research into organizational trust pointed to its benefits (e.g., Deutsch, 1958; Tannenbaum and Davis, 1969). Ekvall and colleagues (1983) found that mutual trust and confidence, support for ideas and open relationships comprised one of four attributes of an organization's climate that favoured creativity and innovation. There has been a resurgence of interest in the concept (cf. Bachmann, 1999; Shaw, 1997), particularly in relation to inter-organizational co-operation, co-ordination and control (cf. Bachmann, 1999). The focus of this research, intra-organizational trust, however, has received relatively less attention (Grey and Garsten, 2001).

There appears to be a consensus that trust between individuals and groups within an organization is important for its long-term stability. For example, McCauley and Kuhnert (1992) identify research which suggests that trust is a prerequisite for group effectiveness, group loyalty, effective group problem solving, managerial and leadership effectiveness, effective organizational processes and organizational effectiveness in general. Mishra and Morrissey (1990) have found that managers see trust as being linked to increased productivity and growth and more effective decision-making as ideas, information and feelings are shared more openly. They argue that it is vital for organizational growth and enhances organizational innovation, loyalty and peace. On the other hand, they found that distrust was correlated with failure to follow company policies, failure to care about performance, vicious competition, inter-departmental bickering and office politics. Lack of trust was linked to the failure of management techniques such as total quality management (Ray, 1994). More recent research by Dirks and Ferrin (2001) suggests that trust and the mechanisms through which it is created may vary with organizational context. Equally, it is argued that trust benefits are not always transmitted in a straightforward manner. There is consensus that trust is a vital ingredient in the success of any change initiative, but trust has been described as being most vulnerable during change processes (Harris and McGrady, 1999; Turnley and Feldman, 1998). Much of this work focuses on trust in leadership, where there is an explicit control and power element in the relationship (e.g., Braun, 1997; Mishra and Morrissey, 1990). This paper, in contrast, focuses on the peer-to-peer trust relationships among senior members of the university involved in the development of strategy.

Higher education institutions (colleges and universities) in the mid- and late-1990s were under intense pressure to change. In the early 1990s there was a widely-held belief in higher education in the UK that change to technological infrastructures and information management in universities would be gradual. An influential government report stated that 'whilst technology has the potential fundamentally to change information provision in higher education, even its most optimistic advocates suggest that change will take place gradually' (Joint Funding Councils' Library Review Group, 1993).

This view prevailed for only a short period. By the mid-1990s the consensus, in the USA and the UK, was that IT would have a rapid, 'profound effect on the future of higher education' (Joint Information Systems Committee, 1995). Indeed, many argued that traditional academic structures were no longer functional (Wolfe, 1996) and must be transformed. A continual strand in the literature was the call for radical and discontinuous approaches to change: the 're-engineering' of HEIs. This was most fervently promulgated in the USA (cf. Grotevant, 1998), but also accepted in the UK (e.g., Hicks, 1997). The concept was promulgated by a number of professional associations in the USA, most prominently the Association for Managing and Using Information Technology in Higher Education (Heterick, 1993; Penrod and Dolence, 1992). It was also echoed in academic literature (Privateer, 1999; Tsichritzis, 1999). Much of this literature was technologically deterministic, positing that technology is the principal driver of this radical change, but also, paradoxically, the predominant solution to the problems created by change (Ernst et al., 1994; May et al., 1994). This literature had a USA provenance and orientation, but clearly resonated with the views of many practitioners in the UK (Ford et al., 1996; Hicks, 1997). During this period, the view that the future of the university was electronic and technological predominated (MacFarlane, 1994; 1995; 1998). As the decade progressed, the literature became more radical and increasingly full of dire warnings. In an article aimed at vice-chancellors of HEIs, Dunderstadt stated:

> Those institutions that can step up to this process of change will thrive. Those who bury their heads in the sand, that rigidly defend the status quo or – even worse – some idyllic vision of a past that never existed, are at very great risk. . . . The real question is not whether higher education will be transformed but rather how and by whom. (Dunderstadt, 1998, 1)

The impact of these changes is brought into relief by the process of information strategy formation in universities – the formal process by which universities in the UK were expected, by the higher education funding councils, to develop strategies for the management of information systems and information services. While information strategy meant different things to different universities, most universities developed one and, for most, it became a process by which they could legitimize the discussion of topics that had not previously been addressed: from the question of who owned information that was seen as academics' intellectual property to the development of administrative information systems. These strategies were intended to resolve many of the information management issues that universities faced, but recent research by Marcella and Knox (2004) indicates that many of the fundamental problems which the information strategies attempted to address remain.

The research reported here indicated that one of the factors that impeded or supported the development of such strategies was the organizational climate of the university and the sensitivity of the developers of the strategy to the local climate. In this chapter I reflect upon one aspect of this lateral trust or mistrust between individuals in the formation of information strategies.

Methodology and theoretical position

The epistemological position taken in the research was interpretative and interactionist following Strauss's view that 'phenomena do not just automatically unfold, nor are they straightforwardly determined by social, economic, political, cultural, or any other circumstances; rather they are in part shaped by the interactions of concerned actors' (Strauss, 1993, 53–4). The research was longitudinal, focusing on cross-case analysis (Eisenhardt, 1989) of 12 sites. Multiple respondents were interviewed, documentation relating to the information strategy process was gathered and analysed and (where possible) strategy meetings were attended. In-depth, iterative interviews were conducted with approximately 20 informants in each organization. Informants were selected because they were perceived as taking lead positions in their organization, as taking lead positions in the change process or as being significantly affected by the change. Informants ranged from the heads of information services (library, management information services, computer centre) to senior managers (deans, pro-vice chancellors, heads of finance, personnel, planning and vice-chancellors). The focus of the interview was on gathering rich, detailed data full of 'thick' (Geertz, 1973) descriptions. A number of research projects in this field have been criticized for taking a 'managerial perspective'; therefore, an explicit attempt was made to address this issue by interviewing dissenting voices, those cut from the process and those uninvolved in the process but affected by it.

The research approach techniques used to analyse the data were drawn from grounded theory. Key elements include an inductive approach, theoretical sampling, a distinct approach to coding of data, and the 'iterative approach to the collection and analysis of data' (Starr, 1998, 218). The first three elements of the approach were used in this research, but an iterative approach was not used and, instead, a cross-case analysis of the research was undertaken (Eisenhardt, 1989). Following Eisenhardt, the data for one case were analysed to gain familiarity with them and to allow some preliminary theory generation. A significant problem was the management of data generated by the research process, for which ATLAS.ti (Software, 1999) was used.

As the research progressed it became increasingly difficult to harvest meaningful data from certain sites. Collecting data was complicated by the reluctance of some of the stakeholders to discuss the process openly because of its highly political nature. This was overcome by assuring anonymity to all participants, and by emphasizing that the researcher was independent and uninvolved in the strategy process. As a result, all names of HEIs were changed and names of individuals omitted. To protect the participants, the researcher has been vaguer about details of events than would have been preferred. In this paper data were utilized from two HEIs: Old Collegial and New Managerial. Old Collegial is a relatively small institution moving from a collegial to a more managerial form of organization. New Managerial is, as the name implies, a large, highly managerial organization which gained the title of university in 1992.

Trust and mistrust in management information services and systems

In the last few years rapid technological advances have made it less feasible for organizations to maintain all the technological expertise they need internally (Heckman, 1999), but this was the model used in universities in the UK in the 1990s. Despite universities' increasing reliance on advanced information technologies there was no standard model of provision. Approaches ranged from having one converged and centralized academic and management information service through to completely devolved models with IT support being organized at departmental level. The role of management information services and systems should be pivotal in the formation of an information strategy; indeed, the relationship between the information systems organization and the business organization has been identified as being of critical importance (Peppard, 2001). This research showed, however, that with few exceptions, IT services were not trusted and were often marginalized in the information strategy formation process. The following example demonstrates this.

Old Collegial University provides a clear example of a university with a lack of trust in its management information services, and the systems developed and managed. In Old Collegial the key factor, which undermined the trust that academic staff and managers had in Computing Services, was the legacy of a past IT initiative. Computer Services had bought a proprietary system for teaching and learning. They made this investment based on the assurances of the vendor that it would be supported. However, with the move to a PC-based, distributed computing environment the vendor abandoned the system. The University then had to discard the system at a cost of hundreds of thousands of pounds. Consequently, Computer Services lost credibility and the perceived failure of the system was memorable to academics many years after the event. As the chair of the Information Strategy Group pointed out, this constrained the ability of Computer Services, and in particular the Head of Computer Services, to make strategic decisions:

> [T]his [IT system] thing was palpably a mistake and an expensive mistake. So this University is not in a good shape to drive through an IT strategy that is not universally accepted. It has to be more tactical than that. I think it is terrible, but, that's the way it's got to be.

The result of this perception of lack of competence was that they were unable to gain political support. As one senior manager noted:

> Computer Services have been trying to implement an information services strategy for a number of years. It had been through the University senate, but it was not acted on, it was not actually implemented. . . . It was strange, because these strategies were reasonably competent at the time, but because they did not come from the appropriate committee and so on they were never driven home.

The service manager was also seen as being both cut out of and as removing himself from the political structures of the HEI, as one senior manager noted: 'The computer services manager does not find it easy to make those sort of strategic decisions because he's not involved in the politics'.

The consultant brought in by the Vice-Chancellor noted that this lack of political support, combined with the fact that there was a general lack of understanding of the terms or language used by Computer Services, had led to a general feeling of frustration with the service. As a result, senior management largely ignored it. This lack of empathy, understanding and political support for Computer Services resulted in it being under-resourced and understaffed. The understaffing, combined with the demands of trying to implement and support the Vice-Chancellor's technological vision for the future of the university, in turn resulted in Computer Services spending much of its time fire-fighting rather then being proactive. Its Director acknowledged this himself: 'It's strange in a way, the usual sort of fire-fighting situation, in that there are lots of things that I would like to do in terms of consolidating where we are but you never really get the time.'

The result was that Computer Services was often unable to progress developments, which meant that development of systems of strategic importance to the HEI, such as management information systems, was ineffective:

> [T]here is so much time fire-fighting and doing ordinary jobs . . . that to actually push something out that is new and challenging in itself, . . . you just do not find the time. . . . That is not just . . . general doubts and cynicism by the university about the MAC initiative, but . . . that even our technical people do not have enough time.

The result was a lack of trust in the competence of the IT services on the part of academic departments in an environment where the existing information systems were perceived as inadequate and where departments were largely autonomous. This led departments to develop their own IT resources and IT support staff. One senior academic noted:

> I think that they are not highly regarded within the University. That has to be qualified in a number of ways. They tend to be perceived as a very bureaucratic organization so a lot of departments have made their own arrangements in terms of the technology, while they need the computer centre there for running the network and managing the network connections and so on.

The Chair of the ISG recognized this problem:

> I am aware that the limitations of the use of the systems in the departments and the central administration is currently causing problems . . . departments are developing the skills to do it themselves and that is inefficient and wasting resources.

The departments were able to fund the technology primarily because much of their funding came from outside sources. As the librarian noted:

A lot of departments obtain their own money from research grants, . . . so they have their own LANs and they have their own machinery and their own software which they run within that. Their own LAN will be connected to the campus network, and be on that to JANET and the internet, . . . and they don't see that the computer centre has a role as far as they are concerned, in the strategic sense.

Indeed, in Old Collegial, academic departments were noticeably reluctant to support central services. As the Chair of the ISG noted: 'The whole power in this University is in the departments, the centre doesn't have much power. It is there to co-ordinate but as soon as it does any real top-slicing the departments start to get ratty'.

This impacted further on IT services: demands upon them increased but they were unable to secure further resources. Any attempts made by Computer Services to manage IT across the HEI in a strategic manner were largely ignored, not only by senior management but also by academic departments.

Computer Services found itself at the centre of a political battle, with academic departments arguing for the devolution of computing budgets to departments and the maintenance of only a skeleton service at the centre to manage the network. The impact of the lack of trust in computing services in the Old Collegial was profound. They found themselves in a vicious downward circle: lack of trust in their credibility eroded their ability to gain resources and provide an acceptable standard of service, this undermined their credibility, which in turn further eroded their ability to gain resources.

Trust between academic staff and administrative staff

The data gathered suggest that the issue of trust between different academic staff and administrative staff significantly affected the process of strategic change. This was particularly significant in HEIs where one or other of the two groups took a dominant role in governance. Some commentators have argued that the harsh external environment in which universities exist and, in particular, the financial pressures, have ended the norm of suspicion and distrust and instead brought faculty and administrators together to discuss system-wide issues (Damrosch, 1995, 203). In contrast to this view, this research demonstrates that, generally, the gulf between academic staff and administrative staff has never been wider. In New Managerial, for example, the political environment created by the Vice-Chancellor was one in which power and authority had been removed from the instruments of academic self-government (deans and schools), and placed in the hands of a professional administrative bureaucracy. As Rourke and Brooks pointed out as early as 1964:

In the context in which faculty members are less privileged and in which they often feel oppressed beneath the weight of administrative authority, the innovation wrought by the new devices of management may widen the gulf between faculty and administration and thus intensify the antagonism, latent and overt, which has traditionally existed between the administrative and academic cultures.

(Rourke and Brooks, 1964, 157)

This seemed to be the case in New Managerial. As one respondent noted:

I think, if I remember the figures correctly, something like only 7% of the staff on the previous staff feedback . . . said that they thought that the management essentially understood what they were doing. About 70 odd percent said . . . it was bad or very bad. . . . Whatever the terminology, there was an enormous polarisation which suggested that the staff were not 'on side'.

Another respondent reinforced this: 'If you actually have to draw a line somewhere in the university then you'd probably put the management team on one side and almost everybody else on the other.' One senior academic commented:

There has certainly been a concern about the relationship of the schools to the senior management team, which now actually has not got anybody in the first tier of that who's got an earned higher degree, which is interesting. So there is tension there and there is concern amongst the directors, of course, that they are not represented academically on the management team itself, and so on.

He was one of a number of interviewees to express concern about the competence and coherence of the SMT based on the view that they were not academics (they did not have an earned higher degree) and so did not have a deep understanding of how the HEI worked.

This quotation also illustrates the concern of many academics interviewed in New Managerial about the lack of representation of academics in the decision-making process. Indeed, it could be suggested that the issue of representation was an important issue because of the general lack of trust in New Managerial's management.

At the other extreme, Old Collegial placed power in the hands of the academics: academics controlled decision-making processes and resources, and theirs were the dominant cultural values. Within Old Collegial there was distrust between the service directors and the academics, and between the executive and the academic heads of departments. The service directors questioned the competence, openness, concern, benevolence and reliability of academics involved in the process (including the Vice-Chancellor). Many expressed the opinion that academics were ill-suited to the task of management. Indeed, there seemed to be a consensus between the different service directors that the SMT (composed of academics) did not understand the difficulty managers faced in attempting to implement their ideas for running the HEI:

> But there is a big difference between one or two academics doing something in a pilot scheme or advising others how to do it . . . and actually doing it yourself on a large scale in your own organization on a day-to-day basis. . . . It's very well sitting down and producing all sorts of theoretical models of how universities should be run under high technology and what have you, but when you come back to this room, there is a real University here to be run.

In Old Collegial, the Vice-Chancellor had provided a radical and dramatic vision for the future of the HEI. This had been embraced by some academics. The service directors felt that these academics did not understand the practical difficulties of implementing the vision:

> [In] practice as we all know, . . . what the technology can do in a pilot scheme is one thing, but getting that into [an actual] working system, which real people can use and benefit from, is a hell of a difference . . . in terms of funding and resources and support and just general development. You can define a wonderful system in theory but when it comes down to practical terms it is a failure.

Another aspect of the perception that academics lacked competence was the belief that, because the Vice-Chancellor had imposed a vision of radical transformative change, the process was 'out of control' and moving too fast. A service director commented:

> There are so many factors that are changing at once, the uncertainty of the funding and the inadequacy of the funding and the general sort of time scales on which these papers and changes are imposed means that you have to be reactive all of the time. While the whole ethos of this idea is that it is proactive, the ethos is that you think ahead and take advantage of the technology and you exploit it proactively rather than retrospectively, I mean everyone can do it five years later, can't they?

The service directors also felt that the senior academic managers lacked professionalism. One service director described the way in which he was told to develop a strategic plan for his service, but found it impossible to get the necessary financial plans from the senior management:

> What's happened in the last few years is that we have . . . gone to the funding authority . . . the Executive Board itself [which has] turned around and said: 'Oh Christ we can't afford that!' They don't even come back and say, that's no good we can't afford it, what they do is put it on the shelf. If they were to come back to me and say, 'That's a good idea, here's the money we have, see what you can do, pick out the best bits and do it.' Instead it just sits in limbo so we go through several years without really knowing whether the University really wants a strategy or can afford it.

The two HEIs have very different approaches to governance. New Managerial HEI is primarily a 'machine bureaucracy' with a managerial culture, while Old Collegial is a professional bureaucracy which retains elements of its collegial culture and structures. Yet in both there was a lack of trust between administrators and academic departments that has most commonly been noted in 'administered universities'. As Birnbaum points out, in these types of HEI, 'administrators are separated from the rest of the university. As a consequence, university executives and faculty form separate and isolated conclaves in which they are likely to communicate only with people similar to themselves' (Birnbaum, 1998, 42).

At the level of lateral trust between academic staff and administrative staff the key factors identified were those of competence, coherence and reliability. Competence and coherence specifically focused on the issue of ability: in both Old Collegial and New Managerial the academic staff and administrative staff did not trust each other because they were concerned about the ability of their counterparts. This was expressed in terms of concerns about the academics' professionalism, which indicated concerns about the ability of the academics to step outside their own areas of expertise and become involved in management. Lack of trust in administrators focused on their ability to understand and value the academic culture. The fact they had not been 'initiated' into the culture of academia by earning a higher degree was seen as undermining their legitimacy. Low levels of trust in ability seemed to be based on an interaction between the emotional response of 'they aren't one of us' reinforced by experience of actions taken, which was seen as illustrating that 'they do not understand us'. Low levels of trust in reliability were shown to be based on experience; for example, in New Managerial HEI the academics described the administrators as unreliable and cited examples of them being inconsistent, not fulfilling promises and being unpredictable.

Conclusion

In common with many other sectors (cf. Barrett, 1999, on the insurance sector) higher education is now at a point where the pressures of the neo-liberal, free-market economy and the 'promise' of new information technologies make further radical change almost inevitable. The findings of this chapter suggest that in such turbulent environments the critical questions are not about whether informal, incremental approaches or formal comprehensive approaches to strategic planning for information systems are more effective: the more fundamental issue is how to build and maintain trust between organizational members during the strategic change process. Indeed, in common with other research (e.g., Scarbrough, 1995) this research reinforces the view that the use of formal plans and methodologies is simply the tip of the organizational iceberg. The findings suggest that the development of information strategy is the outcome of negotiated and political relations (Pettigrew, 1977).

Political behaviour infuses all aspects of strategy formation; it is not a dark realm where Machiavellian figures work their black arts but, rather, consists of actions taken by reasonable and responsible women and men. As Mangham points out:

> [S]ince the conduct of organizations . . . implies a degree of choice about direction, reasonable men are likely to differ about it. Reasonable men are likely to differ not only about ends but also about means and such differences are not readily reconciled since the choice of one course of action rather than another may affect the survival of the enterprise. Thus responsible men are obliged to fight for what they are convinced is right and, perhaps more significantly, against that which they are convinced is wrong.   (Mangham, 1979, 545)

The formation of an information strategy is a process by which these different perspectives are reconciled through a process of compromise and negotiation. For this to work effectively a degree of trust must exist within the organization.

14

Heathcare information management and technology strategy: the story so far

Hugh Preston

Introduction

The UK National Health Service's (NHS) strategic switch-back had been well documented prior to the development of a long-term policy (Abbott et al., 1996). Each centrally originated change resulted in various attempts to record the repercussions and predict the outcomes. In September 1998 the UK Department of Health's information strategy was published – the first attempt at a medium- to long-term view. *Information for Health: an information strategy for the modern NHS, 1998–2005* was an ambitious attempt to pre-define the repercussions of information technology change and match outcomes to aims. It enabled an examination of issues in developing an information management and technology (IM&T) strategy at the local level within the changing national requirements for NHS information management. Among the studies and commentaries that appeared immediately before and after the publication of *Information for Health*, the case of an oncology unit in the north-west of England was chosen for an examination of local strategic implementation (Smith and Preston, 2000). The case detailed was the Clatterbridge Centre for Oncology (CCO) on Merseyside, the second largest centre of its type in the UK. The study's initial investigation of information needs preceded the publication of the national strategy and the strategic implementation at CCO straddled the timescale devised by the NHS Information Authority (NHSIA). As such, it could be anticipated that there would be a degree of incompatibility between timescales for the local and the national developments and these were examined within the case. The work of the (then) new NHSIA and its supporting guidance in its circular, *Information for Health: initial local implementation strategies*, was subsequently evaluated as a tool for aligning local and national strategy (NHS Executive, 1998).

The current study

The 1998 strategy was conceived as a means to achieve a range of information management and technology by 2005. It is apposite at this time to examine some of local-level implementation issues that suggested pointers to full completion of the strategy. In this study, the issues are linked to subsequent developments and the achievements to date, nationally and at Clatterbridge. Policies and attitudes to the IM&T strategy are assessed here in the light of intervening policy developments.

The implications of *Information for Health*

Just as corporate information managers often struggle to cope with the remote requirements of central headquarters (e.g., McGrath and Smithson, 2001), those within the health sector have to meet the demands of central government as well as regional and local management. The speculative commentaries of professional journals such as the *Health Service Journal* are punctuated by periodic reviews by analysts of longitudinal change (Tackley et al., 2003).

The 1998–2005 strategy provided a framework for IM&T (Burns, 1998). This focuses on the NHS as a whole, but predictably aimed to ensure strategic implementation at primary care level first. This was inevitable, given *The New NHS* White Paper's commitment to modernization of general practitioner (GP) systems (Mitchell, 1998). The strategy stated the case for electronic patient and electronic health records (EPR and EHR) and for the supporting infrastructure. These included developing clinical information standards and improving use of the (then) new NHSnet. This strategy was initially viewed positively, largely as a result of the long-standing need for central direction (Wyatt and Keen, 1998).

Despite the primary care priorities, standards for EPR and EHR would apply equally to acute providers such as cancer centres. For the case study treatment unit (CCO), the absence of an IM&T strategy since it became a trust in 1992 had hampered the development of information resources, but the 1998 strategy potentially enabled local and national systems development to be in accordance (Fairey, 1999). The issue of implementing the new information strategy alone was broadly addressed within the *Information for Health* strategy document and supported by an NHS Executive circular (NHS Executive, 1998). It was envisaged that local partnerships between trusts, primary care practices and IT suppliers were a necessary feature of managing local priorities within a framework of national standards. Priorities within *Information for Health* were as follows:

- the complete patient record would be available where, when and to whom required (subject to confidentiality)
- data would be requested and captured once and once only

- management information would be derived from data captured routinely during day-to-day operational activities
- IM&T must be recognized as an investment and not a cost. It was recommended that all health authorities should give a higher priority to IM&T investment than was the case at that time (NHS Executive, 1996b).

The 1998 strategy *Information for Health* embodied these in the following tenets:

- development of lifelong electronic health records for every person in the country
- access for all NHS clinicians to on-line patient records and information about best clinical practice
- genuinely seamless care for patients through GPs, hospitals and community services sharing information across the NHS information highway
- fast and convenient public access to information and care through online information services and telemedicine
- the effective use of NHS resources by providing health managers with the information they need (Burns, 1998).

The case

Clatterbridge Centre for Oncology (CCO) is the second largest centre of its type in the UK. It is a specialist regional centre for the treatment of malignant diseases serving a catchment population in the north-west of England and north Wales. Since its inception in 1958 it has established both national and international reputations. The centre became an NHS Trust on 1 April 1992.

Prior to the 1998 strategy, CCO had developed an IM&T strategy based primarily on local needs but remaining in accordance with the five basic principles set out by the NHS Information Management Group in 1992. However, this had never been fully documented. Development of the CCO strategy later had to incorporate the changes brought about by the White Paper of 1997, which introduced the principle of clinical governance (Department of Health, 1997). Within cancer care, all strategies for the provision of services had additionally to incorporate the requirements of the Calman/Hine initiative of 1995 (Calman and Hine, 1995). The delay in publication of the new national IM&T strategy had resulted in some caution at the local level since IM&T managers had not wished to implement local strategic policies without confidence in their conformance to national requirements. At CCO one outcome of this was wariness about replacing the principal information support system that was not meeting current information requirements. At the time of publication, the close match between CCO local information needs and national strategy was unexpected, owing to the problems previously faced by cancer units with incorporating standards developed in accordance with the requirements of general medicine. Related research has highlighted the difficulties met in keeping in step with national policy while still maintaining local benefits (Bowns et al., 1999; Godden et al., 2000). As such, during the early implementation of CCO's IM&T strategy, it was experiencing a range of environmental forces that determined its activities and information about them. These are summarized in Figure 14.1. Most are common to NHS Trusts and cancer treatment centres in particular.

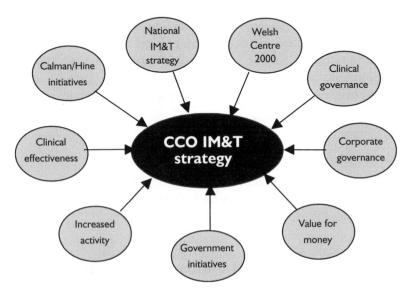

Figure 14.1   Environmental factors affecting cancer centres

Calman/Hine

The Calman/Hine initiative determined that designation as a cancer centre required accreditation, which could only be achieved if minimum quality and service standards were met. This required a shared pool of patients and a flow of aggregated information between individual cancer units and other organizations (Calman and Hine, 1995).

Increased number of cancer cases

The number of new cancer cases at CCO was increasing at the time of the study and all cancer centres were facing increased activity pressures (Smith and Preston, 2000). These developments were frequently not resourced at full cost and therefore required substantial efficiency improvements in the use of staff and resources.

Effective information systems at both the operational and monitoring levels would be essential if additional costs in processing these transactions were to be avoided.

Clinical governance

The concept of clinical governance was introduced in the 1997 White Paper (Department of Health, 1997) and is applicable to all NHS acute provider trusts. The national minimum dataset for cancer registration failed to meet the Calman/Hine requirements in terms of providing a dataset that can be used to monitor the effectiveness of cancer services (Le Maistre and Moseley, 1998). Agencies such as the Commission for Health Improvement (CHI; now the Healthcare Commission) have also been active in monitoring activity. In 2003–4, CCO achieved the maximum three-star rating (Commission for Health Improvement, 2004b).

Corporate governance

The assessment of internal performance varies from trust to trust. Even if the response to increasing activity is discounted, CCO needed to correct its deficiencies which included the following:

- missing and duplicate case notes and investigation results
- multiple telephone calls required in order to obtain investigation results
- use of incomplete and inadequate information to manage a highly complex and dynamic service.

'Cancer Benchmarking Club' data before 1998 indicated that CCO was already very efficient in some areas. Therefore, the scope for improvement without major strategic and organizational change could have been significantly limited compared with other trusts.

Government initiatives

The White Paper published in 1997 indicated a major change in commissioning with the demise of the internal market. The currency of contracting is forever changing, as is the basic principle of contracting itself. The Trust needed information on episode costing and related costing units such as health resource groups (HRGs), 'care packages' or any other defined currency. CHI's Acting Chief Executive, Jocelyn Cornwell, stated in March 2004:

Knowing how to use information well is becoming increasingly important. Massive investment is being made in information systems, but unless the NHS has the right mindset about effective use of information there is a risk that they will not be exploited fully.

(Commission for Health Improvement, 2004a)

As a result, the Commission launched a 'Use of information self-assessment tool' to enable information system prioritization within trusts.

Clinical effectiveness

One of the essential functions for clinical effectiveness is information (NHS Executive, 1996a) but the professions had been slow to implement standards for communication and sharing information in 1998. Structured data collection and entry has been shown to be an effective way of providing decision support for clinical practice (Bowns et al., 1998) but standards and clinical contexts were varied.

Value for money

All NHS organizations had been facing financial pressures for some time before the 1998 strategy (Department of Health, 1996) and the national IM&T strategy aimed to ensure that IM&T gives value for money. Installed in 1992, the principal support system (CIS/R) at CCO was unable to meet the current and future needs of the Trust. Hence £250,000 was spent in 1998–9 on IM&T provision, representing 1.3% of turnover. This expenditure was not excessive for an NHS acute hospital but the functionality received was relatively poor when compared with the functionality and cost of modern systems.

The original study at Clatterbridge

It was apparent that local IM&T strategy could not simply be an implementation of a single set of national guidelines. Consequently, CCO did not assess its information needs solely on the tenets listed, but on the basis of the pressures that clinicians and managers felt in all aspects of their work. The study in 1997–8 outlined the findings and assessed variance from the NHS Information Authority's guidelines. This variance could be the result of the following factors:

- the study preceded the publication of the *Information for Health* strategy
- some environmental factors placed higher priorities on certain data types, communication channels and information formats.

The major issue to be addressed by this exercise was the information needed to support staff in carrying out their day-to-day work. This initially preceded the 1998 strategy, but analysis of the data straddled the publication of the strategy and CCO's aim to fulfil its requirements. It was evident prior to the study that many staff had little idea of their own information needs. One senior clinician had admitted to being very embarrassed at not being able to articulate the information and functionality required to support fellow clinicians in their work. It was evident that the lack of an IM&T strategy had contributed to a very unfocused approach to identification of information needs. Therefore, the method selected to gather data on needs had to be appropriate to investigation in an environment of undirected information use. However, since staff were very conscious of their need for information, the method had to produce results that were directly applicable to a local strategy. Abstract principles of data type, content and communication would not serve the purpose of the exercise. Unstructured interviews were used for senior clinicians and managers. Workshops using a semi-unstructured *aide-mémoire* were used to collect information from other staff. These were arranged on a discipline-by-discipline basis where possible. The focus of the interviews and workshops was system functionality with respect to usefulness and effectiveness as they perceived it and comprised one snapshot of an iterative analysis process. The tools for qualitative research have a good track record (Bryman, 2004).

Information needs

If local implementation of national IM&T requirements was to be successful, the determination of information requirements had to be fundamental, not just a symptomatic exercise in examining current problems. Bias within qualitative data collection (Yin, 1989) was addressed by having a single person conduct the interviews and workshops so that there was an element of consistency.

Research process

The views of directors, senior clinicians and senior managers were established by interviews. Workshops were arranged for all other users on the basis of discipline. Staff at all levels were assured that all comments and opinions were important and confidential.

The method chosen to conduct the original exercise appeared to have been effective, given the following two distinct aspects:

- the results of the exercise formed the foundation of the strategy
- the information gathering exercise increased motivation and commitment to the strategy implementation project at all levels.

While the methodology chosen to carry out this exercise at CCO proved effective it cannot be argued that the issues would be equally applicable in other cancer centres. However, CCO's pre-eminence in its field gives the results some validity as a benchmark.

The procedures for establishing information needs require the involvement of staff in all disciplines and at all levels. The establishment of an information management partnership between managers, end users and IM&T professionals is essential if effective information management is to be achieved (Audit Commission, 1995; Silk, 1991). The aim of the exercise as expressed by Avison and Fitzgerald (2003) is to identify and gain representation of as many views as possible. Features of the three main sample groups and the remaining sampled users can be found in the detail of the original study (Smith and Preston, 2000).

Results

In summary, staff at all levels and across all disciplines expressed a need for information to carry out their regular duties more efficiently and effectively. Existing systems and manual processes were holding staff back from achieving their desire to improve their particular area of service provision. Whether clinical or administrative processes are involved, the end result must be improvement in the quality of care and service to the patient and his/her family. Although these may seem obvious goals, in information terms they pre-empted the national strategy's aim of improving communication of data rather than narrowly refining internal systems. The advancement of information thinking from earlier programmes such as the Resource Management Initiative was clear. The results identified five themes for information needs, drawn from the data of the sample groups. These themes and the expressed needs appear in Table 14.1.

Table 14.1 Thematic information needs

Theme	Information needs
Clinical information needs	Patient clinical histories for a longitudinal record such as an electronic patient record (EPR).
Decision support	Summary data as a tool to:
	• improve understanding of health needs
	• contain costs
	• monitor, review and redistribute resources
	• analyse and compare performance.

Continued on next page

Table 14.1   *Continued*

Theme	Information needs
Education and professional development	Access to: • general information sources such as the internet • specific sources such as Medline and the Cochrane Collaboration databases • computer-based training.
Resource management	Information regarding financial and human resources to: • improve efficiency • meet national audit standards, including new standards relevant to the oncology specialism, such as Calman/Hine assessment.
Performance management and measurement	Internal information regarding performance in the units of: • contract activity • unplanned activity including contract variance such as waiting lists and treatment rates • key financial indicators • case mix profiles of care, clinical audit • staffing numbers and skill mix • outcome measurements related to the Patients' Charter.

Conclusions

Perhaps most notably, the findings included needs around the obvious, but often centrally ignored, patient and staff foci. This was in accord with the new *Information for Health* strategy that appeared after the end of the study. The strategic emphasis on information management expressed through patient and staff needs was apparent. This was to replace previous initiatives including optimization of technology as the priority, rather than its outcomes. The implementation guidance for *Information for Health* took a similarly patient-centred view and placed the EPR at its heart. This match can be linked to the impact of local needs of the type identified at CCO on the development of a national strategy. Much discussion of the insular nature of health sector management had taken place internationally as well as within the UK (Rondeau and Wagar, 1999). Some comments have endorsed this more recently (Kunkler, 2003).

Since 1998: a study in change

As stated earlier, the pace of change in the UK NHS has accelerated rather than steadied or declined. In 1998 the NHS was starting to implement the policies of the Department of Health's White Paper, *The New NHS* (Department of Health, 1997). External comments regarding these changes began immediately after the implementation of *The New NHS* and the Department of Health made no attempt to conceal them. In January 2003 the nature of change appeared in many documents from the Department. Among the objectives for implementing the 1998 IM&T strategy was to 'improve the capacity of the NHS to deliver change and reform' through effective IT procurement (Department of Health, 2003).

In 2002, Mr Richard Granger was appointed Director General of NHS Information Technology. The initial investment of £2.3 billion indicated the importance of IT, but the later and broader strategy attracted £6.2 billion. The NHS Information Authority (NHSIA) was established in 1999 and developed strategic themes for implementation alongside existing agencies, including the National Electronic Library for Health (NeLH). The NHS Network (NHSnet) was to provide a tool that aimed to link primary and secondary care units and also community care. As of March 2005, the NHSIA is being wound up as the main strategic implementation unit and has already been replaced, along with a specific information unit for health and social care, by the NHS National Programme for Information Technology (NPfIT) with resources from the £6.2 billion total. Its implementation guidance already exists (NHS National Programme for Information Technology, 2004). There have been some queries concerning the ability of NPfIT to meet its objectives (Fairey, 2004; Humber, 2004) but it is only at a pilot stage at present. In summary, the aims of NPfIT are 'to procure, develop and implement modern, integrated IT infrastructure and systems for all NHS organizations in England by 2010' (Hextall, 2004). Note the remit of the strategy being limited to England alone within the UK. The facilities intended to achieve this are as follows:

- development of an NHS Care Records Service for a full EPR-based service and the potential for an electronic health record (EHR)
- choose-and-book for electronically booking initial hospital appointments from primary care units such as general practitioner surgeries
- electronic transmission of prescriptions for speed and convenience of medicine collection by patients
- a new national network (N3) to replace NHSnet
- a quality management and analysis system (QMAS) for providing primary care units with measurement feedback regarding national achievement targets
- picture archiving and communication systems (PACS) for digital moving or static medical images
- a secondary uses service (SUS) for system security and confidentiality.

Therefore, since 1998, the implementation of *Information for Health* has expanded in scope and resourcing. It has a leader (Director) with the support of the UK government and with a focus on the patients and staff within the NHS. In this regard it differs from the situation before 1998.

NPfIT as the agency of change

As stated at the start of this chapter, the aim of the current research included the objective of viewing the development of strategic implementation following the publication of Information for Health at the end of 1998. The nature of change, migration of resources and breadth of implementation are apparent from the outline above. It is now necessary to re-examine the themes that emerged in the original 1998 study of local information system policy within CCO, alongside the evolutionary national strategy. One means to achieve this would be to match the 1998 needs alongside the strategy implementation in 2005, the year originally planned for its completion. However, the needs of clinicians and information managers in 1998 were not necessarily expressed in the same terms as those of NPfIT in 2005. Therefore, it would be useful to look at some categories of information need identified by an individual clinician in both his clinical role and as a senior academic. These categories, alongside those of an expert in health informatics, may enable an intermediate perspective to establish whether the CCO themes reflect NPfIT implementation. Two brief articles in the *British Medical Journal* in January 2003 outline the clinician's expressed information needs (Majeed, 2003) and the support of those requirements provided by the health informatics practitioner (de Lusignan, 2003). The latter commentator appreciates all of the clinician's views but places them within the context of a decentralized approach to specific information system development. In this regard, clinical information needs can also fall within resource requirements and priorities. This context reflects the situation at CCO, outlined earlier in this chapter when looking at the case organization itself and the environmental factors that have local significance, replicated in varying degrees elsewhere in England.

Table 14.2 includes the local information themes from the CCO study in 1998, the clinical needs of Majeed on submission of his paper in 2002 (published at the start of 2003) and the NPfIT national strategy. The National Strategic Programme now has a tentative timescale extending to 2010, largely a result of its broadened scope.

Table 14.2   Information needs, themes and strategic facilities

CCO themes 1998	Clinician's needs 2002–3	National Programme for IT in the NHS (NPfIT) facilities 2005 on
Clinical information needs	• Electronic discharge summaries and clinic letters • Electronic hospital diagostic codes • Electronic transfer of records between practices • Improve information sharing • Code outpatient encounters • Improve Lab-Links system • Better speed and reliability of NHSnet	• NHS Care Records Service • Choose-and-book • Electronic transmission of prescriptions • N3 to replace NHSnet • PACS
Decision support	• Electronic discharge summaries and clinic letters • Electronic hospital diagnostic codes • Improve information sharing • Code outpatient encounters • Better speed and reliability of NHSnet • More comparative information activity	• NHS Care Records service • N3 to replace NHSnet • QMAS
Education and professional development	• Improve information sharing • Provide training	• N3 to replace NHSnet • PACS • SUS
Resource management	• Electronic discharge summaries and clinic letters • Electronic transfer of records between practices • Start coding outpatient encounters • Better speed and reliability of NHSnet • Improve Lab-Links system • Transfer maintenance responsibility from practices • More comparative information activity	• NHS Care Records service • Choose-and-book • Electronic transmission of prescriptions • N3 to replace NHSnet • QMAS

Continued on next page

Table 14.2 *Continued*

CCO themes 1998	Clinician's needs 2002–3	National Programme for IT in the NHS (NPfIT) facilities 2005 on
Performance management and measurement	• Electronic discharge summaries and clinic letters • Electronic hospital diagnostic codes • Improve information sharing • Start coding outpatient encounters • Improve Lab-Links system • Better speed and reliability of NHSnet • More comparative information activity	• NHS Care Records service • Choose-and-book • Electronic transmission of prescriptions • N3 to replace NHSnet • QMAS

At present NPfIT is defined in terms of the procurement of its facilities and so there is no stated interpretation of the individual facilities. As such, the Secondary Uses Service for system security and confidentiality will probably be an underlying facility to meet all needs.

Conclusion: implications at the local level

Information systems and policies for implementation at the local level cannot remain static while technical specifications are drawn up and pilot systems trialled prior to roll-out. The specific information needs, themes identified in initial research and the plans for the national programme achieve a degree of match that differs more in terminology changing over time than in its meaning. However, the different environment of different treatment units defines the need for variance in policy implementation. For the case organization at Clatterbridge, the waiting time for initial cancer therapy in 2000 was around 40 days and therefore did not come close to the Department of Health's 14-day target (Department of Health, 2000). Information held within traditional hospital administrative systems, including the paper-based diaries held by consultants was very inflexible (Jones, 2001). In 2002 a new patient administration system was purchased with many of the facilities highlighted in *Information for Health* as vital for its implementation. This is reflected in the CHI Governance Review (Commission for Health Improvement, 2003) carried out shortly beforehand which stated that, at the end of 2001:

- a new PAS system is soon to be introduced
- there is excellent patient information
- there is no electronic booking system for outpatients.

Although it is not yet certain whether it will smoothly dovetail with the N3 network, the new CCO strategy has rapidly reduced the wait-time to 15 days and continues to reduce it. The Centre now fits within the Wirral Health Informatics Service which broadens the regional significance of the information system policy. The anticipated symbiosis lies in the ability to meet local and specialist information needs beyond those of the broad national programme, and also to match the system requirements defined by that strategy (Cross, 2004).

Acknowledgement

The author wishes to thank the Chief Executive, executive directors and all staff at Clatterbridge Centre for Oncology for their co-operation during the original study between 1997 and 1998.

15

National information infrastructure and the realization of the Singapore IT2000 initiative

Cheryl Marie Cordeiro and
Suliman Al-Hawamdeh

Introduction

The aim of this chapter is to review the development of Singapore's plans for its national information infrastructure as an example of the evolution of an information strategy at the national level – albeit one with a strong information technology orientation.

Around the world, government policy is fundamental to steering nations towards the information-based society and economy. Countries are restructuring regulations, financing operations and ownership to meet the demands of new telecommunications and multimedia systems. Plans exist to improve telecommunications channels and to make them more advanced and accessible. Education, staff retraining, health care, productivity, environmental conservation, etc., have potentially brighter futures related to the development of information societies. Singapore is pursuing the Intelligent Island initiative, Japan the Info-Communications for the 21st Century and the European Union (EU) the European Information Society (GIIC Asia Regional Meeting and International Conference, 1995). These various government-led initiatives have become an inter-weave of technologies, economics and politics. New corporate alliances across the globe are making traditional geographical, organizational and technological boundaries irrelevant.

Singapore has prepared to meet the new challenges of the information age. In *A Vision of the Intelligent Island: the IT2000 Report* (National Computer Board of Singapore, 1992), one of the key roles envisaged for the Singapore government was to invest in R&D for leadership positions in the 'locomotive' industry of the next millennium. IT2000 has a ten-year horizon and looks into long-term issues and key trends such as:

- improving price performance of microelectronics, resulting in faster, cheaper, smaller and more user-friendly IT
- increasing the speed and capacity of ICT to achieve availability of broadband and wireless communication networks
- the proliferation of multimedia applications, which means cheap, portable and powerful multimedia systems, reaching out to various public and private spheres, including education; this also includes the convergence of TV, radio and print
- extensive standardization involving the international standardization of information technology driven by market forces and buyers' concerns for the protection of the value of their investment
- integration of ICT with the transportation system, thereby expanding work and lifestyle options.

The National Information Infrastructure Group (NIIG) foresees that information infrastructure planning will be the main social planning direction of the early 21st century. The National Computer Board (NCB) as the national information infrastructure (NII) master-planner, takes on the new function of overseeing and spearheading the implementation of NII. The leading NIIG collaborates with other organizations, mainly Singapore Telecom, Tata Consultancy Services, the Ministry of Information and the Arts (MITA) and the Ministry of Communications, to plan and develop different components of NII. These organizations will design the system architecture and develop functional specifications for common network services. The ultimate goal of the NIIG is to find a balance between integration and flexibility of information infrastructure that enables productive and efficient connectivity.

According to the IT2000 report, there will be a need for multi-agency collaboration as Singapore's society becomes more networked. The implementation of the NII projects also requires the participation of, and has direct impact on, many governmental departments and statutory boards. Singapore's IT visions can only be achieved through synergistic efforts, and a co-ordinated approach at all organizational levels. A high-level steering committee has been formed to implement the NII, charting directions for the development of information infrastructure and addressing policy issues such as data protection, information access, intellectual property and computer security.

Methodology

In all, 76 working professionals volunteered for this study. They came from various working backgrounds: governmental statutory boards such as the National Library Board (NLB), the NCB, MITA, the Ministry of Education (MOE), the Economic Development Board (EDB), and the Telecommunications Authority of Singapore (TAS) and also multi-national corporations and local companies. All participants were taking a graduate study degree in information studies. The participants were asked to discuss and answer an open question: 'Identify areas in which the government can play a role in the development of the information society in Singapore.' The age range of the participants was 24–55.

The participants received the question and discussed it in working groups of four or five for an hour. The groups were formed according to the participants' working background so that educational officers, managers, library officers, IT specialists, etc., all formed distinct groups. After that, each group reported their results through a spokesperson. A week later individual reports on group discussions were collected from all 76 participants.

In order to identify the ideas in the participants' responses, each report was analysed to create a checklist. The checklist enabled comparisons with the IT2000 report, which was used as the framework for this study. This report, as explicated by the NCB, acts as a national standard putting forward the main ideas for IT and IS in Singapore's future development.

Both quantitative and the qualitative methods of analysis were used so that a fair cross-section of responses could be obtained. The quantitative technique was used to collect statistical facts in the responses to evaluate them in relation to the IT2000 report. The qualitative technique was used to investigate each individual's perception of the Singapore government and its efforts in leading Singapore into the information age. The latter method served to seek insight rather than statistics, lending depth to this investigation.

IT2000 as a benchmark

IT2000 as a government initiative outlined the role of government in the development of national information infrastructure in Singapore. The report provided the basic criteria for analysing the responses of the participants. Compared with the IT2000 report, responses helped to determine the extent to which the IT2000 report was able to address the government's role. IT2000 includes five major categories of government involvement:

• Developing global hubs
   — business hub
   — services hub

- — transportation hub
- Boosting the economic engine
  - — manufacturing
  - — commerce
  - — tourism
  - — construction
- Enhancing the potential of individuals
  - — lifelong learning
  - — creativity
  - — skills
  - — knowledge
  - — greater investment in education and training
  - — individual learning pace, place and time
  - — simulated and interactive education: extension of media and cultural institutions, knowledge navigation, extra help for the disadvantaged, interactive distance education and multimedia learning.
- Improving quality of life
  - — easy commuting
  - — teleshopping
  - — one stop, non-stop government and business service
  - — cashless transactions
  - — telecommuting
  - — more options for leisure
  - — intelligent buildings
  - — better healthcare
- Linking communities locally and globally
  - — help create electronic communities of like-minded people
  - — enable Singaporeans to extend and strengthen personal reach
  - — encourage development of a global mindset, blurring the lines between local and global communication
  - — each individual to have access to and actively use various means of electronic communication, to spin their own webs according to affiliations, e.g., clans, old school ties, professional society, etc., via community telecomputing network and Singapore international net.

Findings and analysis

Five tables corresponding to the IT2000 categories were created to show the results of analysis.

More than half of the participants thought that developing Singapore into a global hub served to bring Singapore into the information age. However, more participants saw the globalization of Singapore in terms of business and services rather than transportation (Table 15.1). One participant thought that the Singapore government had done much to position Singapore as a global business and services hub, as evidenced by the number of international conferences, seminars and events held annually in Singapore.

Table 15.1   Developing Singapore as a global hub

Category	Number of transcripts (n = 76)	Percentage of total transcripts
Developing Singapore as a global hub	40	52.6%
— business hub	18	45% (of 40 transcripts)
— services hub	16	40%
— transportation hub	6	15%

The participants also mentioned that multinational companies (MNCs) are encouraged by the government to set up operations in the region, and also to use Singapore as their headquarters or the centre of their Asian region trading zone. One participant gave an example of what Singapore is competing with: Nike has its manufacturing plants located in China to tap the low cost labour market and its R&D division in Silicon Valley, USA. Without the advantage of low labour costs, Singapore has to turn to information technology, R&D, efficiency and a transparent governmental system to attract such organizations and root them in the country.

Regarding 'boosting the economic engine' (Table 15.2), only six of the 76 participants thought that IT2000 is concerned with the manufacturing, commerce and construction sectors — those sectors of the economy traditionally were not related to IT. However, all six mentioned the government's role in the tourism sector, which they deemed a good way to promote Singapore. If tourism figures increase and tourists return to their countries with a good image of Singapore, it can be considered that they left Singapore with a lasting, positive impression.

Table 15.2   Boosting the economic engine

Category	Number of transcripts (n = 76)	Percentage of total transcripts
Boosting the economic engine	6	7.9%
— manufacturing	6	100% (of 6 transcripts)
— commerce	3	50%
— construction	5	83.3%
— tourism	6	100%

IT and NII tend to permeate to the core of Singapore's system. For example, the country's local transport systems provide technology-based, up-to-the-minute information on bus arrivals and departures. Singapore has information kiosks situated along roads to give tourists whatever information they need. One cannot underestimate the power of word-of-mouth or first-hand information. If tourists leave Singapore with the impression of a well-connected and organized country other people will come to experience Singapore's information age.

Of the 76 scripts, 51 mentioned the Singapore government's role in enhancing the potential of individuals and referred to Singaporeans adopting multimedia learning as a way of life in the future. The government encourages Singaporeans to adopt a lifelong attitude towards learning. In recent debates on the age of information technology in Singapore, it was said that the difference between IT 'haves' and 'have-nots' in society is equivalent to the difference between literate and illiterate people in the past (Viewpoints, 2000). Therefore, the Infocomm Development Authority of Singapore (IDA) planned to organize events in March 2000 to make people comfortable with using information and communication technology. They planned to reach housewives, blue-collar workers and disabled persons so that nobody is overlooked or neglected (You too can go Online..., 2000).

Most participants (67.1%) viewed the category 'Enhancing the potential of individuals' (Table 15.3) as the most important. This uncovers the assumption of the participants that computers are tools of economic empowerment to individuals. Enabling easy access to computers gives the under-privileged and the uninformed not only psychological access to power but also democratizes technology in the interests of those who might otherwise be left behind. The IDA's efforts are part of the government's moves to encourage participation in the internet. For example, it has pledged that all students will have access to computers, with a ratio of two students to one PC.

Table 15.3 Enhancing the potential of individuals

Category	Number of transcripts (n = 76)	Percentage of total transcripts
Enhancing the potential of individuals	51	67.1%
— multimedia learning	51	100% (of 51 transcripts)
— interactive distance education	12	23.6%
— extension of media and cultural institutions	22	43.1%
— extra help for the disadvantaged	17	33.3%
— knowledge navigation	14	27.5%

Of the 51 participants, 22 thought that the government could enhance access to media and cultural institutions. To make this a reality, since December 2000, students at the Nanyang Technological University (NTU) have been able to connect to the internet anytime and anywhere within their 'wireless' campus. The university planned to spend nearly $4 million to set up this wireless campus network with 500 access points. It sought tenders for the installation of the network, as mentioned by the NTU president (Soon..., 2000). This was decided in order to keep abreast of the changing education system where computers and the internet play vital roles in expanding students' learning horizons. It also helps to follow global advances in communication. It is not only the tertiary institutions that are moving ahead in terms of ICT. A project entitled *Curriculum Alive* is one of the services made available on Singapore One by Ednovation Pte Ltd. *Curriculum Alive* is multimedia learning and revision software for primary school students and provides about 1800 interactive learning activities with animated stories and educational games. The software complements traditional teaching methods in primary schools so that students can learn in creative and entertaining ways (Virtual Institute..., 2000).

Only 27 participants regarded coming into the information age as a means of improving the quality of life (Table 15.4). All 27 generally thought that a one-stop government business service would be adequate in this aspect. While slightly more than half of the participants conceived of having more leisure time in the information era, few participants saw teleshopping and cashless transactions as a means of improving the quality of life. Few participants mentioned and trusted teleshopping because it is a relatively new phenomenon in Singapore. The NTUC Income Insurance Co-operative Ltd is the first insurance company in Singapore to offer its products and services on Singapore One. It enables the secure buying of policies using credit or cash cards.

Table 15.4: Improving the quality of life

Category	Number of transcripts (n = 76)	Percentage of total transcripts
Improving the quality of life	27	35.5%
— one stop, non-stop government and business service	27	100% (of 27 transcripts)
— teleshopping	3	11.1%
— easy commuting	19	70.4%
— better healthcare	4	14.8%
— intelligent buildings	18	66.6%
— more options for leisure	16	59.3%
— telecommuting	15	55.5%
— cashless transactions	5	18.5%

Singtel Magix, another service offered by Singapore Telecommunications Ltd, sets alternative leisure options for Singaporeans at home: watching movies, playing computer games, etc. (Singapore Techventure, 2000).

Only four participants mentioned improving healthcare administration through the NII. The government has in view the creation of an electronic medical records system recording an individual's medical information history and personal particulars onto a smart card. This card can be used during medical check-ups or emergencies to save time and maybe the individual's life in critical conditions. The NII can also be used to telecast short videoclips on the harm caused by smoking or drug taking anywhere and anytime on the MRTs (mass rapid transits), bus interchanges and shopping centres. With videoconferencing and internet consultations, patients who are housebound or who cannot afford a costly trip to a specialist overseas can use the internet to their advantage (Lee Tsao Yuan, 2000).

All participants agreed that a community network set up by the government would be useful in keeping communities together (Table 15.5). In 2004, 74% of households had computers, with 65% having internet access, compared with 14% in 1997 (Infocomm Development Agency, 2004). It has been said that poverty is the ultimate threat to man and globalization is still the best hope for closing the rich-poor gap (Poverty..., 2000). All participants indicated that globalization should be seen in a positive light and not as 'a blind, potentially malevolent force that needs to be tamed' (Go Global ..., 2000). Emphasizing Singapore's Asian orientation, Singapore's Minister of State for Foreign affairs Ow Chin Hock said in January 2000: 'As Singapore becomes more international and cosmopolitan in the 21st century, let us not forget that we are also Asians. . . . As Asians, we should always strive to preserve our cultural heritage' (Go Global..., 2000).

Table 15.5 Linking communities locally and globally

Category	Number of transcripts (n = 76)	Percentage of total transcripts
Linking communities locally and globally	20	26.3%
— community telecomputing network	20	100% (of 20 transcripts)
— Singapore international net	12	60%

The Minister of State for Foreign affairs has called for Singaporeans to look beyond the monetary and material aspects of life, and to show compassion towards their fellow citizens. He also said that a helping hand should be extended to the needy, and success shared with less fortunate people.

Beyond the scope of the IT2000 initiative

Table 15.6 categorizes the participant responses that are perhaps beyond the scope of or not indicated clearly in IT2000. In some cases the participants wished for more governmental attention and emphasis, or suggested improvements to the IT2000 framework. The issues raised may have affected the participants directly or indirectly (e.g., they may have experienced the issues personally in their working environment or in a personal domain). As indicated in Table 15.6, the top three concerns of the participants were: standardization practices (55.2%); ethical aspects of technopreneurship or technology (27.6%); a secure socio-political and economic environment (23.7%); and tax incentives and subsidy services (23.7%).

Table 15.6   Beyond the scope of IT2000

Category	Number of transcripts (n = 76)	Percentage of total transcripts
Policies and standardization practices	42	55.2%
Ethical aspects of technopreneurship or technology	21	27.6%
Providing a secure socio-political and economic environment	18	23.7%
Providing tax incentives and subsidy services	18	23.7%
Aiding and encouraging private sectors	16	21%
'Human engineering' processes	6	7.9%
Workshops and seminars for IT and information illiteracy for the elderly	5	6.6%
Balance censorship and freedom of expression	3	3.9%

Table 15.7 highlights the participants' responses to IT2000's five major thrusts, with 51 participants or 67.1% emphasizing the importance of enhancing the potential of individuals.

The participants spoke strongly on several issues in both their qualitative and quantitative responses. First, they feel that individuals will benefit most from the Singapore government's efforts to bring the country into the information age. Singaporeans will grow as individuals and government efforts will ensure that they will know how to harvest their own potential and fend for themselves in the information age. Participants defined a variety of governmental roles in the information age: from seeing the government as a 'strategist' and a 'builder' to the government as a 'consumer' of the very IT that they hope to promote and encourage in Singapore. Some insecurity felt by the participants needs attention from the government. Nearly a quarter (23.7%) believed that Singaporeans need to be more open-minded and entrepreneurial and there is a need to re-educate the workforce on IT. Another insecurity revealed by the participants had to do with their general lack of knowledge of the current IT and Infocomm Development Agency (see below for more about infocomm technology) updates in Singapore. And 55.2% believed more work needs to be done in terms of internet security, and of rules and regulations regarding IT usage and exploitation. These issues have been dealt with by the various government ministries.

Table 15.7 Summary of quantitative results of the study

Category	Number of transcripts (n = 76)	Percentage of total transcripts
Developing a global hub	40	52.6%
Boosting the economic engine	6	7.9%
Enhancing the potential of individuals	51	67.1%
Improving the quality of life	27	35.5%
Linking communities locally and globally	20	26.3%

Differing views and expectations

All participants viewed the government as the single most influential body leading Singapore into the information age, mainly responsible for building and providing the means for either the national information infrastructure (NII) or for general information infrastructure. Not all participants agreed with the IT2000 checklist categories. Four participants, who had formed one group, devised their own categories. Six differentiated categories as set forth by this group covered the following governmental roles:

- Strategist – the government as the main body developing a vision for the nation, taking leadership in defining Singapore's future direction of growth and allocating appropriate resources for realizing the information age in Singapore.
- Builder – the government as provider of the physical infrastructure for everyone to access information from around the world, and at the same time developing forward-looking policies to attract global information services and telecommunication players to invest, develop and promote Singapore as the 'gateway of information' on a regional and global scale.

- Regulator and facilitator – the government as facing the challenge of creating a nation of enterprise without stifling innovation through excessive censorship, creating fair business competition (without allowing fraudulent, undesirable businesses to thrive) and an environment for risk-taking in business (without encouraging rampant abuse of the system).
- Investor – the government helping local MNCs, SMEs and individual entrepreneurs to grow in the new information environment; through tax incentives and special grants local enterprises are encouraged to invest in technology and exploit the new medium for trading; SMEs can also take advantage of e-commerce to develop international storefronts without heavy capital investments.
- Integrator – the government ensuring that various programmes and projects (e.g., Singapore ONE, Library 2000, etc.) intended to implement the 'Vision of the Intelligent Island' are well integrated into a cohesive strategy; this requires well-constructed and forward-thinking policies and close co-operation between government, businesses and citizens to respond effectively not only to new opportunities but also to the threats of the information age.
- Educator – the government creating an environment encouraging Singaporeans to adopt the concept of lifelong learning; the education curriculum, schoolwork and information-rich resources (e.g., libraries and the internet) are revised to reflect the change towards a more dynamic and intellectually stimulating mode of learning.

Realization of the IT2000 report

The various governmental statutory boards, from the Singapore Broadcasting Authority to the NCB, have their own rules and regulations for broadcasting and internet use regarding standardization practices and safety. The Electronic Transaction Bill passed in 1998 has also served to address the ethical aspects of internet usage and transactions. Common network services ensure that all users perform electronic transactions in a secured and reliable environment. The services provided by Netscape and Microsoft include secure transactions by secure sockets layer technology, user verification, network security, billing and payment as well as user and service directories. A new certification authority, ID.Safe, launched in June 1999 by Cisco and Singapore Post, promotes further advancement of e-commerce through its public key infrastructure (Up Next..., 2000).

The government has acknowledged Singapore's lack of a nurturing environment for future technopreneurs, and the need to foster such an environment for future e-commerce generations (SM Lee's Talk..., 2000), though governmental organizations such as NCB, the National Science and Technology Board (NSTB) and the Economic Development Board provide subsidies and loans for starting businesses in technopreneurship. There is also extensive online help for smaller-scale businesses about subsidies and tax reduction. For example, Booknet, an internet trading platform for the book and stationery trade, offers services such as point-of-sale, inventory management, order processing and sales analysis. Shopnet, another electronic commerce platform, offers grocery retail shops and suppliers services such as point-of-sales scanning, backend inventory control and electronic data interchange. Many businesses in Singapore are also able to expand operations and utilize opportunities via the internet by making use of the electronic commerce platform put in place by the government in 1996. For example, SMEs can make use of Singapore Connect.

The evidence from national projects, the internet and the mass media supports the opinion that the government is more than just casually involved in leading the country into the information age. 'Infocomm' technology refers to the family of IT and telecommunication technologies such as computers, computer programs, the internet, e-mail, e-commerce, broadband internet access and web-enabled mobile devices and phones. The five-week IDA campaign of March 2000 aimed to demystify infocomm technology for the underprivileged and inexperienced. It also sought to expedite and enhance infocomm qualities for those already experienced in ICT use (e.g., students and professionals). The rate of participants' response that the government could make the greatest impact on enhancing the potential of individuals (67.1%) seems accurate.

Conclusion

To achieve the targets mentioned above Singapore needs to set up a world-class information and communication education system, become the regional e-learning hub and actively recruit foreign talent, including world-renowned researchers and teachers. Foreign talent get their work passes at a much faster rate than others since a separate system has been set up at the Manpower Ministry to process their applications. Singapore also has to boost computer-based schooling so that it makes up one-third of the curriculum.

The Information Society Index (IDC, 2005) now shows that both Sweden and Denmark have edged the USA out of top position in the information revolution. Sweden proved that a small initiative such as an employee purchase scheme (EPS) could have a significant impact upon the information society. This corporate initiative, as opposed to a government programme, demonstrates the ability of corporations to influence the development of the information society. Although the USA has slipped to number two, the International Data Group's global IT Market and Strategies research anticipates that consistent investments in IT will enable it to return to the top. Sweden's movement, however, is proof of the fact that even the strongest information society must remain innovative in terms of both developing IT and integrating it into society. The saturation of PCs in the infrastructure does not secure the strength of a digital economy. Instead, all infrastructures (technology, information and social) must be interwoven into a fabric that supports the information society. Sweden has understood this need for a balanced approach, an approach that Singapore has added to its original plans.

The success of bringing Singapore into the information age depends also on people's attitudes and motivations. While the government can do much to promote IT culture and ideology, the people of Singapore have to embrace it and make IT and infocomm knowledge a part of their lives. Singaporeans have to allow the permeation of such ideologies to the core of their private domains and admit the IT ideology to the crux of their daily lives. Lee reminded Singaporeans that, if Singapore is to succeed in transforming into an information age country, the people must be more open-minded and embrace new ideas and new methods of achieving their goals (What the Players..., 2000). In the information race, foreign players are competing with Singaporeans and the country needs people who will meet the challenge instantly and without hesitation. Singapore has both Hong Kong and the USA to look to as examples of risk takers. Countries such as Japan and Germany are also rethinking old methods of doing business in this new economy. And if exceptionally successful countries go through paradigm shifts, then Singapore has to do so too. Singapore cannot simply produce managers and engineers as it has been doing for the last 30 years. Today, it needs a convincing nucleus of intrinsic entrepreneurial talent.

Bibliography

Abbott, W., Bryant, J. R. and Barber, B. (1996) *Information Management in Health Care: handbook A – introductory themes*, Eastbourne, Health Informatics Specialist Group (HISG) of the British Computer Society.

Abell, A. (1994) Information Use and Business Success: a review of recent research on effective information delivery. In Feeney, M. and Grieves, M. (eds), *The Value and Impact of Information*, London, Bowker-Saur.

Abels, E., Jones, R., Latham, J., Magnoni, D. and Marshall, J. G. (2003) *Competencies for Information Professionals of the 21st Century*, prepared for the Special Libraries Association Board of Directors by the Special Committee on Competencies for Special Librarians, rev. edn, Washington DC, Special Libraries Association, www.sla.org/pdfs/competencies2003_finallocked.pdf [accessed 10 January 2005].

Abram, S. (1997) Post Information Age Positioning for Special Librarians: is knowledge management the answer?, *Information Outlook*, **1** (6), 18–25.

Agor, W. H. (1986) How Top Executives Use their Intuition to Make Important Decisions, *Business Horizons*, **29** (1), 49–53.

Aguilar, F. J. (1967) *Scanning the Business Environment,* New York, NY, Macmillan.

Ahituv, N. Z., Zif, J. and Machlin, I. (1998) Environmental Scanning and Information Systems in Relation to Success in Introducing New Products, *Information & Management,* **33** (4), 201–11.

Aldrich, H. E. (1999) *Organizations Evolving,* Thousand Oaks, CA, Sage Publications.

Alexandersson, M. and Limberg, L. (2003) Constructing Meaning through Information Artefacts, *The New Review of Information Behaviour Research,* **4**, 17–30.

Alfino, M. (1998) Information Ethics in the Workplace: traditional vs. information management theory, *Journal of Information Ethics,* **7** (1), 5–9.

Allen, B. L. (1996) *Information Tasks: toward a user-centered approach to information*, San Diego, CA, Academic Press.

Allen, D. K. (1995) Information Systems Strategy Formation in Higher Education Institutions, *Information Research*, **1** (1), http://informationr.net/ir/1-1/paper3.html [accessed 11 April 2005].

Allison, G. T. and Zelikow, P. (1999) *Essence of Decision: explaining the Cuban missile crisis.* 2nd edn, New York, NY, Addison-Wesley.

American Accounting Association's Financial Accounting Standards Committee (2002) *Comments to the FASB on Nonfinancial Performance Measures,* Sarasota, FL, American Accounting Association, http://aaahq.org/about/committee/fasc/ nonfinancialperformancemeasures.pdf [accessed 10 January 2005].

Andersen, H. V., Lawrie, G. and Savic, N. (2004) Effective Quality Management through Third-generation Balanced Scorecard, *International Journal of Productivity and Performance Measurement,* **53** (7), 634–45.

Andersen, S. S. (1997) *Case-studier og Generalisering: forskningsstrategi og design* [Case Studies and Generalisation: research strategy and design], Bergen, Fagbokforlaget.

Anderton, R. H. (1986) Post-graduate Education for Information Management in the UK: new developments at Lancaster, *International Journal of Information Management*, **6** (4), 247–58.

Andreau, R. and Ciborra, C. (1995) Organisational Learning and Core Capabilities Development: the role of IT, *Journal of Strategic Information Systems*, **5** (2), 111–27.

Ansoff, H. I. (1987) *Corporate Strategy*, rev. edn, Harmondsworth, Penguin.

Argyris, C. and Schoen, D. (1978) *Organizational Learning,* Reading, MA, Addison-Wesley.

Argyris, C., Schoen, D. and Payne, M. (1996) *Organizational Learning II: theory, method, and practice,* Reading, MA, Addison-Wesley.

Armstrong, C., Fenton, R., Lonsdale, R., Stoker, D., Thomas, R. and Urquhart, C. (2001) A Study of the Use of Electronic Information Systems by Higher Education Students in the UK, *Program*, **35** (3), 241–62.

Association of College and Research Libraries (2000) *Information Literacy Competency Standards for Higher Education: standards, performance indicators, and outcomes*, Chicago, IL, Association of College and Research Libraries, www.ala.org/acrl/ilstandardlo.html [accessed 14 May 2001].

Audit Commission (1995) *For Your Information: a study of information management and systems in the acute hospital*, London, HMSO.

Auster, E. and Choo, C. W. (1993a) Enviromental Scanning by CEOs in Two Canandian Industries, *Journal of the American Society for Information Science,* **44** (4), 194–203.

Auster, E. and Choo, C.W. (1993b) Environmental Scanning: preliminary findings of interviews with CEOs in two Canadian industries. In Bonzi, S. (ed.), *Proceedings of the 56th Annual Meeting of the American Society for Information Science, Columbus, OH, Oct. 22–28, 1993*, New Jersey, Learned Information.

Auster, E. and Choo, C. W. (1994a) CEOs, Information, and Decision-making: scanning the environment for strategic advantage, *Library Trends*, **43** (2), 206–55.

Auster, E. and Choo, C. W. (1994b) How Senior Managers Acquire and Use Information in Environmental Scanning, *Information Processing & Management*, **30** (5), 607–18.

Auster, A. and Choo, C. W. (1996) *Managing Information for the Competitive Edge*, New York, NY, Neal-Schuman.

Avison, D. and Fitzgerald, G. (2003) *Information Systems Development: methodologies, techniques and tools*, 3rd edn, London, McGraw-Hill.

Bachmann, R. (1999) *Trust, Power and Control in Trans-organizational Relations*, Cambridge, University of Cambridge, ESRC Centre for Business Research.

Barney, W., Radnor, Z., Johnston, R. and Mahon, W. (2004) The Design of a Strategic Management System in a Public Sector Organisation. In Neely, A. D. and Walters, A. (eds), *Proceedings of the 4th International Conference on Performance Measurement and Management (PMA 2004), Edinburgh, 28–30 July, 2004*, Cranfield, Performance Management Association.

Barrett, M. I. (1999) Challenges of EDI Adoption for Electronic Trading in the London Insurance Market, *European Journal of Information Systems*, **8** (1), 1–15.

Barrionuevo, M. D. (2000) Searching Excellence in the Library System of the University of Cadiz. In Derfert-Wolf, L. and Bednarek-Michalska, B. (eds), *International Conference on Quality Management in Academic Libraries, Bydgoszcz-Gniew, 10–13 September 2000*, EBIB: Conference Proceedings no. 1, Warsaw, Polish Librarians Association, http://ebib.oss.wroc.pl/matkonf/atr/miquel.html [accessed 10 January 2005].

Best, D. P. (ed.) (1996) *The Fourth Resource: information and its management*, Aldershot, Aslib/Gower.

Birnbaum, R. (1998) *How Colleges Work: the cybernetics of academic organization and leadership*, San Francisco, CA, Jossey-Bass.

Black, A. and Brunt, R. (1999) Information Management in Business, Libraries and British Military Intelligence: towards a history of information management, *Journal of Documentation*, **55** (4), 361–74.

Blackler, F. (1995) Knowledge, Knowledge Work and Organizations, *Organization Studies*, **16** (6), 1021–46.

Blair, M. B. (1995) *Ownership and Control: rethinking corporate governance for the twenty-first century*, Washington DC, Brookings Institution.

Boisot, M. (1998) *Knowledge Assets: securing competitive advantage in the information economy*, New York, NY, Oxford University Press.

Bourgeois, L. J. (1980) Strategy and Environment: a conceptual integration, *Academy of Management Review*, **5** (1), 25–39.

Bouthillier, F. and Shearer, K. (2002) Understanding Knowledge Management and Information Management: the need for an empirical perspective, *Information Research*, **8** (1), http://informationr.net/ir/8-1/paper141.html [accessed 11 April 2005].

Bowns, I., Rotherham, G. and Paisley, S. (1999) Factors Associated with Success in the Implementation of Information Management and Technology in the NHS, *Health Informatics Journal*, **5**, 136–45.

Bowns, I., Whitfield, M., Coleman, P., Sampson, F., Stevenson, M. and Bacigalupo, R. (1998) Health Data Marker Research Project. In Richards, B. (ed.), *Current Perspectives in Healthcare Computing Conference, 1998*, Weybridge, BJHC Ltd.

Boynton, A. C. and Zmud, R. W. (1984) An Assessment of Critical Success Factors, *Sloan Management Review*, **25** (4), 17–27.

Braman, S. (1989) Defining Information: an approach for policymakers, *Telecommunication Policy*, **13** (3), 233–42.

Braun, C. (1997) Organizational Infidelity: how violations of trust affect the employee–employer relationship, *Academy of Management Executive*, **11** (4), 94–5.

Brindley, L. J. (1989) *The Electronic Campus – an Information Strategy*, London, British Library.

Broadbent, M. (1977) The Emerging Phenomenon of Knowledge Management, *Australian Library Journal*, **46**, 6–23.

Broadbent, M., Lloyd, P., Hansell, A. and Dampney, C. N. G. (1992) Roles, Responsibilities and Requirements for Managing Information Systems in the 1990s, *International Journal of Information Management*, **12**, 21–38.

Broady-Preston, J. and Hayward, T. (1999) *The Role of Information in the Strategic Management Process*, British Library Research and Innovation Report, 171, London, British Library Research and Innovation Centre, www.dis.aber.ac.uk/dils/research/rfocus5/5sub2/resource/bank0x.htm [accessed 10 January 2005].

Broady-Preston, J. and Hayward, T. (2000) Information Specialists in the Corporate Sector: an analysis of the training and education needs for the 21st century, *Inspel*, **34** (3/4), 141–52.

Broady-Preston, J. and Hayward, T. (2001) Strategy, Information Processing and Scorecard Models in the UK Financial Services Sector, *Information Research*, **7** (1), paper 122, http://informationr.net/ir/7-1/paper122.html [accessed 10 January 2005].

Broady-Preston, J. and Williams, T. (2004) Using Information to Create Business Value: City of London legal firms, a case study, *Performance Measurement and Metrics: the International Journal for Library and Information Services*, **5** (1), 5–10.

Bruce, C. (1997) *The Seven Faces of Information Literacy*, Blackwood Australia, Auslib Press Pty.

Bryman, A. (2004) *Social Research Methods*, 2nd edn, Oxford, Oxford University Press.

Buchanan, S. and Gibb, F. (1998) The Information Audit: an integrated approach, *International Journal of Information Management,* **18** (1), 29–47.

Buckland, M. (1991) Information as Thing, *Journal of the American Society for Information Science,* **42**, 351–60.

Burk, C. F. and Horton, F. W. (1988) *Infomap: a complete guide to discovering corporate information resources,* Englewood Cliffs, NJ, Prentice Hall.

Burns, F. (1998) *An Information Strategy for the Modern NHS 1998–2005, A1103,* Leeds, NHS Executive,
www.imt4nhs.exec.nhs.uk/strategy/full/contents.htm [accessed 10 January 2005].

Calman, K. and Hine, D. (1995) *A Policy Framework for Commissioning Cancer Services: a report by the expert advisory group on cancer to the chief medical officers of England and Wales,* London, Department of Health.

Case, D. O. (2002) *Looking for Information,* San Diego, CA, Academic Press.

Ceynowa, K. (2000) Managing Academic Information Provision with the Balanced Scorecard: a project of the German Research Association, *Performance Measurement and Metrics: the International Journal for Library and Information Services,* **1** (3), 157–64.

Chalmers, A. (1995) Finding Out: use of business information by managers in New Zealand, *Business Information Review,* **12** (1), 43–56.

Chan, Y.-C. L. (2004) Performance Measurement and Adoption of Balanced Scorecards: a survey of municipal governments in the USA and Canada, *International Journal of Public Sector Management,* **17** (3), 204–21.

Chandler, A. D. (1990) *Scale and Scope: the dynamics of industrial capitalism,* Cambridge, MA, Harvard University Press.

Chatman, E. A. (2000) Framing Social Life in Theory and Research, *The New Review of Information Behaviour Research,* **1**, 3–17.

Cheuk, B. W. (1998a) An Information Seeking and Using Process Model in the Workplace: a constructivist approach, *Asian Libraries,* **7** (12), 375–90.

Cheuk, B. W. (1998b) Modelling the Information Seeking and Use Process in the Workplace: employing sense-making approach, *Information Research,* **4** (2),
http:// informationr.net/ir/4-2/isic/cheuk.html [accessed 15 January 2003].

Choo, C. W. (1998a) *Information Management for the Intelligent Organization: the art of scanning the environment,* Medford, NJ, Information Today.

Choo, C. W. (1998b) *The Knowing Organization: how organizations use information to construct meaning, create knowledge, and make decisions,* New York, NY, Oxford University Press.

Choo, C. W. (2001) Environmental Scanning as Information Seeking and Organizational Learning, *Information Research,* **7** (1),
http://informationr.net/ir/7-1/paper112.html [accessed 10 April 2005].

Choo, C. W. (2002) *Information Management for the Intelligent Organisation: the art of scanning the environment,* Medford, NJ, Information Today.

Choo, C. W. and Auster, E. (1993) Environmental Scanning: acquisition and use of information by managers, *Annual Review of Information Science and Technology*, **28**, 279–314.

Choo, C. W. and Bontis, N. (2002) *The Strategic Management of Intellectual Capital and Organizational Knowledge*, New York, NY, Oxford University Press.

Choo, C. W., Detlor, B. and Turnbull, D. (1998) A Behavioral Model of Information Seeking on the Web: preliminary results of a study of how managers and IT specialists use the Web. In Preston, C. M. (ed.), *Proceedings of the 61st Annual Meeting of the American Society for Information Science,* Medford, NJ, Information Today.

Choo, C. W., Detlor, B. and Turnbull, D. (2000a) Information Seeking on the Web: an integrated model of browsing and searching, *First Monday*, **5** (2), www.firstmonday.org/issues/issue5_2/choo/index.html [accessed 15 March 2005].

Choo, C. W., Detlor, B. and Turnbull, D. (2000b) *Web Work: information seeking and knowledge work on the World Wide Web,* Dordrecht, Kluwer.

Choo, C. W. and Marton, C. (2003) Information Seeking on the Web by Women in IT Professions, *Internet Research*, **13** (4), 267–80.

Christensen, C. M. (1997) *The Innovator's Dilemma: when new technologies cause great firms to fail,* Boston, MA, Harvard Business School Press.

Claver E., González, R. and Llopis, C. (2000) An Analysis of Research in Information Systems (1981–1997), *Information & Management*, **37** (4), 181–95.

Cohen, D. and Prusak, L. (2001) *In Good Company: how social capital makes organizations work,* Boston, MA, Harvard Business School Press.

Cohen, M. D., March, J. G. and Olsen , J. P. (1972) A Garbage Can Model of Organizational Choice, *Administrative Science Quarterly*, **17**, 1–25.

Commission for Health Improvement (2003) *Clinical Governance Review: Clatterbridge Centre for Oncology NHS Trust, March 2003*, www.healthcarecommission.org.uk/assetroot/04/00/29/02/04002902.pdf [accessed 11 January 2005].

Commission for Health Improvement (2004a) *CHI Launches a Self-assessment Tool for NHS Organisations to Improve their Use of Information,* news release 11 March 2004, www.chi.nhs.uk/eng/news/2004/mar/11.shtml [accessed 11 January 2005].

Commission for Health Improvement (2004b) *Clatterbridge Centre for Oncology NHS Trust – performance ratings (2003/2004): Trust detail report,* http://ratings2004.healthcarecommission.osrg.uk/reports/acutetrustsummary.asp?trustcode=ren [accessed 11 January 2005].

Commission on Federal Paperwork (1977) *Information Resources Management*, Washington DC, US Government Printing Office.

Compton, J. (2001) Dial K for Knowledge, *CIO Magazine* (15 June), www.cio.com/archive/061501/dial.html [accessed 10 April 2005].

Corrall, S. (2001) *Strategic Management of Information Services: planning handbook*, London, Aslib.

Correia, Z. (1996) *Scanning the Business Environment for Information: a grounded theory approach*, unpublished PhD thesis, Sheffield, University of Sheffield.

Correia, Z. and Wilson, T. D. (1997) Scanning the Business Environment for Information: a grounded theory approach, *Information Research*, **2** (4), http://informationr.net/ir/2-4/paper21.html [accessed 26 February 2005].

Correia, Z. and Wilson, T. D. (2001) Factors Influencing Environmental Scanning in the Organizational Context, *Information Research*, **7** (1), paper 121, http://information.net/ir/7-1/paper121.html [accessed 15 March 2005].

Cronin, B. and Davenport, E. (1993) Social Intelligence, *Annual Review of Information Science and Technology*, **28**, 3–44.

Cross, M. (2004) Clinic Puts End to Waiting Game, *The Guardian e-public supplement*, (27 October), 8.

Cross, R. and Parker, A. (2004) *The Hidden Power of Social Networks: understanding how work really gets done in organizations,* Boston, MA, Harvard Business School Press.

Cross, R., Parker, A., Prusak, L. and Borgatti, S. P. (2001) Knowing What we Know: supporting knowledge creation and sharing in social networks, *Organizational Dynamics*, **30** (2), 100–20.

Culnan, M. J. (1983) Environmental Scanning: the effects of task complexity and source accessibility on information gathering behaviour, *Decision Sciences*, **14** (2), 194–206.

Cyert, R. M., Simon, H. A. and Trow, D. B. (1956) Observations of a Business Decision, *The Journal of Business*, **29** (4), 237–48.

Daft, R. L., Sormunen, J. and Parks, D. (1988) Chief Executive Scanning, Environmental Characteristics, and Company Performance: an empirical study, *Strategic Management Journal*, **9** (2), 123–39.

Daft, R. L. and Weick, K. E. (1984) Toward a Model of Organizations as Interpretation Systems, *Academy of Management Review*, **9** (2), 284–95.

Damrosch, D. (1995) *We Scholars: changing the culture of the university,* Cambridge, MA, Harvard University Press.

Daniel, D. R. (1961) Management Information Crisis, *Harvard Business Review,* **39** (5), 111–21.

Davenport, R. (2005) Why does Knowledge Management still Matter?, *T+D Magazine*, (February), 19–25.

Davenport, T. H. (1994) Saving IT's Soul: human-centered information management, *Harvard Business Review,* **72** (2), 119–31.

Davenport, T. H., Eccles, R. G. and Prusak, L. (1996a) Information Politics, *Sloan Management Review,* (Summer), 53–65.

Davenport, T. H., Jarvenpaa, S. L. and Beers, M. C. (1996b) Improving Knowledge Work Processes, *Sloan Management Review,* (Summer), 53–65.

Davenport, T. H. and Prusak, L. (2000) *Working Knowledge: how organizations manage what they know,* Boston, MA, Harvard Business School Press.

De Alwis, S. M. (1997) *Information as a Tool for Management Decision Making: a case study of Singapore*, Master's thesis, Singapore, Nanyang Technological University.

De Alwis, S. M. and Higgins, S. E. (2001) Information as a Tool for Management Decision Making: a case study of Singapore, *Information Research*, **7** (1), http://informationr.net/ir/7-1/paper114.html [accessed 13 March 2005].

De Heer, A. J. (1999) *Informationsstrategier på Exportmarknaden: problemidentifiering och problemlösning bland finländska stockhusexportörer på den tyska marknaden* [Information Strategy in Export Markets: problem identification and problem solution among Finnish exporters of log houses to the German market], Åbo (Turku) Finland, Åbo Akademis Förlag.

De Lusignan, S. (2003) Commentary: improve the quality of the consultation, *British Medical Journal*, **326**, 205–6.

Degagne, C., Leandri, S. and Puchley, T. (2003) Linking Knowledge and Risk Management: controlling the information flood, *Risky Business*, **7**, 15–20, www.pwc.com/ch/ger/ins-sol/publ/risk/download/pwc_riskybusiness_7_e.pdf [accessed 6 August 2004].

Department of Health (1996) *Implementing the Infrastructure: a handbook for IM&T specialists*, Leeds, NHS Executive.

Department of Health (1997) *White Paper The New NHS – Modern, Dependable*, London, The Stationery Office, www.official-documents.co.uk/document/doh/newnhs/newnhs.htm [accessed 11 January 2005].

Department of Health (2000) *Health Service Circular: cancer referral guidelines*, www.dh.gov.uk/assetroot/04/01/22/53/04012253.pdf [accessed 11 January 2005].

Department of Health (2003) *The National Programme for IT in the NHS: key elements of the procurement approach* (v.1.0 – 31 January), 3.

Dervin, B. (1977) Useful Theory for Librarianship: communication, not information, *Drexel Library Quarterly*, **13**, 16–32.

Dervin, B. and Nilan, M. (1986) Information Needs and Uses, *Annual Review of Information Science and Techology*, **21**, 3–33.

Detlor, B. (2000) The Corporate Portal as Information Infrastructure: towards a framework for portal design, *International Journal of Information Management*, **20** (2), 91–101.

Deutsch, M. (1958) Trust and Suspicion, *Journal of Conflict Resolution*, **2** (2), 65–79.

Dewhirst, H. D. (1971) Influence of Perceived Information-sharing Norms on Communication Channel Utilization, *Academy of Management Journal*, **14** (3), 305–15.

Dill, W. R. (1958) Environment as an Influence on Managerial Autonomy, *Administrative Science Quarterly*, **2** (4), 409–43.

Dill, W. R. (1971) The Impact of Environment on Organizational Development. In Maurer, J. G. (ed.), *Readings on Organizational Theory: open system approaches,* New York, NY, Random House.

Dirks, K. T. and Ferrin, D. L. (2001) The Role of Trust in Organizational Settings, *Organisational Science,* **12** (4), 450–67.

Ditzig, H. and You, P. S. (1988) In Search of the Singapore Managerial Style, *Singapore Management Review,* **10** (2), 35–51.

Dollinger, M. J. (1984) Environmental Boundary Spanning and Information Processing Effects on Organizational Performance, *Academy of Management Journal,* **27** (2), 351–68.

Dresang, E. T. and Robbins, J. B. (1999) Preparing Students for Information Organizations in the Twenty-first Century: web-based management and practice of field experience, *Journal of Education for Library and Information Science,* **40** (4), 218–30.

Drucker, P. (1995) *Managing in a Time of Great Change,* Oxford, Butterworth Heinemann.

Drury, C. (2004) *Management and Cost Accounting,* 6th edn, London, Thomson Learning.

Duncan, R. (1972) Characteristics of Organizational Environments and Perceived Environmental Uncertainty, *Administrative Science Quarterly,* **17** (3), 313–27.

Dunderstadt, J.J. (1998) Can Colleges and Universities Survive in the Information Age? In Katz, R. (ed.), *Dancing with the Devil: information technology and the new competition in higher education,* San Francisco, CA, Jossey-Bass.

Eagleson, G. K. and Waldersee, R. (2000) Monitoring the Strategically Important: assessing and improving strategic tracking systems, *Proceedings of the 2nd International Conference on Performance Measurement and Management* (PMA 2000), Cambridge, July.

Earl, M. (2004) Tantalised by the Promise of Wisdom, *Financial Times,* (26 August), http://news.ft.com/cms/s/b194e66e-f6fc-11d8-a879-00000e2511c8.html [accessed 26 August 2004, requires registration].

Eisenberg, M. B. and Berkowitz, R. E. (2000) *The Big6 Collection: the best of the Big6 Newsletter,* Worthington, OH, Linworth Publishing, Inc.

Eisenhardt, K. (1989) Building Theory from Case Study Research, *Academy of Management Review,* **14** (4), 532–50.

Ekvall, G., Arvonen, J. and Waldenstrom-Lindblad, I. (1983) *Creative Organizational Climate: construction and validation of a measuring instrument,* Stockhom, FA-rådet – The Swedish Council for Management and Organizational Behaviour.

Elefalke, K. (2001) The Balanced Scorecard of the Swedish Police Service: 7,000 officers in total quality management project, *Total Quality Management,* **12** (7/8), 958–66.

Ellis, D. (1992) A Behavioural Approach to Information Retrieval System Design, *Journal of Documentation,* **45** (3), 171–212.

Ellis, D., Allen, D. and Wilson, T. D. (1999) Information Science and Information Systems: conjunct subjects, disjunct disciplines, *Journal of the American Society for Information Science,* **50** (12), 1095–107.

Ellis, D., Barker, S., Potter, S. and Pridgeon, C. (1993) Information Audits, Communication Audits and Information Mapping: a review and survey, *International Journal of Information Management,* **13** (2), 134–51.

Endersby, J. W. (1996) Collaborative Research in the Social Sciences: multiple authorship and publication credit, *Social Science Quarterly,* **77** (2), 375–91.

Ernst, D. J., Katz, R. N. and Sack, J. R. (1994) *Organizational and Technological Strategies for Higher Education in the Information Age,* Bolder CO, CAUSE – The Association for the Management of Information Technology in Higher Education.

Eureka (2004) *Park Research,* www.parc.com/research/spl/projects/commknowledge/eureka.html [accessed 11April 2005].

Euromonitor (2001) *European Marketing Data and Statistics 2001,* 36th edn, London.

European Foundation for Quality Management (2001) *The Business Excellence Model,* Brussels, European Foundation for Quality Management.

Fairer-Wessels, F. A. (1997) Information Management Education: towards a holistic perspective, *South African Journal of Library and Information Science,* **65** (2), 93–103.

Fairey, M. (1999) Missing Pieces: an analysis of the organisational framework for effecting the information strategy, *British Journal of Healthcare Computing & Information Management,* **16** (2), 26–30.

Fairey, M. (2004) BJHC Autumn Forum Reveals Serious Concern about NPfIT's Management, *British Journal of Healthcare Computing & Information Management,* **21** (10), News, 2.

Fayol, J. (1949) *General Industrial Management,* London, Pitman.

Ferguson, S. (2004) The Knowledge Management Myth: will the real knowledge managers please step forward? *ALIA 2004 Biennial Conference: Challenging Ideas, Broadbeech, Queensland, 21–24 September 2004,* Canberra, Australia, Australian Library and Information Association, http://conferences.alia.org.au/alia2004/conference.papers.html [accessed 11 April 2005].

Floyd, S. W. and Wooldridge, B. (1996) *The Strategic Middle Manager: how to create and sustain competitive advantage,* San Francisco, CA, Jossey-Bass.

Ford, N. (1989) From Information-management to Knowledge-management: the role of rule induction and neural net machine learning techniques in knowledge generation, *Journal of Information Science,* **15** (4–5), 299–304.

Ford, P., Goodyear, P., Heseltine, R., Lewis, R., Darby, J., Graves, J. et al. (1996) *Managing Change in Higher Education*, Buckingham, SRHE and Open University Press.

Geertz, C. (1973) *Interpretation of Cultures*, New York, NY, Basic Books.

Ghoshal, S. (1988) Environmental Scanning in Korean Firms: organizational isomorphism in action, *Journal of International Business Studies*, **19** (1), 69–86.

Ghoshal, S. and Kim, S. K. (1986) Building Effective Intelligence Systems for Competitive Advantage, *Sloan Management Review*, **28** (1), 49–58.

GIIC Asia Regional Meeting and International Conference (1995) *National Information Infrastructure for Social and Economic Development in Asia*, organized by the Global Information Infrastructure Commission (GIIC) National Electronics and Computer Technology Center, Thailand, and The World Bank, November 28–30. Carol, A. C. (ed.), Bangkok.

Gilad, B. (1994) *Business Blindspots*, Chicago, IL, Probus Publishing Co.

Ginman, M. (1987) *De Intellektuella Resurstransformationerna: informationens roll i företagsvärlden* [The Transformations of Intellectual Resources: the role of information in the business world], Åbo (Turku) Finland, Åbo Akademis Förlag.

Ginman, M. (1995) Paradigmer och Trender inom Biblioteks och informationsvetenskap [Paradigms and Trends in Library and Information Science]. In Höglund, L. (ed.), *Biblioteken, Kulturen och den Sociala Intelligensen*, Stockholm, Forskningsrådsnämnden.

Glaser, B. G. (1978) *Theoretical Sensitivity*, Mill Valley, CA, Sociology Press.

Glaser, B. G. and Strauss, A. L. (1967) *The Discovery of Grounded Theory*, Chicago, IL, Aldine.

Glazier, J. D. and Powell, R. R. (eds) (1992) *Qualitative Research and Information Management*, Englewood CO, Libraries Unlimited.

Go Global but Keep Asian Values (2000) *The Straits Times, Home*, (10 January), 31.

Godden, S., Pollock, A. and Pheby, D. (2000) Information on Community Health Services, *British Medical Journal*, **320**, 265.

Goldsmith, N. (1991) Linking IT Planning to Business Strategy, *Long Range Planning*, **24** (6), 67–77.

Gorman, G. E. (2004) The Uniqueness of Knowledge Management – or the Emperor's New Clothes, *Library Management & Information Services*, (April), http://titania.emeraldinsight.com/vl=2370950/cl=159/nw=1/rpsv/librarylink/management/ [accessed 10 April 2005].

Gourlay, S. (2000) Frameworks for Knowledge: a contribution towards conceptual clarity for knowledge management, *Knowledge Management: concepts and controversies conference, Warwick University, 10–11 February 2000*, http://bprc.warwick.ac.uk/km013.pdf [accessed 10 April 2005].

Granovetter, M. S. (1973) The Strength of Weak Ties, *American Journal of Sociology*, **78**, 1360–80.

Greene, F., Loughridge, B. and Wilson, T. D. (1999) The Management Information Needs of Academic Heads of Department in Universities: a critical success factors approach, *Information Research*, **4** (3), http://informationr.net/ir/4-3 [accessed 2 March 2005].

Grey, C. and Garsten, C. (2001) Trust, Control and Post-bureaucracy, *Organization Studies*, **22** (2), 29–250.

Griffiths, P. (2004) *Managing your Internet and Intranet Services*, London, Facet Publishing.

Grimshaw, A. (ed.) (1995) *Information Culture and Business Performance*, Hatfield, University of Hertfordshire Press.

Grönhaug, K. and Haukedal, W. (1988) Environmental Imagery and Strategic Actions, *Scandinavian Journal of Management*, **4** (1/2), 5–17.

Grotevant, S. M. (1998) Business Engineering and Process Redesign in Higher Education: art or science?, In *Proceedings of CAUSE 98: Seattle, Washington. December 8, 1998,* www.educause.edu/ir/library/html/cnc9857/cnc9857.html [accessed 11 April 2005].

Gummesson, E. (1988) *Qualitative Methods in Management Research*, Lund, Sweden, Studentlitteratur.

Hall, E. A., Rosenthal, J. and Wade, J. (1994) How to Make Re-engineering Really Work, *McKinsey Quarterly*, **2**, 107–28.

Hamel, G. and Prahalad, C. K. (2000) Competing for the Future, *Harvard Business Review,* **72** (4), 122–28.

Harris, L. and McGrady, A. (1999) Local Government Reorganisation – Rules, Responsibilities and Renegotiating Relationships, *Strategic Change*, **8** (5), 287–97.

Heckman, R. (1999) Organizing and Managing Supplier Relationships in Information Technology Procurement, *International Journal of Information Management*, **19** (2), 141–55.

Heinström, J. (2002) *Fast Surfers, Broad Scanners and Deep Divers: personality and infor-mation-seeking behaviour,* Åbo (Turku) Finland, Åbo Akademis Förlag.

Heterick, R. C. (ed.) (1993) *Reengineering Teaching and Learning in Higher Education: sheltered groves, Camelot, windmills and malls*, Professional Paper Series #10, Boulder, CO, Cause.

Hewins, E. T. (1990) Information Need and Use Studies, *Annual Review of Information Science and Technology (ARIST),* **25**, 145–72.

Hextall, G. (2004) *The National Programme for IT, makingITwork,* www.npfit.nhs.uk/news/all_images_and_docs/making_it_work_dec04.pdf [accessed 11 January 2005].

Hicks, P. J. (1997) *Re-engineering Higher Education: discussion paper*, Manchester, UMIST, www.umist.ac.uk/future/re-he.htm [accessed 15 May 2005].

Hlupic, V., Pouloudi, A. and Rzevski, G. (2002) Towards an Integrated Approach to Knowledge Management: 'hard', 'soft', and 'abstract issues', *Knowledge and Process Management*, **9** (2), 90–101.

Hobohm, H. (ed.) (2004) *Knowledge Management: libraries and librarians taking up the challenge*, Munich, Saur, IFLA Publications.

Hofstede, G. (1991) *Kulturer og Organisationer: overlevelse i en graensoverskridende ver-den* [Cultures and Organizations: survival in a boundary-crossing world], Copenhagen, Schultz.

Houser, R. J. and Shamir, B. (1993) Toward the Integration of Transformational, Charismatic, and Visonary Theories. In Chemers, M. and Ayman, R. (eds), *Leadership Theory and Research: perspectives and directions,* San Diego, CA, Academic Press.

Huber, G. P. and Daft, R. L. (1987) The Information Environments of Organizations. In Jablin, F. M. (ed.) *Handbook of Organizational Communication,* Newbury Park, CA, Sage.

Humber, M. (2004) National Programme for Information Technology: is sorely needed and must succeed, but is off to a shaky start, *British Medical Journal,* **328**, 1145–6.

Huotari, M.-L. (1995) Strategic Information Management: a pilot study in a Finnish pharmaceutical company, *International Journal of Information Management,* **15** (4), 295–302.

Huotari, M.-L. (1997) *Information Management and Competitive Advantage. The Case of a Finnish Publishing Company*, Finnish Information Studies 7, Tampere, University of Tampere, Department of Information Studies.

Huotari, M.-L. (1998) Human Resource Management and Information Management as a Basis for Managing Knowledge: a synthesis of three case studies, *Swedish Library Research,* **3–4**, 53–71.

Huotari, M.-L. (1999) Social Network Analysis as a Tool to Evaluate IM in the Public Sector: a pilot study at the University of Tampere. In Wilson, T. D. and Allen, D. (eds), *Exploring the Contexts of Information Behaviour*, London, Taylor Graham.

Huotari, M.-L. (2000) Information Behaviour in Value Constellation: an example from the context of higher education, *Swedish Library Research*, **3–4**, 3–20.

Huotari, M.-L. (2001) *Information Management and Competitive Advantage. Case II: A Finnish pharmaceutical company*, Finnish Information Studies 19, Tampere, University of Tampere, Department of Information Studies.

Huotari, M.-L. and Chatman, E. (2001) Using Everyday Life Information Seeking to Explain Organizational Behavior, *Library & Information Science Research,* **23** (4), 351–66.

Huotari, M.-L. and Iivonen, M. (2001) University Library – a Strategic Partner in Knowledge and Information Related Processes? In Aversa, E. and Manley, C. (eds), *Information in a Networked World: harnessing the flow: proceedings of the 64th ASIST Annual Meeting*, vol. 38, Medford NJ, Information Today.

Huotari, M.-L. and Iivonen, M. (2005) Trust in Knowledge-based Organizations. In Khosrow-Pour, M. (ed.), *Encyclopedia for Information Science and Technology, Vols. I–V*, Hershey, Idea Group Publishing.

Huotari, M.-L. and Wilson, T. D. (1996) The Value Chain, Critical Success Factors and Company Information Needs in two Finnish Companies. In Ingwersen, P. and Pors, N. O. (eds), *Information Science: integration in perspective,* Copenhagen, The Royal School of Librarianship.

Huotari, M.-L. and Wilson, T. D. (2001) Determining Organizational Information Needs: the critical success factors approach, *Information Research,* **6** (3), paper 108, http://informationr.net/ir/6-3/paper108.html [accessed 2 March 2005].

IDC (2005) *Information Society Index,* www.idc.com/groups/isi/main.html [accessed 11 April, 2005].

Infocomm Development Agency (2004) *Annual Survey on Infocomm Usage in Households and by Individuals for 2004,* Singapore, IDA, www.ida.gov.sg/idaweb/factfigure/infopage.jsp?infopagecategory=&infopageid=133 50&versionid=4 [accessed 11 April 2005].

Ingwersen, P. (1996a) Cognitive Perspectives of Information Retrieval Interaction: elements of a cognitive IR theory, *Journal of Documentation,* **52** (1), 3–50.

Ingwersen, P. (1996b) Information and Information Science in Context. In Olaisen, J., Munch-Petersen, E. and Wilson, P. (eds) *Information Science: from the development of the discipline to social interaction,* Oslo, Scandinavian University Press.

Irwin, D. (2002) Strategy Mapping in the Public Sector, *International Journal of Strategic Management,* **35** (6), 563–672.

Jenkins, C. P. (1997) Downsizing or Dumbsizing, *Brigham Young Magazine,* **51** (1), http://magazine.byu.edu/article.tpl?num=26-spr97 [accessed 11 April 2005].

Johannessen, J. A. and Olaisen, J. (1993) The Information Intensive Organisation: a study of governance, control and communication in a Norwegian shipyard, *International Journal of Information Management,* **13**, 341–54.

Johnsen, A. (2001) Balanced Scorecard: theoretical perspectives and public management implications, *Managerial Auditing Journal,* **16** (6), 319–30.

Joint Funding Councils' Library Review Group (1993) *A Report for HEFCE, SHEFC, HEFCW and DENI,* Bristol, HEFCE.

Joint Information Systems Committee (1995) *Exploiting Information Systems in Higher Education,* Bristol.

Jones, O. (2003) The Persistence of Autocratic Management in Small Firms: TCS and organizational change, *International Journal of Entrepreneurial Behaviour & Research,* **9** (6), 245–67.

Jones, R. (2001) Quick, Quick Slow, *Health Service Journal,* (25 October), 20–23.

Jones, R. (2003) Measuring the Benefits of Knowledge Management at the Financial Services Authority: a case study, *Journal of Information Science,* **29** (6), 475–87.

Julien, H. E. (1996) A Content Analysis of the Recent Information Needs and Uses Literature, *Library and Information Science Research,* **18** (1), 53–65.

Juuti, P. (1994) *Yrityskulttuurin Murros* [Breaking Business Cultures], Oitmäki Finland, Aavaranta.

Kakabadse, N. K., Kouzmin, A. and Kakabadse, A. (2001) From Tacit Knowledge to Knowledge: leveraging invisible assets, *Knowledge and Process Management,* **8 (3),** 137–54.

Kanter, R. M. (1991) Transcending Business Boundaries: 12,000 world managers view change, *Harvard Business Review,* **69** (3), 151–64.

Kaplan, R. S. and Norton, D. P. (1992) The Balanced Scorecard: measures that drive performance, *Harvard Business Review,* **70** (1), 71–9.

Kaplan, R. S. and Norton, D. P. (1993) Putting the Balanced Scorecard to Work, *Harvard Business Review,* **71** (5), 134–47.

Kaplan, R. S. and Norton, D. P. (1996a) Using the Balanced Scorecard as a Strategic Management System, *Harvard Business Review,* **74** (1), 75–85.

Kaplan, R. S. and Norton, D. P. (1996b) *The Balanced Scorecard: translating strategy into action,* Cambridge, MA, Harvard Business School Press.

Kaplan, R. S. and Norton, D. P. (2001a) *The Strategy-focused Organization,* Cambridge, MA, Harvard Business School Press.

Kaplan, R. S. and Norton, D. P. (2001b) Transforming the Balanced Scorecard from Performance Measurement to Strategic Management: part 1, *Accounting Horizons,* **15** (1), 87–104.

Kaplan, R. S. and Norton, D. P. (2001c) Transforming the Balanced Scorecard from Performance Measurement to Strategic Management: part 2, *Accounting Horizons,* **15** (2), 147–60.

Kaplan, R. S. and Norton, D. P. (2004) The Strategy Map: guide to aligning intangible assets, *Strategy and Leadership,* **32** (5), 10–17.

Katzer, J. and Fletcher, P. T. (1992) The Information Environment of Managers. In Williams, M. E. (ed.) *Annual Review of Information Science and Technology, Vol. 27,* New Jersey, Learned Information.

Keane, D. (1999) The Information Behaviour of Senior Executives. In Wilson, T. D. and Allen, D. K. (eds), *Exploring the Contexts of Information Behaviour: proceedings of the Second International Conference on Research in Information Needs, Seeking and Use in Different Contexts, 13–15 August 1998, UK,* London, Taylor Graham.

Keegan, W. J. (1974) Multinational Scanning: a study of the information sources utilized by headquarters executives in multinational companies, *Administrative Science Quarterly,* **19** (3), 411–21.

Kennerley, M. and Neely, A. D. (2000) Performance Measurement Frameworks – a Review. In *Proceedings of the 2nd International Conference on Performance Measurement and Management (PMA 2000), Cambridge, 19–21 July,* Cranfield, Performance Measurement Association, Cranfield School of Management.

Kim, C.-S. and Davidson, L. F. (2004) The Effects of IT Expenditure on Banks' Business Performance: using a balanced scorecard approach, *Managerial Finance,* **30** (6), 28–45.

Kirk, J. (1999) Information in Organisations: directions for information management, *Information Research,* **4** (3), paper 57, http://informationr.net/ir/4-3/paper57.html [accessed 20 February 2005].

Kirk, J. (2002) *Theorising Information Use: managers and their work,* PhD thesis, Sydney, University of Technology, unpublished.

Koenig, M. (1998) *Information Driven Management Concepts and Themes,* Munich, Saur.

Kotter, J. P. (1982) *The General Managers,* New York, NY, Free Press.

Kudernatsch, D. (2000) Die Einfuhrung der Balanced Scorecard im Customer Care Management der Direkt Anlage Bank AG [The Adoption of the Balanced Scorecard in Customer Care Management of the Direkt Anlage Bank AG]. In Engelbach, W. and Meier, R. (eds), *Customer Care Management,* Munich, Gabler Verlag.

Kuhlthau, C. C. (1991) Inside the Search Process: information seeking from the user's perspective, *Journal of the American Society for Information Science,* **42** (5), 361–71.

Kuhlthau, C. C. (1993) *Seeking Meaning: a process approach to library and information services,* Norwood, NJ, Ablex.

Kuhlthau, C. C. (2004) *Seeking Meaning. a process approach to library and information services,* 2nd edn, Westport, CT, Libraries Unlimited.

Kunkler, I. (2003) Rethinking Management, *British Medical Journal,* **326,** 221.

Kurik, S., Lumiste, R., Terk, E. and Heinlo, A. (2002) *Innovation in Estonian Enterprises 1998–2000,* (Innovation studies 2), Tallinn, Enterprise Estonia.

Langley, A., Mintzberg, H., Pitcher, P., Posada, E. and Saint-Macary, J. (1995) Opening Up Decision Making: the view from the black stool, *Organization Science,* **6** (3), 260–79.

Lawrie, G. and Cobbold, I. (2004) Third-generation Balanced Scorecard: evolution of an effective strategic control tool, *International Journal of Productivity and Performance Measurement,* **53** (7), 611–23.

Le Maistre, J. C. and Moseley, P. T. (1998) Developing Quality Information in Oncology: a region-wide approach. In *Current Perspectives in Healthcare Computing Conference 1998,* Weybridge, BJHC Ltd.

Lee Tsao Yuan (ed.) (2000) *Perspectives: 2000 and beyond,* Singapore, Times Academic Press for IPS.

Leidecker, J. K. and Bruno, A. V. (1984) Identifying and Using Critical Success Factors, *Long Range Planning,* **17** (1), 23–32.

Lester, R. and Walters, J. (1989) *Environmental Scanning and Business Strategy,* BL Library and Information Research Report 75, London, British Library Board.

Library 2000 - Investing in a Learning Nation: report of the Library 2000 Review Committee (1994) Singapore, SNP Publishers.

Lim, L. L. K. and Dallimore, P. (2004) Intellectual Capital: management attitudes in service industries, *Journal of Intellectual Capital*, **5** (1), 181–94.

Limberg, L. (1999) Three Conceptions of Information Seeking and Use. In Wilson, T. D. and Allen, D. K. (eds), *Exploring the Contexts of Information Behaviour: proceedings of the Second International Conference on Research in Information Needs, Seeking and Use in Different Contexts*, London, Taylor Graham.

Limberg, L. (2000) Phenomenography: a relational approach to research on information needs, seeking and use, *The New Review of Information Behaviour Research*, **1**, 51–67.

Loasby, B. J. (1991) Long Range Formal Planning in Perspective. In Mintzberg, H. and Quinn, J. B. (eds), *The Strategy Process: concepts, contexts, cases*, Englewood Cliffs, NJ, Prentice Hall.

Lucas, W. (1998) Effects of E-mail on Organization, *European Management Journal*, **16** (1), 18–30.

Luthans, F., Hodgetts, R. and Rosenkrantsz, S. A. (1988) *Real Managers*, Cambridge MA, Ballinger.

Lytle, R. H. (1988) Information Resource Management: a five-year perspective, *Information Management Review*, **3** (3), 9–16.

Macevičiūtė, E. (2002) Information management in the Baltic, Nordic, and UK LIS schools, *Library Review*, **51** (3/4), 190–99.

MacFarlane, A. (1994) *Future Patterns of Teaching and Learning*, London, Society for Research in Higher Education.

MacFarlane, A. (1995) Future Patterns of Teaching and Learning. In Schuller, T. (ed.), *The Changing University?* Buckinghamshire, SRHE and Open University Press.

MacFarlane, A. (1998) Information, Knowledge and Learning, *Higher Education Quarterly*, **52** (1), 77–92.

Maes, R. (2003) On the Alliance of Executive Education and Research in Information Management at the University of Amsterdam, *International Journal of Information Management*, **23** (3), 249–57.

Majeed, A. (2003) Ten Ways to Improve Information Technology in the NHS, *British Medical Journal*, **326**, 202–4.

Malmi, T. (2001) Balanced Scorecards in Finnish Companies: a research note, *Management Accounting Research*, **12** (2), 207–20.

Mangham, I. (1979) *The Politics of Organizational Change*, London, Associated Business Press.

Marcella, R. and Knox, K. (2004) Systems for the Management of Information in a University Context: an investigation of user need, *Information Research*, **9** (2), paper 172, http://informationr.net/ir/9-2/paper172.html [accessed 12 March 2005].

March, J. and Simon, H. (1993) *Organizations*, 2nd edn, Cambridge, MA, Blackwell.

Marchionini, G. (1995) *Information Seeking in Electronic Environments*, Cambridge, Cambridge University Press.

Marr, B., Gray, D. and Neely, A. (2003) Why Do Firms Measure their Intellectual Capital?, *Journal of Intellectual Capital,* **4** (4), 441–64.

Martensson, M. (2000) A Critical Review of Knowledge Management as a Management Tool, *Journal of Knowledge Management,* **4**, 204–16.

Marti, J. M. V. (2004) Strategic Knowledge Benchmarking System (SKBS): a knowledge-based strategic management information system for firms, *Journal of Knowledge Management,* **8** (6), 31–49.

Marton, F. (1994) Phenomenography. In Husén, T. and Postlethwaite, T. N. (eds), *The International Encyclopedia of Education Vol. 8,* 2nd edn, Oxford, Pergamon.

Marton, F. and Booth, S. (1997) *Learning and Awareness,* Mahwah, NJ, Lawrence Erlbaum.

Marton, F. and Trigwell, K. (2000) Variatio est Mater Studiorum, *Higher Education Research & Development,* **19** (3), 381–95.

Matthews, J. R. (2002) *The Bottom Line: determining and communicating the value of the special library,* Westport, CT, Libraries Unlimited.

May, L., Arzt, N., Beck, R. and Gordon, J. (1994) *Chasing the Boulder Down the Hill: reengineering and architecture at the University of Pennsylvania,* unpublished paper presented at CAUSE 94, Orlando, Florida.

Mayo, E. (1933) *The Social Problems of an Industrial Civilization,* New York, NY, Macmillan.

McAdam, R. and Bailie, B. (2002) Business Performance Measures and Alignment Impact on Strategy: the role of business improvement models, *International Journal of Operations and Production Management,* **22** (9), 972–6.

McCauley, D. P. and Kuhnert, K. W. (1992) A Theoretical Review and Empirical Investigation of Employee Trust in Management, *Public Administration Quarterly,* **16** (2), 265–85.

McGonagle, J. and Vella, C. (2003) *The Manager's Guide to Competitive Intelligence,* Westport, CT, Greenwood Press.

McGrath, K. and Smithson, S. (2001) Organisational Culture as a Regime of Truth: a critical perspective. In *Proceedings of the 6th United Kingdom Academy for Information Systems Conference,* Manchester, Zeus Press, 47–51.

McKinnon, S. M. and Bruns, W. J. (1992) *The Information Mosaic: how managers get the information they really need,* Boston, MA, Harvard Business School Press.

Meadow, C. T., Boyce, B. R. and Kraft, D. H.(2000) *Text Information Retrieval Systems,* 2nd edn, San Diego, CA, Academic Press.

Mendoza, G. (1991) *Management: the Asian way,* Manila, Asian Institute of Management.

Migliorato, P., Natan, N. and Norton, D. (1996) A Scoring System for Creating JVs that Survive, *Mergers and Acquisitions,* **30** (4), 45–50.

Miles, R. E. and Snow, C. C. (1978) *Organizational Strategy, Structure and Process,* New York, NY, McGraw-Hill.

Miller, D. and Friesen, P. H. (1977) Strategy-Making in Context: ten empirical archetypes, *Journal of Management Studies,* **14** (3), 253–80.

Miller, D. and Friesen, P.H. (1983) Strategy Making and Environment: the third link, *Strategic Management Journal,* **4** (3), 221–35.

Miller, F. (2002) I=0 (Information has no Intrinsic Meaning), *Information Research,* **8** (4), paper 140,
http://informationr.net/ir/8-1/paper140.html [accessed 6 August 2004].

Miller, J. P. (1994) The Relationship Between Organizational Culture and Environmental Scanning: a case study, *Library Trends,* **43** (2), 170–205.

Min, C. (1995) *Asian Management Systems: Chinese, Japanese and Korean styles of business,* London, Routledge.

Mintzberg, H. (1975) The Manager's Job: folklore and fact, *Harvard Business Review,* **53**, 49–61.

Mintzberg, H. (1983) *Structure in Fives: designing effective organizations,* Englewood Cliffs, NJ, Prentice-Hall.

Mintzberg, H. (1994) *The Rise and Fall of Strategic Planning,* London, Prentice-Hall.

Mintzberg, H. (1998) *The Nature of Managerial Work,* London, Haymarket.

Mintzberg, H., Ahlstrand, B. and Lampel, J. (1998) *Strategy Safari: a guided tour through the wilds of strategic management,* New York, Free Press.

Mintzberg, H., Raisinghani, D. and Theeoret, A. (1976) The Structure of the 'Unstructured' Decision Processes, *Administrative Science Quarterly,* **21** (2), 246–75.

Mishra, J. and Morrissey, M. (1990) Trust in Employee/Employer Relationships: a survey of West Michigan managers, *Public Personnel Management,* **19** (4), 443–63.

Mitchell, K. D. (2000) Knowledge Management: the next big thing, *Public Manager,* **29** (2), 57–60.

Mitchell, P. (1998) Net Values; *Health Service Journal: IT update,* (29 October), 2–5.

Mizruchi, M. S. (1994) Social Network Analysis: recent achievements and current controversies, *Acta Sociologica,* **37**, 329–43.

Morgan, G. (1986) *Images of Organisation,* Beverly Hills, CA, Sage.

Murphy, M. F. (1987) *Environmental Scanning: a case study in higher education,* EdD thesis, University of Georgia, unpublished.

Narver, J. C. and Slater, S. F. (1990) The Effect of a Market Orientation on Business Profitability, *Journal of Marketing,* **54**, 20–35.

National Computer Board of Singapore (1992) *A Vision of an Intelligent Island: The IT2000 Report,* Singapore, SNP Publishers.

Newcombe, T. (1999) Knowledge Management: new wisdom or passing fad?, *Government Technology,* (June),
www.govtech.net/magazine/gt/1999/june/magastory/feature.php

Newgren, K. E., Rasher, A. A. and LaRoe, M. E. (1984) An Empirical Investigation of the Relationship Between Environmental Assessment and Corporate Performance, unpublished paper presented at the *Proceedings of the 44th Annual Meeting of the Academy of Management*, Washington, DC.

NHS Executive (1996a) *Promoting Clinical Effectiveness: a framework for action in and through the NHS*, London, NHS Executive.

NHS Executive (1996b) *Seeing the Wood, Sparing the Trees: efficiency scrutiny into the burdens of paperwork in NHS Trusts and health authorities*, NHS Executive, Leeds.

NHS Executive (1998) *Information for Health: initial local implementation strategies*, Health Service Circular HSC 1998/225 (27 November).

NHS National Programme for Information Technology (2004) *Implementing the Programme*, www.npfit.nhs.uk/implementation/ [accessed 11 January 2005].

Niven, P. R. (2002) *Balanced Scorecard Step by Step: maximizing performance and maintaining results,* New York, NY, Wiley.

Nonaka, I. (1991) The Knowledge-creating Company, *Harvard Business Review,* (November–December), 96–104.

Nonaka, I. (1994) Dynamic Theory of Organizational Knowledge Creation, *Organization Science,* **5** (1), 14–37.

Nonaka, I. and Takeuchi, H. (1995) *The Knowledge Creating Company: how Japanese companies create the dynasties of innovation*, Oxford and New York, Oxford University Press.

Normann, R. and Ramírez, R. (1994) *Designing Interactive Strategy: from value chain to value constellation,* Chichester, John Wiley & Sons.

Norreklit, H. (2000) The Balance on the Balanced Scorecard – a critical analysis of some of its assumptions, *Management Accounting Research,* **11** (1), 65–88.

Norreklit, H. (2003) The Balanced Scorecard: what is the score? A rhetorical analysis of the balanced scorecard, *Accounting, Organizations and Society,* **28**, 591–619.

O'Brien, F. and Meadows, M. (2003) Exploring the Current Practice of Visioning: case studies from the UK financial services sector, *Management Decision,* **41** (5), 488–97.

O'Reilly, C. A. (1980) Individuals and Information Overload in Organizations: is more necessarily better? *Academy of Management Journal,* **23** (4), 684–96.

O'Reilly, C. A. (1982) Variations in Decision Makers' Use of Information Sources: the impact of quality and accessibility of information, *Academy of Management Journal,* **25** (4), 756–71.

O'Reilly, C. A. (1983) The Use of Information in Organizational Decision Making: a model and some propositions. In Cummings, L. L. and Staw, B. M. (eds), *Research in Organizational Behavior, Vol. 5,* Greenwich, CT, JAI Press.

Olve, N., Roy, J. and Wetter, M. (1999) *Performance Drivers: a practical guide to using the balanced scorecard*, Chichester, Wiley.

Oluic-Vukovic, V. (2001) From Information to Knowledge: some reflections on the origin of the current shifting towards knowledge processing and further perspective, *Journal of the American Society for Information Science and Technology,* **52** (1), 54–61.

Oppenheim, C. (1997) Managers' Use and Handling of Information, *International Journal of Information Management,* **17** (4), 239–48.

Oppenheim, C., Stenson, J. and Wilson, R. M. S. (2001) The Attributes of Information as an Asset, *New Library World,* **102** (1170/1171), 458–63.

Orna, E. (2004) *Information Strategy in Practice,* Aldershot, Gower.

Ottum, B. D. and Moore, W. L. (1997) The Role of Market Information in New Product Success/Failure, *Journal of Product Innovation Management,* **14** (4), 258–73.

Owens, I. and Wilson, T. D. (1997) Information and Business Performance: a study of information systems and services in high-performing companies, *Journal of Librarianship and Information Science,* **29** (1), 19–28.

Owens, I., Wilson, T.D. and Abell, A. (1996) *Information and Business Performance: a study of information systems and services in high performing companies,* London, Bowker Saur.

Palmer, A. (2005) *Principles of Services Marketing,* 4th edn, London, McGraw-Hill.

Parmenter, D. (2002) Implementing a Balanced Scorecard in 16 weeks, *Chartered Accountants Journal,* **81** (3), 19.

Patton, M. Q. (1990) *Qualitative Evaluation and Research Methods,* 2nd edn, Newbury Park CA, Sage.

Pellow, A. and Wilson, T. D. (1993) The Management Information Requirements of Heads of University Departments: a critical success factors approach, *Journal of Information Science,* **19** (6), 425–37.

Penenberg, A. L., and Barry, M. (2000) *Spooked: espionage in corporate America,* Cambridge, MA, Perseus Publishing.

Penrod, J. I. and Dolence, M. G. (1992) *Reengineering: a process for transforming higher education,* Boulder, CO, CAUSE: The Association for the Mangement of Information Technology in Higher Education.

Peppard, J. (2001) Bridging the Gap between the IS Organisation and the Rest of the Business: plotting a route, *Information Systems Journal,* **11** (3), 249–70.

Perry, W. G. (1970) *Forms of Intellectual and Ethical Development in the College Years: a scheme,* New York, NY, Holt, Rinehart and Winston, Inc.

Pettigrew, A. M. (1977) Strategy Formation as a Political Process, *International Studies of Management and Organization,* **7** (2), 78–87.

Pfeffer, J. and Salancik, G. R. (1978) *The External Control of Organizations: a resource dependence perspective,* New York, NY, Harper & Row.

Pitts, J. (1994) *Personal Understandings and Mental Models of Information: a qualitative study of factors associated with the information seeking and use of adolescents,* PhD thesis, Tallahassee, FL, The Florida State University, unpublished.

Poh, K. W. (2001) Singapore's Strategy to Become a Knowledge-based Economy. In Chee, Y. N. and Griffy-Brown, C. (eds), *Trends and Issues in East Asia, 2001,* Tokyo, Foundation for Advanced Studies on International Development.

Polanyi, M. (1958) *Personal Knowledge: towards a post-critical philosophy,* Chicago, IL, University of Chicago Press.

Porter, M. (1980) *Competitive Strategy,* New York, NY, Free Press.

Porter, M. (1985) *Competitive Advantage: creating and sustaining superior performance,* New York, NY, Free Press.

Porter, M. (1990) *The Competitive Advantage of Nations,* New York, NY, Free Press.

Porter, M. (1996) What is Strategy? *Harvard Business Review,* **74** (6), 61–78.

Porter, M. (2002) *Singapore Competitiveness: a presentation to the IIR Leading Minds Conference,* (30 July), www.isc.hbs.edu/caon%20singapore%2007-22-02%20(final)%20ck.pdf [accessed January 18 2003].

Porter, M. and Millar, V. E. (1985) How Information Gives You Competitive Advantage, *Harvard Business Review,* **85** (4), 149–60.

Poverty the 'Ultimate Threat' to Man (2000) *The Straits Times – Prime News,* (14 February), 2.

Powell, W. W., and DiMaggio, P. J. (eds) (1991) *The New Institutionalism in Organizational Analysis,* Chicago, IL, University of Chicago Press.

Privateer, P. M. (1999) Academic Technology and the Future of Higher Education: strategic paths taken and not taken, *Journal of Higher Education,* **70** (1), 60–72.

Ptaszynski, J. G. (1989) *Ed Quest As an Organizational Development Activity: evaluating the benefits of environmental scanning,* PhD thesis, University of North Carolina at Chapel Hill, unpublished.

Radford, K. J. (1981) *Modern Managerial Decision Making,* Englewood Cliffs, NJ, Prentice-Hall.

Radnor, Z. and Lovell, W. (2003) Defining, Justifying and Implementing the Balanced Scorecard in the National Health Service, *International Journal of Medical Marketing,* **3** (3), 174–88.

Ray, D. W. (1994) The Missing T in TQM . . . trust, *Journal for Quality & Participation,* **17** (3), 64–7.

Redding, G. (1996) Management in Pacific Asia. In Warner, M. (ed.), *International Encyclopedia of Business and Management, Vol. 3,* London, Routledge.

Reuters Business Information (1994) Information in Organisations: new research from Reuters Business Information, *Business Information Review,* **11** (2), 48–52.

Roberts, N. and Clifford, B. (1986) *Regional Variations in the Demand and Supply of Business Information: a study of manufacturing firms,* Sheffield, University of Sheffield, Department of Information Studies.

Rockart, J. F. (1979) Chief Executives Define their Own Data Needs, *Harvard Business Review,* **57** (2), 81–93.

Rondeau, K. V. and Wagar, T. H. (1999) Hospital Choices in Times of Cutback: the role of organizational culture, *Leadership in Health Services,* **12** (3), xiv–x.

Rosenbaum, H. (1996) *Managers and Information in Organizations: towards a structura-tional concept of the information use environment of managers*, PhD thesis, New York, Syracuse University, unpublished.

Rourke, F. E. and Brooks, G. E. (1964) The 'Managerial Revolution' in Higher Education, *Administrative Science Quarterly*, **9** (2), 154–81.

Rowley, J. (1998) Towards a Framework for Information Management, *International Journal of Information Management*, **18** (5), 359–69.

Ruohotie, P. (1998). *Motivaatio, tahto ja oppiminen* [Motivation, Willingness, and Learning], Helsinki, Edita.

Savolainen, R. (2000) Incorporating Small Part and Gap-bridging: two metaphorical approaches to information use, *The New Review of Information Behaviour Research*, **1**, 35–50.

Scarbrough, H. (1995) Strategic Change in Financial Services: the social construction of strategic IS, paper presented at the *IFIP WG8.2 working Conference on Information Technology and Changes in Organizational Work*, Judge Institute of Management Studies, Cambridge University.

Schein, E. (1994) Innovative Cultures and Organisations. In Allen, T. J. and Morton M. S. S. (eds), *Information Technology and the Corporation of the 1990s: research studies*, New York, NY, Oxford University Press.

Schlögl, C. (2003) Wissenschaftslandkarte Informationsmanagement [Knowledge Map of Information Management], W*irtschaftsinformatik*, **45** (1), 7–16.

Schneider, S. C. (1989) Strategy Formulation: the impact of national culture, *Organizational Studies*, **10** (2), 149–68.

Schneider, S. C. and de Meyer, A. (1991) Interpreting and Responding to Strategic Issues: the impact of national culture, *Strategic Management Journal*, **12** (4), 307–20.

Schutz, A. (1967) *The Phenomenology of the Social World*, Evanston, IL, Northwestern University Press.

Scott, W. R. (1987) The Adolescence of Institutional Theory, *Administrative Science Quarterly*, **32**, 493–511.

Seldén, L. (2001) Academic Information Seeking: careers and capital types, *The New Review of Information Behaviour Research*, **2**, 195–215.

Self, J. (2004) Metrics and Management: applying the results of the balanced scorecard, *Performance Measurement and Metrics: the International Journal for Library and Information Services*, **5** (3), 101–5.

Senge, P. M. (1990) *The Fifth Discipline: the art and practice of the learning organization*, New York, NY, Currency Doubleday.

Shaw, R. B. (1997) *Trust in the Balance: building sucessful organizations on results, integrity and concern*, San Francisco, CA, Jossey-Bass.

Sievewright, M. (2001) Charting the Future of Financial Services, *Credit Union Magazine*, **67** (4), 4–6.

Silk, D. J. (1991) *Planning IT: creating an information management strategy*, Oxford, Butterworth-Heinemann.

Simon, H. (1957) *Models of Man,* New York, NY, John Wiley.

Simon, H. (1960) *Administrative Behaviour*, Basingstoke, Macmillan.

Simpson, C. W. and Prusak, L. (1995) Troubles with Information Overload Moving from Quantity to Quality in Information Provision, *International Journal of Information Management,* **15**, 413–25.

Singapore Economic Review Committee (2003) *New Challenges, Fresh Goals: toward a dynamic global city,* Singapore, Ministry of Trade.

Singapore Ministry of Trade and Industry. The Economic Planning Committee (1991) *The Strategic Economic Plan: toward a developed nation*, Singapore, National Printers.

Singapore Techventure 2000 Conference (2000) *The Straits Times – Prime News*, (11 March), 2.

SM Lee's Talk at NTU (2000) *The Straits Times – Home*, (16 February), 44.

Smith, L. and Preston, H. (2000) Information Management and Technology Strategy in Healthcare: local timescales and national requirements, *Information Research*, **5** (3), http://informationr.net/ir/5-3/paper74.html [accessed 11 January 2005].

Software, S. (1999) *ATLAS:ti*, London, Sage Publications Ltd.

Soon ... Surf the Net Anywhere in NTU (2000) *The Straits Times – Home*, (17 February), 46.

Souder, W. E. and Moenaert, R. K. (1992) Integrating Marketing and R&D Project Personnel within Innovation Projects: an information uncertainty model, *Journal of Management Studies*, **29** (4), 485–512.

Speckbacher, G., Bischof, J. and Pfeiffer,T. (2003) A Descriptive Analysis on the Implementation of Balanced Scorecards in German-speaking Countries, *Management Accounting Research*, **14** (4), 361–87.

Starr, S. L. (1998) Grounded Classification: grounded theory and faceted classification, *Library Trends,* **47** (2), 218.

Stenmark, D. (2003) Knowledge Creation and the Web: factors indicating why some intranets succeed where others fail, *Knowledge and Process Management,* **10** (3), 207–16.

Straits Knowledge (2002) *Knowledge Based Leadership in Singapore Organisations,* Singapore.

Strauss, A. (1987) *Qualitative Analysis for Social Scientists*, Cambridge, Cambridge University Press.

Strauss, A. (1993) *Continual Permutations of Action*, New York, NY, Aldine De Gruyter.

Strauss, A. and Corbin, J. (1990) *Basics of Qualitative Research: grounded theory procedures and techniques*, London, Sage.

Subramanian, R., Fernandes, N. and Harper, E. (1993) Environmental Scanning in US Companies: their nature and their relationship to performance, *Management International Review,* **33** (3), 271–86.

Subramanian, R., Kumar, K. and Yauger, C. (1994) The Scanning of Task Environments in Hospitals: an empirical study, *Journal of Applied Business Research,* **10** (4), 104–15.

Sundin, O. (2002) Nurses' Information Seeking and Use as Participation in Occupational Communities, *The New Review of Information Behaviour Research,* **3,** 187–202.

Sundin, O. (2005) Webbaserad Användarundervisning: ett forum för förhandlingar om bibliotekariers professionella expertis [Web-based User Education: a forum for negotiation on the professional expertise of librarians], *Human IT,* **7** (3), 109–68.

Sutcliffe, K. M. (1991) *Determinants and Outcomes of Top Managers' Perceptions and Interpretations of the Environment,* unpublished PhD thesis, Austin, TX, University of Texas at Austin.

Sveiby, K. E. (1998) *Measuring Intangibles and Intellectual Capital – an Emerging First Standard,* Brisbane, Sveiby Knowledge Associates, www.sveiby.com/articles/emergingstandard.html.

Sveiby, K. E. (1997) *The New Organizational Wealth: managing and measuring knowledge-based assets,* San Francisco, CA, Berrett-Koehler.

Sveiby, K. E. (2001) *What is Knowledge Management?* Brisbane, Sveiby Knowledge Associates, www.sveiby.com/faq.html# [accessed 11 August 2004].

Sveiby, K. E. (2003) *Creating Value with the Intangible Assets Monitor,* Brisbane, Sveiby Knowledge Associates, www.sveiby.com/articles/companymonitor.html [accessed 13 August 2004].

Sveiby, K. E. (2004) *Methods for Measuring Intangible Assets,* Brisbane, Sveiby Knowledge Associates, www.sveiby.com/articles/intangiblemethods.htm [accessed 13 August 2004].

Tackley, R., Jones, S., Madden, A. and Dunnill, R. (2003) Making the Most of the National Programme for IT in the NHS – Learning from Experience, *British Journal of Healthcare Information Management & Technology,* **20** (10), 25–7.

Talja, S. (1997) Constituting 'Information' and 'User' as Research Objects: a theory of knowledge formations as an alternative to the information man-theory. In Vakkari, P., Savolainen, R. and Dervin, B. (eds), *Information Seeking in Context. Proceedings of an International Conference on Research in Information Needs, Seeking and Use in Different Contexts,* London, Taylor Graham.

Tan, J.-S. (1996) Management in Singapore. In Warner, M. (ed.), *International Encyclopedia of Business and Management, Vol. 3,* London, Routledge.

Tannenbaum, R. and Davis, S. A. (1969) Values, Management, and Organizations, *Industrial Management Review,* **10** (2), 803–15.

Taylor, F. W. (1911) *The Principles of Scientific Management,* New York, NY, Harper Bros.

Taylor, R. S. (1986) *Value-added Processes in Information Systems*, Norwood, NJ, Ablex Publishing.

Teo, T. (2000) Using the Internet for Competitive Intelligence in Singapore, *Competitive Intelligence Review*, **11** (2), 61–70.

Thurow, L. (1996) *The Future of Capitalism: how today's economic forces shape tomorrow's world*, London, Nicholas Brealey.

Tiamiyu, M. A. (1992) The Relationships Between Source Use and Work Complexity, Decision-maker Discretion and Activity Duration in Nigerian Government Ministries, *International Journal of Information Management*, **12** (2), 130–41.

Tibar, A. (2000) Information Needs and Uses in Industry: the implications for information services, *New Review of Information Behaviour Research*, **1**, 185–200.

Tibar, A. (2002) Critical Success Factors and Information Needs in Estonian Industry, *Information Research*, **7** (4), paper 138, http://informationr.net/ir/7–4/paper138.html [accessed 2 March 2005].

Toh, M. H., Tang, H. C. and Choo, A. (2002) Mapping Singapore's Knowledge-based Economy. In *Economic Data, Feature Articles,* Singapore, Ministry of Trade and Industry, www.mti.gov.sg/public/pdf/cmt/nws_2002q3_kbe1.pdf?sid=165&cid=1416 [accessed 1 March 2005].

Trauth, E. M. (1988) Information Resource Management, *Encyclopedia of Library and Information Science*, **43**, 93–112.

Tsichritzis, D. (1999) Reengineering the University, *Communications of the ACM,* **42** (6), 93–100.

Tsoukas, H. and Vladimirou, E. (2000) On Organizational Knowledge and its Management: an ethnographic investigation, unpublished paper presented at the *Knowledge Management: concepts and controversies conference, Warwick University, 10–11 February 2000.*

Turnley, W. H. and Feldman, D. C. (1998) Psychological Contract Violations during Corporate Restructuring, *Human Resource Management,* **37** (1), 71–83.

Tyson, K. (1998) Perpetual Strategy: a 21st century essential, *Strategy and Leadership,* **26** (1), 14–18.

Up Next: Dot.com-ing each home in Singapore (2000) *The Straits Times – Home*, (19 February), 49.

Vakkari, P., Savolainen, R. and Dervin, B. (eds) (1997) *Information Seeking in Context*, London, Taylor Graham.

Van Riel, A. C. R., Lemmink, J. and Ouwersloot, H. (2004) High-technology Service Innovation Success: a decision-making perspective, *Journal of Product Innovation Management,* **21** (5), 348–59.

Viewpoints (2000) *The Sunday Times* [Singapore] – *Review*, (27 February), 42.

Virtual Institute to Promote E-learning (2000) *The Sunday Times* [Singapore] – *Home*, (5 March), 1.

Wallach, E. J. (1983) Individuals and Organizations: the cultural match, *Training and Development Journal*, **2**, 29–36.

Wasserman, S. and Faust, K. (1994) *Social Network Analysis: methods and applications*, Cambridge, Cambridge University Press.

Webber, A. M. (2000) New Math for a New Economy, *Fast Company*, (31) www.fastcompany.com/magazine/31/lev.html [accessed 20 February 2005].

Weick, K. E. (1979) *The Social Psychology of Organizing*, 2nd edn, New York, NY, Random House.

Weick, K. E. (1995) *Sensemaking in Organizations*, Thousand Oaks, CA, Sage Publications.

Wenger, E. (2002) *Cultivating Communities of Practice: a guide to managing knowledge*, Boston, MA, Harvard Business School Press.

West, J. J. (1988) *Strategy, Environmental Scanning, and Their Effect Upon Firm Performance: an exploratory study of the food service industry*, PhD thesis, Virginia Polytechnic Institute and State University, unpublished.

What the Players Say (2000) *The Straits Times – Home*, (16 February), 48.

White, D. A. (1986) Information Use and Needs in Manufacturing Organizations: organizational factors in information behaviour, *International Journal of Information Management*, **6** (3), 157–70.

White, D. A. and Wilson, T. D. (1988) *Information Needs in Industry: a case study approach*, Sheffield, University of Sheffield, Department of Information Studies.

White, G. P. and Jacobs, F. R. (1998) Perceived Importance of the Internet as an Information Channel for OM Professionals, *International Journal of Operations & Production Management*, **18** (12), 249–70.

Widén-Wulff, G. (2001) *Informationskulturen som Drivkraft i Företagsorganisationen* [Information Culture as a Driving Force in Business Organizations], Åbo (Turku) Finland, Åbo Akademi University Press.

Widmier, S. (2002) The Effects of Incentives and Personality on Salesperson's Customer Orientation, *Industrial Marketing Management*, **31** (7), 609–15.

Wiig, K.M. (1999) Introducing Knowledge Management into the Enterprise. In Liebowitz, J. (ed.), *Knowledge Management Handbook*, New York, NY, Boca Raton, FL, CRC Press, 3.1–3.41.

Wilensky, H. (1967) *Organisational Intelligence: knowledge and policy in government and industry*, New York, NY, Basic Books.

Wilson, P. (1983) *Second-hand Knowledge: an inquiry into cognitive authority*, Westport, CT, Greenwood Press.

Wilson, T. D. (1981) On User Studies and Information Needs, *Journal of Documentation*, **37** (1), 3–15.

Wilson, T. D. (1989) Towards an Information Management Curriculum, *Journal of Information Science*, **15** (4–5), 203–9.

Wilson, T. D. (1994a) Information Needs and Uses: fifty years of progress? In Vickery, B. (ed.), *Fifty Years of Information Progress: a Journal of Documentation review,* London, Aslib.

Wilson, T. D. (1994b) *The Nature of Strategic Information and its Implications for Information Management.* In Alvares-Ossorio, J. R. and Goedegebuure, B. G. (eds), *New Worlds in Information and Documentation: proceedings of the 46th F.I.D. Congress and Conference, Madrid, October 1992,* Amsterdam, Elsevier.

Wilson, T. D. (1994c) Tools for the Analysis of Business Information Needs, *Aslib Proceedings*, **46** (1), 19–23.

Wilson, T. D. (1999) Models in Information Behaviour Research, *Journal of Documentation*, **55** (3), 249–70.

Wilson, T. D. (2000) Human Information Behaviour, *Informing Science*, **3** (2), 49–55.

Wilson, T. D. (2002) The Nonsense of Knowledge Management, *Information Research*, **8** (1), paper 144,
http://informationr.net/ir/8-1/paper144.html [accessed 11 April 2005].

Wilson, T. D (2003) Information Management. In *International Encyclopedia of Information and Library Science*, 2nd edn, London, Routledge.

Wilson, T. D. and Allen, D. K. (eds) (1999) *Exploring the Contexts of Information Behaviour*, London, Taylor Graham.

Wolfe, A. (1996) The Feudal Culture of the Postmodern University, *The Wilson Quarterly,* **20** (1), 54–68.

Wyatt, J. and Keen, J. (1998) The NHS's New Information Strategy, *British Medical Journal,* **317**, 900.

Yin, R. (1989) *Case Study Research: design and methods*, rev. edn, London, Sage.

You too, can go Online. Don't worry about IT (2000) *The Straits Times – Prime News*, (2 March), 3.

Zeithaml, V. A. and Bitner, M. J. (2003) *Services Marketing,* 3rd edn, Boston, MA, McGraw Hill.

Index